Understanding the Symbols, Covenants, and Ordinances of the TEMPLE

AMY HARDISON

Covenant Communications, Inc.

Cover image *Salt Lake Sacred Doors* © Robert A. Boyd, www.RobertABoyd.com.

Published by Covenant Communications, Inc.
American Fork, Utah

Printed in the United States of America
First Printing: May 2016

18 17 16 15 14 13 12 11 10 9

ISBN 978-1-68047-241-7

Understanding the Symbols, Covenants, and Ordinances of the TEMPLE

To Steve

The sine qua non of this book and my life

Table of Contents

List of Illustrations

Introduction

Joseph Smith declared, "We need the temple more than anything else."[1] President Howard W. Hunter asked members of the Church to take the temple as the symbol of our discipleship.[2] He entreated, "Let us truly be a temple-attending and a temple-loving people. We should hasten to the temple as frequently, yet prudently, as our personal circumstances allow."[3] President Gordon B. Hinckley pled:

> I hope that everyone gets to the temple on a regular basis. . . . I know your lives are busy. I know that you have much to do. But I make you a promise that if you will go to the House of the Lord, you will be blessed; life will be better for you. Now, please, please, my beloved brethren and sisters, avail yourselves of the great opportunity to go to the Lord's house and thereby partake of all of the marvelous blessings that are yours to be received there.[4]

At the dedication of the San Diego temple, Elder David E. Sorenson said, "I testify to you that the key to spiritual maturity is the endowment."[5]

---

1 *History of the Church*, 6:230, quoted in Truman G. Madsen, "The Temple and the Atonement," in *Temples of the Ancient World: Ritual and Symbolism*, ed. Donald W. Parry (Salt Lake City: Deseret Book and FARMS, 1994), 65.

2 See Howard W. Hunter, *The Teachings of Howard W. Hunter*, ed. Clyde J. Williams (Salt Lake City: Bookcraft, 1997), 239.

3 Ibid., 236.

4 Gordon B. Hinckley, *Teachings of Gordon B. Hinckley* (Salt Lake City: Deseret Book Company, 1997), 624.

5 David E. Sorensen, quoted in "San Diego Temple Dedication: Temples—Linking Heaven and Earth," *Church News*, May 8, 1993.

Such are the words of our leaders. Such is the promise of the temple. However, it is not what every temple patron experiences. Previous to the construction of the Los Angeles temple, President McKay met with stake presidents in the Los Angeles area. He shared with them his deep feelings about the temple. He also shared with them the feelings of his niece when she first attended the temple. Before she received her endowments, she had participated in a sorority initiation—she preferred the sorority initiation. Andrew F. Ehat relates:

> President McKay was open and frank with them about the experience of one in his own family with the endowment. He wasn't worried about their audible gasps. With characteristic aplomb, he paused, and then said, "Brothers and sisters, she was disappointed in the temple. Brothers and sisters, I was disappointed in the temple. And so were you." Then he said something incredibly important that should be engraven on all our souls. "There are few, even temple workers, who comprehend the full meaning and power of the temple endowment. Seen for what it is, it is the step-by-step ascent into the Eternal Presence." Then he added, "If our young people could but glimpse it, it would be the most powerful spiritual motivation of their lives!"[6]

Clearly, our task, if we are to be a temple-loving people, is to comprehend the meaning and the power of the temple endowment.

If we made a continuum for the temple experience, we could place on it the following points representing the differing attitudes of temple patrons: those who find their initial temple experience so strange they never return, those who occasionally go to the temple, those who regularly go to the temple out of duty and obligation, those who enjoy the peace and spirit present in the temple, those who experience the rich outpouring of the Spirit, and those who experience exquisite joy and transcendent communion with God. The operative question is what do we need to do to move more to the right on our personal continuum? Among the many possible answers, creating appropriate

---

6 Andrew F. Ehat, "'Who Shall Ascend into the Hill of the Lord?' Sesquicentennial Reflections of a Sacred Day: 4 May 1842," *Temples of the Ancient World*, 58.

expectations, increasing our understanding of the temple, and keeping the temple fresh and new must surely be on the list.

Appropriate Expectations

For those who are born into the Church, preparation to go to the temple begins early. As children, they sing "I love to see the temple. I'm going there someday." They have numerous lessons in their classes in the Young Women and Young Men organizations on the importance of the temple and how they need to live their lives to be worthy to enter therein. If they live close to a temple, they may attend morningsides at the temple, do baptisms for the dead, and go to the visitors' center. They will hear about the importance of the temple from prophets and apostles in general conference. Because of the justifiable concern of speaking too openly of sacred things and of saying things we ought not, they may have a solid understanding of how to *get* to the temple but no significant understanding of what happens once they are there. John A. Widtsoe wrote, "It is not quite fair to let the young girl or young man enter the temple unprepared, unwarned, if you choose, with no explanation of the glorious possibilities of the first fine day in the temple."[7] Unprepared and unwarned, their expectations may be very different from what they experience. Converts may not experience as many years of temple mystique, but what they miss in longevity is made up in intensity as ward members lovingly guide converts to "the crowning blessings the Church has to offer."[8]

Attending the temple is different than attending any other church meeting. Our regular Sunday meetings are simple and reserved. There is minimal ceremony and formality. In this, we resemble Protestant churches, who lost or eliminated a great part of the high ritual, ceremonies, and elaborate attire of the Catholic Church. However, the Catholic rites that appear so foreign to Latter-day Saints are based on "the sacred ceremonies of the Jews and the early Christians, even though the Catholic ritual is said to have 'undergone additions, deletions, and alterations, which have modified their character' over the centuries."[9]

---

7 John A. Widtsoe, "Symbolism in the Temples," in *Saviors on Mount Zion*, ed. Archibald F. Bennett (Salt Lake City: Deseret Sunday School Board, 1950), 168.

8 Gordon B. Hinckley, "New Temples to Provide 'Crowning Blessings' of the Gospel," *Ensign*, May 1998, 88.

9 Marcus von Wellnitz, "The Catholic Liturgy and the Mormon Temple," *BYU Studies* 21 (Winter 1981), 4.

The Church of Jesus Christ of Latter-day Saints is neither Protestant nor Catholic. It is restored. As such, it "claims a divine restoration of ancient modes and ordinances,"[10] ancient modes that were marked by ritual and ceremony. Therefore, it is not surprising that "there should be some resemblances and connections between the ceremonial aspects of the Latter-day Saint ordinances and the Catholic traditions and practices."[11] Nevertheless, first-time temple patrons accustomed to the simple and reserved worship of our Sunday meetings are often not prepared for the shift to the greater amount of ritual and ceremony.

In addition to expecting a different style of worship, we might expect a different kind of spiritual experience than that which is usually had in the temple. After attending the temple, my daughter and I routinely ask each other, "Did you see any angels today?" Inevitably, the other responds, "Not today." While our question is a lighthearted way to express the real possibility of visitors from heavenly realms, it also reveals a common expectation for the temple to provide spiritual experiences that are unique, even spectacular—something commensurate with the exquisite holiness of the temple. This expectation may leave one feeling disappointed with his or her temple experience. To preclude this kind of disappointment, it is helpful to remember that there are two reasons we go to the temple: for eternal blessings and for blessings in the here and now.

Eternal Blessings

In the temple, we participate in ordinances and receive knowledge that will be a supernal blessing to us in the eternities. Brigham Young explains:

> Let me give you a definition in brief. Your endowment is, to receive all those ordinances in the house of the Lord, which are necessary for you, after you have departed this life, to enable you to walk back to the presence of the Father, passing the angels who stand as sentinels, being enabled to give them the key words, the signs and tokens, pertaining to the holy Priesthood, and gain your eternal exaltation in spite of earth and hell."[12]

10 Ibid, 3.

11 Ibid, 3.

12 Brigham Young, *Discourses of Brigham Young*, ed. John A. Widtsoe (Salt Lake City: Deseret Book Company, 1954), 416.

This idea of walking back to God and passing by angels in the next world may be an unfamiliar one to many Latter-day Saints who have not received their endowments. It's not a doctrine we speak about regularly from the pulpit. However, I believe Brigham Young's statement is literal. On the course back to God, there will apparently be gates, doors, or other checkpoints where we will need to say certain words and do certain things. This idea, like many truths taught in the temple, is not unique to Latter-day Saint temples.

In the ancient temple in Jerusalem, one had to pass through a series of stairs, doors, and gates to reach the most holy spot, the Holy of Holies—the place of Divine Presence and the throne room of God. Each passageway was more restrictive than the previous one. The pilgrims coming to worship in the temple would first pass through the Double Gate of the Temple Mount, where they would then ritually purify themselves before actually entering the Temple Mount and the Court of the Gentiles. In this court there was a balustrade, called the *soreg*, which served as a barrier beyond which Gentiles could not pass on penalty of death. Israelites could pass by this railing and enter into the Court of the Women. Fifteen curved steps led from the Court of the Women up to the Nicanor Gate. Only the men of Israel could pass through this gate into the Court of the Men. From here, only priests and authorized persons could enter into the Court of the Priests. Only authorized priests could pass from the Court of the Priests through two large twin pillars into a place that functioned as a kind of porch or vestibule and then through doors of cypress wood into the Holy Place. Only the High Priest could pass through the veil into the most sacred room of all, the Holy of Holies.

References to gates, points of passage, keywords, and tokens also show up in many ancient documents, particularly Egyptian ones. The earliest literary corpus was originally carved into the walls of the pyramids in Egypt and was therefore appropriately called "the Pyramid Texts." These writings "assured the happy afterlife of the deceased."[13] Later, these texts also appeared on the coffins of those who could afford them. The text's main purpose is to give the dead the knowledge they need to pass by "the 2 ways, the 7 gates, the 21 portals . . . the

13 James R. Harris, "The Book of Abraham Facsimiles," in *Studies in Scripture, Volume 2: The Pearl of Great Price*, eds. Robert L. Millet and Kent P. Jackson (Salt Lake City: Randall Book Company, 1985), 252.

door-keepers and heralds."[14] In order to pass through all these gates and portals, the deceased must have been washed and clothed in the appropriate clothing. The gates were guarded by gatekeepers who, in the Egyptian texts, were demons or apotropaic gods, gods designated to avert evil. They were depicted with animal masks and knives, identifying them as dangerous and terrifying beings. "The deceased wards off their threat by calling them by name but also by knowing the names of the gates; he secures unhindered passage by showing proof of his purity."[15] The terror these doorkeepers engender is meant to repel evil, but once the worthy initiate passes through the gates, these creatures guard and protect him from evil.[16]

The ability to walk back into the presence of God is but one of the eternal blessings available in the temple. It is the blessing that deals with our personal eternal salvation. But salvation without those we love would be incomplete. Eternal marriage is the pinnacle of the ordinances available in the temple. To be sealed eternally to the one to whom you have given your heart and soul and with whom you are willing to walk through life with all its joys and vicissitudes is a gift beyond measure. Indeed, we might join with Parley P. Pratt in saying that such an eternal union is "at the very foundation of everything worthy to be called happiness."[17] Along with the blessing of eternal marriage is the blessing of eternal families, of having the sweet sociality of family extend into the eternal realms, there coupled with eternal glory.

After receiving these supernal blessings for ourselves, we may help extend these great blessings to those who have passed from this life unendowed. This is an occasion of great joy for those in the spirit world. The *Utah Genealogical and Historical Magazine* records the experience

14 Jan Assmann, "Death and Initiation in the Funerary Religion of Ancient Egypt," in *Religion and Philosophy in Ancient Egypt* (New Haven, Conn.: Yale Egyptological Seminar, 1989), 143; quoted in John Gee, "The Keeper of the Gate," in *Temple in Time and Eternity*, eds. Donald W. Parry and Stephen D. Ricks (Provo, Utah: The Foundation for Ancient Research and Mormon Studies at Brigham Young University, 1999), 238.

15 Ibid., 241.

16 Ibid.

17 Parley P. Pratt, *Autobiography of Parley P. Pratt,* 3rd ed., Deseret Book, 1938, 297–298; quoted in Truman G. Madsen and Steven R. Covey, *Marriage and Family: Gospel Insights* (Salt Lake City: Bookcraft, 1983), 4.

of a brother who was helping with baptisms for the dead in the Manti temple. As he served as a witness, he saw the spirits of those for whom the baptisms were being performed.

> The spirits stood awaiting their turn, and, as the recorder called out the name of a person to be baptized for, . . . [the brother] noticed a pleasant smile come over the face of the spirit whose name had been called, and he would leave the group of fellow spirits and pass over to the side of the recorder. There he would watch his own baptism performed by proxy, and then with a joyful countenance would pass away, mak[ing] room for the next favored person who was to enjoy the same privilege.[18]

As this brother was observing this remarkable scene, he noticed that those spirits waiting their turns suddenly turned away with great sorrow in their faces. He looked around and saw that the room was nearly empty and the recorder was gathering up his records and stepping down from his desk. The day's work was complete. The remaining baptisms would have to be performed on another day. Such experiences fill the histories of the temples and are poignant reminders that the ordinances of the temple bring eternal blessings and joy.

The Here and Now

The eternal blessings of the temple are glorious, superlative, and beyond full comprehension. But they are not only for the hereafter. There are a multitude of blessings for the here and now, blessings that touch our everyday lives. Even those blessings that are primarily eternal in nature have temporal benefits. Regarding genealogical research and vicarious work for the dead, John A. Widstoe said, "I have the feeling . . . that those who give themselves with all their might and main to this work receive help from the other side, and not merely in gathering genealogies. Whoever seeks to help those on the other side

---

18 *Utah Genealogical and Historical Magazine,* vol. 11, July 1920, 119; quoted in Joseph Heinerman, *Temple Manifestations* (Salt Lake City: Joseph Lyon and Associates, Inc., 1974), 110–111.

receives help in return in all the affairs of life."[19] It may be that as we do temple work for our ancestors, we empower them, which in turn grants them more power to aid us.[20] George Q. Cannon points out that since we have been chosen to be saviors to the children of men, to stand as a medium through which salvation is offered to our ancestors, our ancestors pray for us in the spirit world, beseeching our Heavenly Father that we might remain faithful and true.[21]

Eternal marriage is another eternal blessing that has immediate benefits. Obviously, an eternal commitment creates a different perspective than a till-death-do-you-part commitment or the equally common until-things-get-too-hard commitment. But there is more than that. According to Doctrine and Covenants 19:10–12, "eternal" describes both quantity (forever) and quality (like God).[22] When we enter into an eternal marriage, we are entering into a relationship that will last forever and will, at its ideal, be godlike in character and nature. This does not happen magically, instantaneously, or without effort. An eternal marriage "is always a triumph of spiritual principles, a product of selfless, sustained effort on behalf of both partners, a victory arising out of the will to love."[23] The temple is integral in making us the kind of people who can sustain this type of love. President Hinckley stated, "I am satisfied that if our people would attend the temple more, there would be less of selfishness in their lives. There would be less absence of love in their relationships. There would be more of fidelity on the part of husbands and wives. There would be more of love and peace and

19 John A. Widstoe, "Genealogical Activities in Europe," *Utah Genealogical and Historical Magazine* 22 (July 1931): 104; quoted in Byron R. Merrill, *Elijah: Yesterday, Today, and Tomorrow* (Salt Lake City: Bookcraft, 1997), 137.

20 I am indebted to my dear friend Charlotte Grant, who has devoted her heart and her life to family history work, for this insight.

21 See George Q. Cannon, *Gospel Truth*, ed. Jerreld L. Newquist (Salt Lake City: Deseret Book Company, 1974), 2:107.

22 "Those who are married in the temple for all time and eternity obtain the blessing of eternal lives. I put stress on eternal lives. Eternal life is God's life, that is, to be like him." Joseph Fielding Smith, *Answers to Gospel Questions* (Salt Lake City: Deseret Book, 1963), 4:197. "Now eternal life is the name of the kind of life which God our Eternal Father lives. Eternal life is God's life, and God's life is eternal life. Thus, if we gain eternal life it will be because we advance and progress and become like him." Bruce R. McConkie, Conference Report, April 1970, 26.

23 M. Catherine Thomas, *Spiritual Lightening* (Salt Lake City: Bookcraft, 1996), 62.

happiness in the homes of our people."[24] The temple ordinances and temple worship have the power to change our natures, to make us more loving and less ego driven. In short, as we internalize what the temple offers, we become better spouses. In addition, in a temple marriage, a husband and wife enter into a covenant not only with each other but also with God. He is a covenant partner in their marriage. As such, husband and wife have covenant access to a divine counselor of infinite wisdom and omniscience. Douglas Brinley put it this way: "Is there any marriage or marital problem that the Father, Son, or Holy Ghost cannot fix? Can you imagine God saying, 'I've built a lot of worlds, but I've never seen a marriage problem like this one!'"[25]

While proxy work for the dead and eternal marriage bless us both eternally and immediately, there are many other blessings whose primary focus is the here and now. One of the oft-overlooked blessings of the temple is simply living worthy to enter the temple. In and of itself, this can profoundly alter the quality of our lives.

One of the greatest of blessings of the temple is detailed in Doctrine and Covenants 109:15. Those who attend the temple are promised that "they may grow up in thee, and receive a fulness of the Holy Ghost." When we are baptized and confirmed, we receive the gift of the Holy Ghost, but we are a long way from receiving the fullness of the Holy Ghost. That comes as we grow in spiritual and physical maturity, gain essential experience, purify our lives, overcome the natural man, and above all, consistently yearn for greater spiritual power. Receiving our temple endowments is a significant step toward a fullness of the Holy Ghost. "Members who go to the temple have access to a fullness of the Holy Ghost that is not available to those who have only received the gift of the Holy Ghost."[26] However, much of the time, we may not even notice this increase—any more than we could feel ourselves growing when we were children. Occasionally, a child might have leg aches or growing pains—and at times the Spirit is poured out profusely

24 Gordon B. Hinckley, *Regional Representatives' Seminar*, April 6, 1984; quoted in Dean L. Larsen, "The Importance of the Temple for Living Members," *Ensign*, April 1993, 12.

25 Douglas Brinley, "How the Doctrine and Covenants Can Strengthen Marriages," Church Educational System Religious Educators Conference at Brigham Young University, August 2002, 13–15.

26 Glenn L. Pace, *Spiritual Revival* (Salt Lake City: Deseret Book, 1993), 128.

and His presence is unmistakable. But there are many times we go to the temple and experience only the gentler, softer expressions of the Spirit, such as peace and a quiet sense of spiritual well-being. Even in moments like these, we are definitely and undeniably still growing up in the Spirit.

The temple is also a place of revelation. John A Widstoe stated, "That is the gift that comes to those who enter the temple properly, because it is a place where revelations *may be expected.* I bear you my personal testimony that this is so."[27] President Ezra Taft Benson promised: "Now by virtue of the sacred priesthood in me vested, . . . I promise you that, with increased attendance in the temples of our God, you shall receive increased personal revelation to bless your life as you bless those who have died."[28]

In addition to being a place of revelation, the temple is a haven of peace, a refuge from the world and from our worldly concerns. It is a place where we are reminded about what is important and that there is more to our existence than this thin slice of mortality. Peering into eternity, we are reminded that there are worlds without number but it is our own life on this earth that is our primary interest (see Moses 1:33, 35). The temple is a place where we are taught metaphorically and symbolically how to live our lives, about our relationships with one another, and how to return to the presence of God. It is for these and other blessings that we need the temple.

Increasing Our Understanding

Whether we understand the temple or not, the temple works. As we enter the temple, we may enjoy an outpouring of the Holy Ghost, bask in being in the holiest place on earth, receive important personal revelation, and experience a sorely needed respite from the world. As

27 John A. Widstoe, "Temple Worship," *Utah Genealogical and Historical Magazine* 12 (April 1921); quoted in Alan K. Parrish, "Modern Temple Worship through the Eyes of John A. Widtsoe, A Twentieth-Century Apostle," in *The Temple in Time and Eternity*, eds. Donald W. Parry and Stephen D. Ricks (Provo, Utah: The Foundation for Ancient Research and Mormon Studies at Brigham Young University, 1999), 157; italics added.

28 Ezra Taft Benson, "The Book of Mormon and the Doctrine and Covenants," *Ensign*, May 1987; quoted in David B. Haight, "Come to the House of the Lord," *Ensign*, May 1992, 16.

rich as these blessings are, our temple experience can be sweeter and fuller with a greater understanding of the temple and its symbols. Shortly after becoming President of the Church, Spencer W. Kimball spoke to the youth in the Salt Lake Valley at a fireside held in the Tabernacle on Temple Square—a fireside deemed important enough to be broadcast live on TV. Andrew F. Ehat writes, "As I listened to the fireside, I was awed by his assurance: 'If you understood the ordinances of the House of the Lord, you would crawl on your hands and feet for thousands of miles in order to receive them!'"[29] Understanding the temple is an important key in helping us move from sometime temple attendees to people who would do anything and pay any price to be in God's holy house.

Why is the meaning of the temple so elusive, so difficult to grasp? It may be that the complexity of the symbols is commensurate with the spiritual riches that are available. Eternal treasures don't yield to superficial curiosity. However, I have come to believe there is another reason. Don Norton wrote in the preface to Hugh Nibley's *Temple and Cosmos*, "The temple is indeed a very 'different' experience—as well it ought to be, reflecting, as it does, the realities of another world."[30] While this other world may be the world of spiritual things, I believe it applies equally to the ancient world. The temple, its rites, and its symbols are far more at home in the cultural milieu of the ancient world than in the modern, western world. In a world of computers, cell phones, air travel, and democracy, we are at a decided disadvantage when it comes to understanding the symbolism associated with kingship, ancient Israel's high priests, and pilgrimages to offer sacrifices at a temple. Even if we get the broad-brush symbolism of the temple, the finer details frequently elude us. One of the purposes of this book is to shine a light on the ancient world as it relates to the temple.

Keeping the Temple Fresh and New

Anything that is done over and over is in danger of becoming meaningless or at least less meaningful. Newness itself piques our interest and rivets our attention. But as repetition and familiarity replace awe and wonder,

29 Ehat, 58–59.

30 Don E. Norton, in *The Collected Works of Hugh Nibley*, vol. 12, ed. Don E. Norton, *Temple and Cosmos* (Salt Lake City and Provo, Utah: Deseret Book Company and FARMS, 1992), xvi.

it is easy to slip into autopilot, to become unengaged. We are lured into the "difficulty [of] getting beyond what we think we already know."[31] This is true of all things, both secular and spiritual. Consider how few people actually listen to flight attendants as they tell passengers what to do in case of an emergency.

The first several times you went through the temple, you were probably alert and focused, hungrily taking in everything you saw and eagerly anticipating what would come next. You were probably challenged by the newness of it all. Even finding your way to the dressing room might have been a little intimidating. However, as we return to the temple month after month and year after year, we no longer wonder where the dressing room is or what is going to happen. We meet a different challenge, the challenge of familiarity. How do we avoid slipping into the kind of familiarity that results in meaningless participation or even boredom? How do we avoid having temple attendance become merely a responsibility? How do we bring newness and fascination to something we could repeat by memory?

The best answer, for both secular and spiritual things, is crisis. If an airline pilot announces the plane is having a mechanical failure and you are in danger of crashing and then tells you to listen to the flight attendant's instructions, you would listen like your life depended on it, for indeed it might. Moving from the hypothetical to the real, perhaps you experienced a heightened ardor and solemnity when seeing an American flag flying or singing the national anthem after 9/11. The death of a loved one might be the crisis that awakens us to the power and importance of the temple. But since crises are mercifully the exception rather than the rule and are a rather uncomfortable way to be awakened, there are other, preferable ways.

Today in Jerusalem you can still climb the stairs leading up to the Double Gate, which was the entrance into the Second Temple, the temple at the time of Jesus. These steps are not uniform. They have different depths (see figure 1-1). The steps were purposefully built this way to make them difficult to ascend hurriedly, thoughtlessly, or mechanically. The ascending pilgrim would, of necessity, have to

---

31 James E. Faulconer, *Scripture Study: Tools and Suggestions* (Provo, Utah: FARMS, 1999), 11.

Figure 1-1. Steps at the Temple Mount.

slow down and focus on the task at hand—entering the temple.[32] The equivalent for us is thoughtful and prayerful preparation. Preparation can begin the night before by getting a good night's sleep to help us be alert and attentive. We can also begin to ponder and pray about the issues in our lives for which we need guidance from God. We can think about some aspect of the endowment we would like to understand better. As we travel to the temple, we can allow ample time so we are not rushed and frantic. We might want to listen to music that invokes the Spirit. We need to put our temporal concerns on hold and follow Brigham Young's counsel when he said, "Say to the fields, . . . flocks, . . . herds, . . . gold, . . . silver, . . . goods, . . . chattels, . . . tenements, . . . possessions, and to all the world, stand aside; get away from my thoughts, for I am going up to worship the Lord."[33] Above all, we need to punctuate our preparations with prayer. Such preparation moves us out of autopilot and into intentionality. Intentionality is always more riveting.

Another way to re-create a newness and fascination for the temple is to be mentally engaged, learning new things and deepening our understanding. This is what High Nibley calls "the most exhilarating

32 Leen and Kathleen Ritmeyer, *Secrets of Jerusalem's Temple Mount* (Washington, DC: Biblical Archeology Society, 1998), 32.

33 Brigham Young, *Deseret News*, Jan 5 1985; quoted in Neal A. Maxwell, "The Tugs and Pulls of the World," *Ensign*, November 2000, 37.

aspect of the whole thing . . . the purest form of fun."[34] Without it, our time in the temple will lack meaning and we "might as well send bags of sand through the endowment while running up the most satisfying statistics on our computers."[35] It is to this end that this book is written: to bring to light aspects of the temple that will empower you to rivet your attention and engage your intellect and thus make your temple experience an exhilarating delight.

34 Hugh Nibley, *Collected Works of Hugh Nibley*, ed. Don E. Norton, vol. 9, *Approaching Zion* (Salt Lake City and Provo, Utah: Deseret Book Company and FARMS, 1989), 265–266.

35 Ibid., 265.

Understanding the Physical Temple

"God teaches with symbols; it is his favorite method of teaching."[1] Nowhere is this truer than in the temples of the Lord. The temple endowment is replete with symbolism. So integral is symbolism to the endowment that it could be said that if we miss the symbolism, we miss the endowment. "No man or woman can come out of the temple endowed as he should be, unless he has seen, beyond the symbol, the mighty realities for which the symbols stand."[2] But symbolism is not reserved for the endowment alone. Everything in, around, and about the temple is purposefully there to teach us. It begins before we even walk inside and extends to the very structure of the building. However, the messages aren't blatant or pushy, for God does not work that way. Rather, the lessons are taught in the understated eloquence of symbols. They are available to those who are committed to noticing and pondering.

Before examining some of the symbolism of the physical temple, it is fitting to make a few remarks about symbols in general. Most symbols are multifaceted. There is not one definitive, correct interpretation for a symbol. There are many. We should be cautious anytime we think we have learned *the* meaning of a symbol. Such thinking puts our learning

---

1 Orson F. Whitney, "Latter-day Saint Ideals and Institutions," *Improvement Era* (August 1927); quoted in Richard G. Oman, "Exterior Symbolism of the Salt Lake Temple: Reflecting the Faith That Called the Place into Being," *BYU Studies*, vol. 36, no. 4 (1996–97), 22.

2 John A. Widstoe, "Temple Worship," address given in Salt Lake City, October 12, 1920; quoted in Ezra Taft Benson, *The Teachings of Ezra Taft Benson* (Salt Lake City: Bookcraft, 1988), 250–251.

at risk. Once we think we know something, we tend to look no further and miss some of the more subtle and sometimes more mature and significant symbolism. For instance, it is well-known that a snake symbolizes evil and Satan. But because most snakes shed their skin four to eight times a year, a snake is also one of the most ancient symbols for resurrection. As a symbol of the renewal of life, the snake is also a symbol for healing, eternity, and Christ.[3] Had the early Israelites insisted on one and only one symbolic meaning for the snake—evil, or Satan—they would have been quite befuddled when Moses placed a bronze serpent on a pole and commanded those who had been bitten by real serpents to look to the bronze serpent and live.

Each time we discover the meaning of a symbol, it would be wise to remember we have discovered *a* meaning of that symbol. This is true even in the temple when we are given the symbolic meaning of certain things. Even a revealed interpretation may not be the only interpretation. It may even be that God is not as intent upon giving us the meaning of a symbol as He is trying to teach us how to think, listen, and learn. In this book, I will present several interpretations for any one symbol. Sometimes the interpretations will even be conflicting, like the serpent symbolizing both Satan and Christ. Rather than choosing one interpretation, consider holding all the meanings. Symbols are meant to be like prisms that reflect several different colors. Each color is beautiful, but the most beautiful of all is the rainbow.

The Design of Temples

Today we are building temples all over the world. Often these new temples reflect the culture and architecture of the country in which they are built. The new, smaller temples must provide everything essential to temple worship that is provided by the larger temples but in less space. Such considerations have impacted the design of modern temples. The temples built today look quite different from the Salt Lake Temple and other early temples. Nevertheless, all our temples are

---

3 See Andrew Skinner, "Savior, Satan, and Serpent: The Duality of a Symbol in the Scriptures," in *The Disciple As Scholar: Essays on Scripture and the Ancient World in Honor of Richard Lloyd Anderson*, eds. Stephen D. Ricks, Donald W. Parry, and Andrew H. Hedges (Provo, Utah: FARMS, 2000), 359–360. For the snake as a symbol of healing, consider the medical symbol of a serpent entwined around a staff, the rod of Asclepius.

strikingly beautiful. All are designed to teach eternal truths not only within their sacred walls but also by their very design.

"Our early LDS temples were all designed as fortresses, with their buttresses and their battlements, their gates, their walls—always the surrounding wall."[4] This fortress image is easy to see in the Salt Lake, Manti, St. George, and Logan temples. Even the Washington D.C. and San Diego temples bear resemblance to a fortress, though they are more stylized and modern. The fortress motif of these temples is applicable to all temples, regardless of their design. A fortress is an image of safety, protection, and war. Moroni, a man of perfect understanding, erected many small forts around his land to give his people places of refuge. In our day, many small temples have been built around the world as places of spiritual refuge. As the war between good and evil rages, "we must come to the temple for light and safety. Only in the house of the Lord will we find quiet, sacred havens where the storm cannot penetrate. There unseen sentinels watch over us."[5]

Another symbolic motif is the circle and the square. We see this in the Manti temple with the square building and the beautiful freestanding circular staircase. The Ogden temple (before the 2014 remodel) and the Provo temple appear, from a geometric standpoint, to be a circle poised upon a square base. The square symbolizes the earth and our earthly existence. The four corners evoke the four elements (earth, air, fire, and water), the four seasons, and the "four corners," or the entirety, of the earth. The circle, which has no beginning and no end, represents eternity.[6] The circle with the square is heaven and earth, time and eternity. What better describes the temple than the place where time meets eternity?

But the circle and the square both embody other symbols that are pertinent to the temple. The square denotes honesty, integrity, and morality. In addition, "it is the fixation of death as opposed to the dynamic circle of life and movement. . . . In sacred architecture it signifies

---

4 Nibley, "The Meaning of the Temple," *CWHN*, 12:34.

5 Vaughn J. Featherstone, *The Incomparable Christ: Our Master and Model* (Salt Lake City: Deseret Book Company, 1995), 3–4.

6 The symbolism of the circle can also be applied to the compass, the instrument that makes a circle.

transcendent knowledge."[7] The circle signifies recurrence, which entails not only the act of recurring but the return to a previous condition. This is a major theme of the temple endowment: providing us with everything we need to return to the Edenic state of being in the presence of God. "The circle also depicts the Precious Pearl, or the Pearl of Great Price."[8] The architectural circle of the Provo and Ogden temples is not a perfect circle. Rather, it appears to be a rounded square. Hugh Nibley quips, "It would have been nice had they made up their minds whether they wanted it square or round."[9] But this fusion of circle and square is appropriate temple architecture, for the squaring of the circle symbolizes the transformation of the earth into heaven and the bringing down of heaven to earth.

Several temples resemble each other, but most have features and symbols that are unique to them. The seven floors of the Washington D.C. Temple represent the six days of creation and a day of rest.[10] Also, to enter the Washington D.C. Temple, members must cross a bridge that connects the annex and the entrance, symbolically leaving the world behind in order to enter the presence of God.[11] The Mount Timpanogos temple has prisms embedded in the glass windows that "refract light into its colorful spectrum, symbolizing God's influence radiating down upon His children."[12]

Sometimes the unique features of a temple are due to unique challenges. For instance, real estate is limited and costly in New York City as it is in Hong Kong. The solution in both instances was to build temples not as stand-alone buildings but with meetinghouses and other church buildings occupying other floors. The Manhattan temple was built in an existing building, and the inner walls of the temple were connected to the outer walls at only a few points. As a result, the

---

7 J. C. Cooper, *An Illustrated Encyclopaedia of Traditional Symbols* (London: Thames and Hudson, 1978), 157–158.

8 Ibid., 36.

9 Nibley, "The Circle and the Square," *CWHN*, 12:149.

10 See Kathy England, "The Washington D.C. Temple," *Ensign*, October 1977, 88.

11 See ibid.

12 "Thousands Visit Newest Utah Temple, 49th in the Church, During Open," *Church News*, August 17, 1996.

temple is a haven of quiet peace in the midst of a busy and noisy city.[13] What is true of the physical building is also true in our lives. No matter how loud the world or how hectic our lives, we can find peace and tranquility in the temples of the Lord.

Each temple is beautiful. Each has a sense of the numinous and inspires quiet dignity and sacred reverence. The architecture of the temple reflects the transcendent work that goes on inside. After touring the San Diego temple during its open house, Rabbi Wayne Dosick wrote, "The entire Temple is built for the purpose of using earthly materials to construct a place that inspires heavenly awe."[14] He went on to note, "This Mormon Temple uses sweeping architecture to create a space that invokes the celestial heavens that is awesome, that transcends the place and the moment, transporting people from the here and now to thoughts and images of God's presence."[15] Thus the design of the temple echoes the purpose of the temple, to bring us into the presence of God.

The Orientation

The early Latter-day Saint temples, as well as many ancient temples, were constructed along an east-west orientation. East is the sacred direction. It is the direction of the rising sun and thus the direction of life. In ancient times, the east commonly represented God's abode or God's presence. Consequently, an Israelite in Biblical times oriented himself by facing east. As the abode of God, the east was a place of refuge[16] and the direction from whence divine manifestations came. People from the east were often respected for wisdom, as in the case of the "wise men from the east" (Matthew 2:1) that came to pay homage to the Christ child. The east wind is called "the Wind of Yahweh" because it comes from God and is often an instrument of His judgment. It was an east wind that separated the waters of the Red Sea (see Exodus 14:21) and afflicted Jonah as he sat fuming at the Ninevites and the Lord (see Jonah 4:8).

---

13 See David R. Stone, "Zion in the Midst of Babylon," *Ensign*, May 2006, 92.

14 Rabbi Wayne Dosick, "How Goodly Is Your Temple, O Mormons," *San Diego Jewish Times*, March 25, 1993, 15.

15 Ibid.

16 "Under all circumstances the east provides refuge." Jacob Neusner, *Genesis Rabbah, The Judaic Commentary to the Book of Genesis* (Atlanta, Georgia: Scholars Press, 1985), 1:236.

Temples on an east-west axis could have entrances on the east or the west. Those that had entrances on the east opened their doors to the rising sun. "On the equinoctial day (either March 21 or September 21), [the sun] sent the earliest rays—considered 'the glory of the Lord'—to shine through the temple doors, which were opened for the occasion, directly into the holiest part."[17] Temples with entrances on the west side allowed the king or priest (or today, the temple patron) to move from darkness into light. When a modern temple has this orientation, the temple patron enters from the region of darkness, the temporal world. As he moves toward the celestial room, or toward God, he moves eastward, toward wisdom and the region of light where the sun arises.[18] Moving toward light is also moving toward truth and knowledge (D&C 93:36).

The Fence

The first thing we come to when we approach many temples is a fence demarcating the property line. While the fence is not a significant deterrent to anyone determined enough to scale it, it is significant in its symbolism. The fence reminds us that the world has no access to the temple and to the sacred ordinances.[19] This is true even when the endowment is illegitimately published on the Internet. Even when it is exposed to prying and unauthorized eyes, the world still has no access to it. Its significance and its saving power are missed.

The fence also teaches us that if we are to enter into the temple and enjoy its sacred blessings, we ourselves must be cut off from the world. "The first order God gave to his people was to remove themselves utterly from the world, to be completely different, holy, set apart, chosen, special, peculiar . . . not like any other people on the face of the earth."[20] We are to be sanctified, consecrated, and holy. The Latin and Greek roots of these words, as well as the meaning of the Hebrew word for *holy*, all convey the sense of separation. Hugh Nibley notes

17 John W. Welch, "The Temple in the Book of Mormon: The Temples at the Cities of Nephi, Zarahemla, and Bountiful," *Temples of the Ancient World*, 324.

18 See Von Wellnitz, 7.

19 See Nibley, "What Is Zion? A Distant View," *CWHN*, 9:27–28.

20 Hugh W. Nibley, "On the Sacred and the Symbolic," in *Temples of the Ancient World* (Salt Lake City and Provo, Utah: Deseret Book Company and FARMS, 1994), 543.

that to be holy is to be "set off or cut off by a fence, an insurmountable wall, an unbridgeable gap."[21]

Early in Israel's history, the people petitioned Samuel for a king "that we also may be like all the nations" (1 Samuel 8:20). Though God granted their petition, it appears that He was not pleased.[22] The children of Israel had been called to be a special community, divinely favored and uniquely privileged. They were willing to set this aside to be like everyone else. They wanted to be ordinary. Being holy had become too great a burden. In essence, they wanted to take down the fence that set them apart from the world. If we are going to be a holy and consecrated people, we must decide which world we are going to live in—a decision we are reminded of each time we see the fence around the temple.

Reflecting Pools

Many temples have beautiful reflecting pools at their doors. Like other aspects of the temple grounds, this is rich in symbolism. In the courtyards of Israel's tabernacle and temple was a bronze laver.[23] This magnificent washbasin was made from mirrors donated by the women of Israel. (In the ancient world, mirrors were not made of glass but of burnished metal, especially copper.) According to the description in 1 Kings, the laver sat upon an incredibly ornate bronze base decorated with lions, oxen, and cherubim in relief (see 1 Kings 7:29). On its base, the laver was taller than the average person. It held approximately 243 gallons of water, which was used for purification. The priests would take the water to wash their hands and feet preparatory to performing their ritual duties. As we approach the temples, the reflecting pools should remind us of the moral purity required to enter the temple and that "becoming clean is a key step on our path back to God's presence."[24]

---

21 Ibid.

22 It must be noted that there is a conflicting attitude in the Old Testament regarding kingship. On one hand, the people's desire for a king expressed a lack of faith in God and a rejection of Him, choosing instead the ways of the world. On the other hand, the text also suggests that God appointed kings in Israel to bless them and to teach them about the King of Kings.

23 1 Kings 7:38 describes ten bronze lavers, each supported by an elaborate stand.

24 Richard O. Cowan, "Sacred Temples Ancient and Modern," *The Temple in Time and Eternity*, 102.

In addition to the laver, 1 Kings 7:23 mentions a "molten sea," or an enormous basin of metal, near the temple's entrance. It was fifteen feet in diameter and seven-and-a-half feet high. This impressive laver symbolized the original waters that covered the earth, the "face of the deep" in Genesis 1:2, which Ancient Near Easterners thought were the waters of chaos. In the creation process, God imposed order and bounds upon the waters by placing a "firmament in the midst of the waters" (Genesis 1:6). By implication, He restrained the threat of chaos. Ancient temples were viewed as being built upon these cosmic waters. The waters that issued forth from the temple were the sacred waters of creation, rebellious and chaotic, but when controlled by God, life giving and saving. The molten sea signifies both the sacred waters of creation and the power and presence of God, who subdued them.[25] The reflecting pools at the entrances of our temples are modern equivalents to the molten sea and all its symbolism. Particularly, they represent the transformation of our lives from chaotic and rebellious into calm and life giving when we obey God's word and accept His bounds. The reflecting pools also symbolize the power of God that is in the temples, including the power of godliness (see D&C 84:21) or the power to become godly. They represent the eternal life-giving power of the ordinances performed therein.

The waters of the temple are not only significant in regard to the beginning of creation; they will again be prominent in the last days, as several scriptures attest. The scriptures vary slightly, but the composite picture drawn from Ezekiel, Joel, and Zechariah reveals a river that flows from "under the threshold of the house" (Ezekiel 47:1), in other words from beneath the temple. The waters will flow through the courtyard of the temple, through the city of Jerusalem, and to the Dead Sea, where they will heal the salty waters. So thorough will be the transformation of the Dead Sea that it will sustain an abundance of fish (see Ezekiel 47:8–9). Zechariah mentions two rivers, one flowing eastward, the other westward (see Zechariah 14:8), and Joel says that a "fountain shall come forth of the house of the Lord, and shall water the valley of Shittim" (Joel 3:18), or in other words, it will transform the desert.

25 See Carol Meyers, "Sea, Molten," *The Anchor Bible Dictionary*, ed. David Noel Freedman (New York: Doubleday, 1992), 5:1062.

It appears that these scriptures will be fulfilled literally at some future time. However, the healing waters that will one day flow literally from the temple in Jerusalem already flow spiritually from the temples of the Restoration.[26] Whatever the rivers touch, be it as barren as a desert or as desolate as the Dead Sea, is healed and vivified. Sometimes our lives and our relationships become barren, like deserts. Sometimes our marriages and our family relationships become strained and bitter, even dead. The spirit of Elijah that attends temple work and turns the hearts of the children to the fathers and the fathers to the children is very real. We usually think of it in terms of instilling the desire to search out our ancestors and do their temple work,[27] but the spirit of Elijah also applies to family members who are still alive—to husbands and wives, parents and children, brothers and sisters. President Benson promised, "When you attend the temple and perform the ordinances that pertain to the house of the Lord, certain blessings will come to you: You will receive the spirit of Elijah, which will turn your hearts to your spouse, to your children, and to your forebears. You will love your family with a deeper love than you have loved before."[28]

Finally, the reflecting pools of the temple remind us that the temple is a return to Eden. Genesis 2:10 tells us that "a river went out of Eden . . . and from thence it was parted and became into four heads." If one were to return to Eden, he would have to walk past these waters, past the cherubim with flaming swords, and past the tree of knowledge of good and evil to the tree of life and back into the presence of God. In ancient Israel, once a year on Yom Kippur, the holiest day of the year, the high priest ceremonially reenacted this journey back to Eden

---

26 See S. Michael Wilcox, "The Temple: Taking an Eternal View," *Every Good Thing: Talks from the 1997 BYU Women's Conference*, eds. Dawn Hall Anderson, Susette Fletcher Green, Dlora Hall Dalton (Salt Lake City: Deseret Book Company, 1998), 296–297.

27 The turning of hearts also applies to the hearts of our ancestors turning to us. President George Q. Cannon said, "You cannot tell the interest felt in eternity for you by those of our dead who have gone before us. Their hearts yearn after us, their constant desire being that we may be faithful and maintain our integrity and be prepared to bring salvation to them and redeem them by going forth and obeying every ordinance which God has established in the Church for the salvation of the living and the dead." Cannon, 2:107–108.

28 Benson, *The Teachings of Ezra Taft Benson*, 254.

by walking past the laver (the river), past the images of cherubim that were woven into the fabric of the veil, past the candlestick, or menorah, which was the stylized tree of life, and to the mercy seat of God, which sat on top of the ark of the covenant and was believed to be the place where God would appear were He to come.[29] The culmination of the ancient high priest's journey was his arrival in the Holy of Holies (see figure 2-1). Today, we reenact this same journey each time we return to the temple. We walk past the waters at the entrance of the temple and past the guardians at the entrance of the temple. As part of the endowment, we ceremonially and vicariously travel past the tree of knowledge of good and evil. We pass celestial beings who guard the tree of life. The pinnacle of our journey is our arrival in the celestial room, the place of the presence of God.

What is significant about returning to Eden? Before the Fall, the world existed as a terrestrial state. This will basically be the state that will exist during the Millennium, that respite from the wickedness, war, and troubles of the telestial world. When we enter the temple, we can enjoy for a few hours the peace and bliss of the Millennium. Although we must eventually reenter the telestial world, we can take some of the millennial world with us. One way we do so is through our covenants. The covenants we make in the temple raise us above the telestial world. They can help us create a personal world where peace and love prevail over enmity, where consecration and obedience are the essence of our lives, and where, to some degree, Satan is bound and his pernicious influence limited. When we go to the temple, we not only walk into Eden, we walk out with it.

Holiness to the Lord

Inscribed on every temple are the words *Holiness to the Lord.* This familiar phrase is somewhat enigmatic. Does it apply to the temple, the patrons, or the work that goes on inside? What exactly is "Holiness *to* the Lord?" Understanding this phrase begins with understanding the nature of holiness in its Old Testament setting. As previously discussed, the word *holiness* suggests separation. In the Old Testament, God is the

---

29 See Donald W. Parry, "Garden of Eden: Prototype Sanctuary," *Temples of the Ancient World*, ed. Donald W. Parry (Salt Lake City: Deseret Book and FARMS, 1997), 134-135.

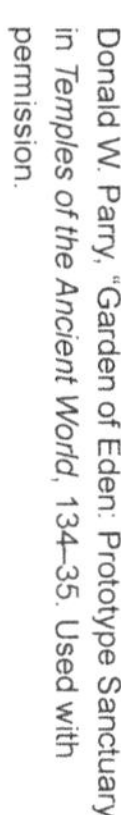

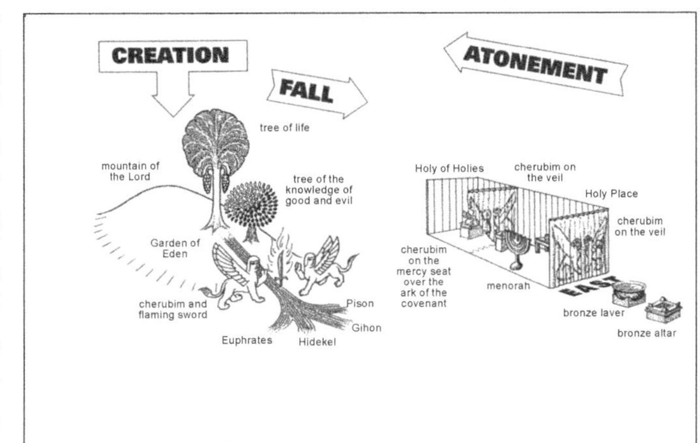

Figure 2-1. Journey of High Priest as Reversal of Fall.

embodiment of holiness. He is wholly other, wholly set apart from the world. However, His holiness can be imparted to places, things, time, and persons by anointing them with oil or by dedicating them to the Lord (i.e., setting them apart). Items also became holy when they were brought into direct contact with the temple. Places became holy by the presence of God (consider Mount Sinai or the Sacred Grove).

People became holy through three means: obedience, ritual, and contact with God. The ordinary Israelite could become more holy by obedience to God's laws, which set him apart from the world. Higher degrees of holiness were available to prophets, priests, and kings. This was done through a ritual anointing with oil and, in the case of priests and kings, by donning special clothes. The high priest was the most holy person of ancient Israel. The anointing and the sacred clothing which set him apart were more elaborate than those associated with ordinary priests.[30] Moses is a good example of a person who became holy through contact with God. After being in God's presence on Mount Sinai, Moses's face glowed with glory. This was so disconcerting to the Israelites, Moses donned a veil when speaking to them (see Exodus 34:29–35).

In the phrase "Holiness to the Lord," the word *to* can indicate different things. First, it can be directional—toward the Lord. In this

30 See David P. Wright, "Holiness," *The Anchor Bible Dictionary*, 3:238.

sense, "holiness to the Lord" is becoming more like the Lord. Second, it can convey the idea of holiness offered to the Lord. In the temple, we offer our holiness to the Lord. In other words, we offer our hearts, our talents, and our current level of righteousness to the Lord so that He might use us as He will to do His work. Third, *to* may express the idea of belonging. In Hebrew, saying something is *to* something else indicates possession. For instance, "David's house" might literally read, "the house to David." Accordingly, *holiness to the Lord* could be translated, "The Lord's holiness." When we enter into the temple, we have the singular privilege of entering not only into the Lord's house but also into His holiness. Elder Jeffrey R. Holland explains that when we participate in the sacred ordinances of the temple (as well as in sacred ordinances outside the temple like the sacrament and blessing a baby), we actually take some of God's divinity to ourselves. In other words, we take on some of His holiness.[31]

The phrase "holiness to the Lord" (or "holiness unto the Lord") occurs six times in scripture. Twice it refers to the gold plate worn by Aaron and the ancient high priests as part of their headdress. Wearing the gold plate placed Aaron in God's favor and granted him God's protection. The same may be said of those who enter the sacred building which bears the same inscription. Elder Boyd K. Packer stated, "Our labors in the temple cover us with a shield and a protection, both individually and as a people."[32] Since one of the meanings of "to be holy" is to dedicate or consecrate, this gold plate also dedicated Aaron to God. Thus, the inscription *Holiness to the Lord* on the temple dedicates the temple, all the work that goes on within it, and the patrons to the Lord.

Dressing Rooms

The dressing rooms, or changing rooms, are ultimately practical and functional. Yet even they convey an important spiritual lesson. As we change from our street clothes into white clothing, we are reminded that we are leaving the world behind. The white clothes are a symbol of purity and represent robes of righteousness. It is the color of the

---

31 See Jeffrey R. and Patricia T. Holland, *On Earth as It Is in Heaven* (Salt Lake City: Deseret Book Company, 1989), 193–194.

32 Boyd K. Packer, *The Holy Temple* (Salt Lake City: Bookcraft, 1980), 265.

clothing worn by exalted beings. Since all temple patrons—rich and poor, ordinary member and prophet of God—dress in simple white clothing, it is a reminder that God is no respecter of persons. In addition to all this, changing from our street clothes into robes of righteousness is a reminder that the temple can change our very natures. President Benson taught that the "temple ceremony was given by a wise Heavenly Father to help us become more Christlike."[33] Marion D. Hanks explains:

> What really matters is the kind of people we are, the kind of people we become as we return to the temple to serve others. . . . The mature experience of temple worship ideally has the power to produce—and sometimes does—a new and different kind of person who knows the path of principles followed by the Savior and gives them application in his or her personal life.[34]

Each time we enter the temple and change from our street clothes into the white clothing of temple worship, we are reminded of the more significant change that is to take place while we are in the temple, the change of nature.

Levels of Sacredness

The ancient temple in Jerusalem was composed of concentric circles of holiness. The outer court was the Court of the Gentiles and was the least restrictive. Jew and Gentile, men and women, moneychangers and vendors of sacrificial animals could all enter this court. The innermost court was the Holy of Holies. Only the high priest could enter this most sacred room and only once a year on the Day of Atonement. The closer one moved to the center, the more sacred the space. Many early Latter-day Saint temples reflect this concentric design with the celestial room being in the center of the temple. Levels of sacredness, in both ancient and modern temples, are expressed not only by moving inward but also by moving upward. The farther you progress, the higher you climb until you reach the celestial room, which is the highest room in the temple. Before temple films were in use, this inward and upward

33 Benson, *Teachings of Ezra Taft Benson*, 250.

34 Marion D. Hanks, "Christ Manifested to His People," *Temples of the Ancient World*, 24.

progression was literal and physical. Today, it is more subtle, but it is still present.

This journey upward and inward approximates the ascent up a mountain, an image frequently associated with temples. Many cultures of the Ancient Near East (hereafter ANE) considered a mountain the place most conducive for making contact with the divine. "With its peak reaching into the skies, it represents the closest connection in the environment between earth, the domain of humanity, and heaven, the realms of the gods."[35] Moses, Elijah, Nephi, the brother of Jared, Peter, James, John, and the Savior all had momentous spiritual experiences on a mountain. Ultimately, temples replaced mountains as the primary place to make contact with the divine.[36] Many temples were built to be a visual representation of a mountain and were even regarded as artificial mountains. Indeed, the temple of Solomon is "little more than the architectural realization and the ritual enlargement of the Sinai experience."[37]

In ancient thought, the mountain linked the three cosmic regions. It stood on the earth, its top reached into the heavens, and its base, it was believed, reached down into the subterranean waters of the underworld, or Sheol, the abode of the dead. As the point where all three regions intersected, the mountain was extremely sacred.

In our temples, the baptismal fonts are beneath the surface of the earth, symbolic of the dead who are in their graves[38] or as it might be said in the Old Testament, in Sheol, the spirit world. The endowment rooms represent our life upon the earth, and the celestial room signifies heaven, the abode of God. The temple is the place that connects all three realms. For us as well as the ancients, this point of intersection is holy ground.

The experience of climbing a mountain is much like going through the temple endowment. As we ascend a mountain, we move away from

---

35 Theodore Hiebert, "Theophany in the OT," *The Anchor Bible Dictionary,* 6:506.

36 Joseph Smith said, "The rich can only get them [the endowment keys] in the temple, the poor may get them on the mountaintop as did Moses" (quoted in Ehat, 52).

37 John M. Lundquist, "What Is a Temple? A Preliminary Typology," *Temples of the Ancient World,* 85.

38 See Joseph Fielding Smith, *Church History and Modern Revelation: A Course of Study for the Melchizedek Priesthood Quorums* (Salt Lake City: Deseret Book Company, 1949), 4:86–87.

the world toward the domain of God. This ascent grants us a new perspective. Cars, homes, businesses, and other things that dominate our physical and mental landscape become less significant. As we climb, we experience a quiet peace not present in the noisy, frantic world below. Moreover, climbing a mountain is not a casual walk through a park. It is physically demanding. It may leave us breathless and with quivering muscles. Often, it is steepest right before the summit. So it is with the temple. The covenants we make therein are increasingly demanding. Having entered into these covenants, casual obedience does not suffice. As a student once said to me, "The gospel is not a passive religion. I think we ought to break a sweat doing the best we can."[39]

The Pillars

Even a cursory glance at some of the ancient temples of the world reveals that pillars were an important part of temple architecture (see figures 2-2, 2-3). These pillars were both structural and aesthetic. Their appearance suggested grandeur, strength, and power. Pillars show up in Facsimile 1 in the Pearl of Great Price (see figure 2-4, cf. figure 2-5). The vertical lines at the bottom of the facsimile are "designed to represent the pillars of heaven, as understood by the Egyptians" (explanation figure 11). Many of the earliest tombs in Egypt had a long line of false doors flanked by square pillars. The central panel is the gate to the other world, and the pillars flanking them are the

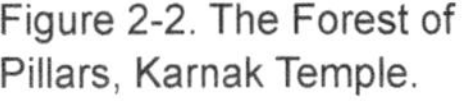

Figure 2-2. The Forest of Pillars, Karnak Temple.

Figure 2-3. Temple of Hatshepsut, Egypt.

39 Personal correspondence with Cory Fairchild, December 9, 2003.

Figure 2-4. Facsimile 1, book of Abraham.

Explanation

1. The Angel of the Lord.
2. Abraham fastened upon an altar.
3. The idolatrous priest of Elkenah attempting to offer up Abraham as a sacrifice.
4. The altar for sacrifice by the idolatrous priests, standing before the gods of Elkenah, Libnah, Mahmackrah, Korash, and Pharaoh.
5. The idolatrous god of Elkenah.
6. The idolatrous god of Libnah.
7. The idolatrous god of Mahmackrah.
8. The idolatrous god of Korash.
9. The idolatrous god of Pharaoh.
10. Abraham in Egypt.
11. Designed to represent the pillars of heaven, as understood by the Egyptians.
12. Raukeeyang, signifying expanse, or the firmament over our heads; but in this case, in relation to this subject, the Egyptians meant it to signify Shaumau, to be high, or the heavens, answering to the Hebrew word, Shaumahyeem.

Figure 2-5. Temple of Hatshepsut, Egypt.

pillars of heaven.[40] In the Pyramid Texts, "on each side [of the expanse of heaven] is a doorway that keeps out commoners and foreigners but through which the gods and the king can gain access to the sky."[41]

Solomon's temple had two magnificent and finely crafted pillars that flanked the entrance of the temple proper (see 1 Kings 7:21). These two pillars had names: Jachin, which means "He [God] shall establish," and Boaz, which means "In him [God] is strength." These pillars were symbolic rather than functional. They were made of bronze and decorated with exquisitely carved floral capitals. Since ordinary Israelites had no access into the temple, these beautiful pillars provided a visual link to the unseen grandeur within. Standing at the doorway of the temple, these pillars also marked the boundary between profane and sacred space. They mirrored the idea that one reaches God by passing through a series of doors and gates. Finally, the ancient temple was a residence for God. The pillars were the gateposts to the courtyard of God's house, the entryway into the presence of God.[42]

Today, many of our temples feature stylized pillars. In praising the beauty of the temples, President Hinckley said, "I have appreciated architectural masterpieces across this world, but I have never seen more beautiful workmanship than is found in the House of the Lord."[43] As one of the examples of fine craftsmanship, he cites the "many fluted columns with delicately carved floral pieces at their crown."[44] Such columns are stylized pillars. In the Mesa Arizona Temple, they are part of the motif and are recurrent in the celestial room. These pillars occur in pairs and are placed close together, reminding us that the path that leads to God is strait and narrow. They also remind us that temples are "the gates of heaven."[45] It is well to remember that the gate swings both ways.

---

40 See Hugh Nibley, "A New Look at the Pearl of Great Price," *Improvement Era*, September 1969, 87.

41 Gee, 235.

42 See Carol L. Meyers, "Jachin and Boaz in Religious and Political Perspective," *The Temple in Antiquity: Ancient Records and Modern Perspectives*, ed. Truman G. Madsen (Provo, Utah: Religious Studies Center, 1984), 142–143.

43 Gordon B. Hinckley, *Teachings of Gordon B. Hinckley* (Salt Lake City: Deseret Book Company, 1997), 627.

44 Ibid.

45 Franklin D. Richards, *Journal of Discourses* 25:231; quoted in Heinerman, *Temple Manifestation,* 9. See also Howard W. Hunter, 235.

There are many stories of people in the temple who have seen, felt, or heard those who have passed out of this life. Sometimes it is a relative; other times it is the person for whom the temple work is being done. A friend shared with me her experience of attending a session in the St. George temple with her mother. In the middle of the session, her mother let out a quiet but surprised, "Oh." My friend turned to her mother, who whispered, "Someone just kissed me on the cheek."[46] On one occasion while I was doing washings and anointings in the temple, the temple worker helping me shared how much she loved serving in the temple. Her husband had died a year previously, and she felt nearest to him while in the temple. She proceeded to tell me that her husband had frequently given her flowers. On their last wedding anniversary, the first since he passed away, she had walked into the washing and anointing booth and for a brief moment was overcome with the scent of roses. Stories like these abound in Church history, in temple records, and in individuals' hearts and journals. It is well to keep in mind that while they are real, they are the exception. Hugh Nibley explains:

> There have been many manifestations in the temples, but one does not expect them as the order of the day. Heavenly visitors have always been few and far between, for the purpose of our being here is to test us when we are left on our own. The founders of the dispensations have a virtual monopoly on the major visitations. And that is as it should be. One comet in a hundred years is quite adequate to prove beyond a doubt that comets really exist; it is not necessary to repeat their visitations every month.[47]

The Altar

According to the *Dictionary of Biblical Imagery*, the altar is one of the most prominent images of worship and religious allegiance in the Old Testament. Indeed, building an altar or traveling to an altar to offer sacrifices may have been the most visible sign of one's devotion to God.[48] Today, sacred altars hold a prominent place in the endowment

46 I'm indebted to Arnell Ver Hoef for sharing this experience with me.

47 Nibley, "On the Sacred and the Symbolic," 569.

48 See Leland Ryken, James C. Wilhoit, Tremper Longman III, eds. *Dictionary of Biblical Imagery* (Downers Grove, Illinois: InterVarsity Press, 1998), 20.

and sealing rooms. To understand their significance, we need to once again look to the Old Testament.

From the very beginning, altars have been associated with making covenants. The first altar mentioned in the Bible is in Genesis 8, where Noah, upon exiting the ark, builds an altar unto the Lord. God responds by establishing a covenant with Noah in which He promises that He will never again destroy all mankind with a flood. Some Jewish authorities believe Noah's altar was not the first altar. Rather, Noah rebuilds the altar that was first built by Adam but destroyed in the flood.[49] The book of Moses confirms that Adam offered sacrifices to God, and the temple teaches that his sacrifices were connected with altars and with covenants.

The next occurrence of altars we read about in the Old Testament are those built by the patriarchs. Abraham, Isaac, and Jacob built altars at places where God appeared or spoke to them. Building these altars was an act of homage and a profession of loyalty, but mostly it marked a place that had been made sacred by the presence of the divine. Later, in Exodus 29:42 we read that sacrifices were to be offered on altars at the door of the tabernacle, "where I will meet you, to speak there unto thee." Thus, altars were places of divine presence and of contact with God.

Sometimes, the patriarchs built altars at places known to be sacred to pagans. In doing so, the patriarchs deliberately claimed that spot as the God of Israel's. In these instances, building an altar was like planting a flag to claim a territory. Sometimes these claims were contested. The showdown between Elijah and the priests of Baal at the altar on Mount Carmel may reflect this. Carmel stood on the border between the kingdom of Israel and the kingdom of Tyre. In ancient thought, gods were believed to have power only in the territories of the people who worshipped them. When one crossed into another country, he passed from the territory of one god into the territory of another. Since Mount Carmel was on the border of Israel and Tyre, both peoples could have claimed that their god had dominion on this mountain. The fact that Elijah "repaired the altar of the Lord that was broken down" (1 Kings 18:31) before he could offer his bullock suggests that at one time the

49 See Kenneth A. Mathews, *The New American Commentary: Genesis 1–11:26*, vol. 1A (USA: Broadman and Holman Publishers, 2002), 391.

Israelites had claimed the territory as Yahweh's. The priests of Baal might have demolished Yahweh's altar as an assertion of the supremacy of their gods.[50]

With the construction of the tabernacle and later the temple, two altars gain prominence: the altar of incense and the altar of burnt offering.[51] The altar of incense stood in the Holy Place immediately before the veil that separated the Holy Place from the Holy of Holies. Offerings of incense were to be made at this altar twice a day, morning and evening. The smoke that ascended from the incense symbolized the prayers of the righteous ascending to God. Thus, altars are a place of prayer.

While the altar of incense stood inside the sacred temple, the altar of burnt offering was located in the courtyard in front of the tabernacle and temple. This was the altar upon which animal sacrifices were offered. Today, many people have a hard time understanding the beautiful and sacred nature of animal sacrifice. For many of us, the animals we interact with are pets not sustenance. When we eat animal flesh, we obtain it in neat little packages wrapped in cellophane. No wonder many modern people find animal sacrifice distasteful. This would not have been the case for ancient Israelites. Slaughtering an animal was no more distasteful to them than going to the grocery store is to us. Moreover, it may seem to us that the Israelites were running to the altar every day, burning up their sheep or goats.[52] That was not the case. Ordinary Israelites only ate meat occasionally as part of a rite of religious devotion or on occasions of great significance or celebration, such as the return of a prodigal son or the visit of an important guest. In cases of ritual sacrifice, a family usually presented an offering only once or twice a year on a special occasion, such as one of the three great annual feasts, like Passover, or at the birth of a child. The rarity of these

50 See Merrill, 29.

51 Some scholars consider the table of shewbread a kind of altar. The ark of the covenant could also be considered an altar inasmuch as the high priest sprinkled blood and made covenants with the Lord for all Israel on the Day of Atonement. See Bruce H. Porter, "Altar," in *Encyclopedia of Mormonism*, ed. Daniel H. Ludlow (New York: Macmillan Publishing Company, 1992), 37.

52 See Edward J. Brandt, "The Law of Moses and the Law of Christ," in *A Witness of Jesus Christ: The 1989 Sperry Symposium on the Old Testament*, ed. Richard D. Draper (Salt Lake City: Deseret Book Company, 1990), 23.

occasions made the offering of a sacrifice and the subsequent feast an occasion for great celebration and joy. In modern terms, it was much more like a Thanksgiving Day feast than a weeknight meal.

Many of us relate animal sacrifices only with offerings for sin. This keeps us from understanding the rich symbolism of sacrifices and altars. There were actually two kinds of offerings: expiatory offerings and sweet savor offerings. Expiatory offerings were to atone for sin and to satisfy justice. They were to seal one's repentance, not replace it. Ancient prophets leveled harsh denunciations at those who looked at sacrifices as a mere "get-out-of-jail-free card" (see Micah 6:6–8; Hosea 6:6). Expiatory offerings were to be accompanied with sorrow for sins and a change of heart.

Sweet savor offerings were divided into three categories: burnt offerings, cereal offerings, and peace offerings. These were voluntary offerings and were offered by one who was hungering and thirsting for greater intimacy with God. In the case of the burnt offering, the offerer would bring a prescribed animal to the altar in the forecourt of the tabernacle. He then put his hands upon the head of the animal, signifying the transfer of his identity to the animal. The animal was then slaughtered and completely burned upon the altar. This represented the complete self-surrender of one's whole soul to God.

The cereal offering (called "meat offering" in the Old Testament) was an offering of grain. However, simple grain was not acceptable; it had to be ground into fine flour. It could then be offered with oil and frankincense or made into "cakes or wafers"—pitas or tortilla-like flat bread (see Leviticus 2:4–7). Since frankincense was quite costly, the baked cereal offering was a merciful concession for the poor. The cereal offering was offered along with the burnt offering or could serve as a surrogate for the burnt offering for those who were too poor to offer up an animal.[53] A small part of the cereal offering was burned on the altar, but most of it was given to the priests. Both the burnt offering and the cereal offering represented man's devotion and commitment to God. However, the burnt offering was given directly to God, while the cereal offering was given to God indirectly; it was given to the offerer's fellowman. In other words, the burnt offering and the cereal offering

53 See Jacob Milgrom, *Leviticus 1–16*, Anchor Bible (New York: Doubleday, 1991), 182–183.

fulfill the two great commandments: loving God with all one's heart and loving one's neighbor.[54]

Peace offerings were offered on special occasions, such as births and marriages, or at times of thanksgiving. Such times might include the recovery from an illness or the safe return from a voyage or, in the case of Lehi, the safe return of his sons from their errand to get the brass plates (see 1 Nephi 5:9.) Peace offerings were performed at moments of great happiness, whatever the cause. With peace offerings, the fat was given to God and burned completely on the altar. A portion of the meat was given to the priest, and most of the meat was returned to the offerer for a feast with his family. These meals were sacred feasts with Jehovah. It was a joyful time of intimate fellowship with God and family.

The different kinds of sacrifices demonstrate that animal sacrifices were far more than restitution for sin alone. "When the three offerings—sin, burnt, and peace—were offered together, they symbolized respectively the progression from atonement through sanctification to fellowship with the Lord."[55] This progression describes man's journey back to God, one of the main lessons of the temple. While the temples of the Restoration teach the lesson spatially and didactically, sacrifices at the altar taught it experientially.

In addition to being the locus of sacrifice, an altar is a place where covenants are made and sealed. In today's world, when we want to seal an agreement, we shake hands or sign our name on a contract. In the ancient world, a covenant was sealed by the shedding of blood or, in other words, with a sacrifice. Offering a sacrifice may have entailed first building an altar upon which to perform that sacrifice. After receiving the covenant on Mount Sinai, Moses performed several ritual actions, including building an altar and offering burnt offerings and peace offerings unto the Lord (see Exodus 24). The covenant was

54 It is noteworthy that although the cereal offering was to benefit man, it was offered to God. Herein is an essential distinction. If our labor, love, and service for our fellow man are offered to God, it doesn't matter if our offering is slighted, misunderstood, or even rejected. It is accepted by Him to whom we offer it. We can continue in our labor unmiffed and undeterred.

55 M. Catherine Thomas, "The Sermon on the Mount: The Sacrifice of the Human Heart," *Studies in Scripture*, vol. 5: *The Gospels*, eds. Kent P. Jackson and Robert Millet (Salt Lake City: Deseret Book Company, 1986), 5:241.

then considered ratified and binding. In this instance, Moses also took the blood of the sacrifice and sprinkled it on the altar and then on the people. This did at least two things. First, it showed that both God and the people were mutually bound by the covenant—God to support and defend the people, the people to love and obey God. Second, it identified the people with the sacrificed animal. If they failed to live up to their covenants, they might expect the same fate that met the animal. This was a common feature of Ancient Near Eastern covenants. Another part of the Sinai covenant ceremony was a covenant meal. Moses, Aaron, Nadab and Abihu (two of Aaron's sons), and seventy elders of Israel ascended Mount Sinai, where "they saw God, and did eat and drink" (Exodus 24:11). This meal further ratified or sealed the covenant. This, too, is related to the altar, for the altar is the table of the Lord (see Malachi 1:7). Animals that were placed upon the altar were the main course of the meal of fellowship shared by God and the offerer.

Seeing the altar in its Old Testament context allows us a deeper understanding of the altars in the temple. For both ancient and Latter-day Saints, the altar is the place for making and sealing covenants, the place of God's presence, the place of prayer, and the place of sacrifice. The altar is the place where we offer up our whole souls to God as we strive for greater intimacy and devotion. It is the place where our will is completely consumed by the fire of obedience and consecration. It is the place where we allow God to be sovereign in our lives, to rule and reign in our hearts. It is the place where we offer up our talents and our time. We lay them on the altar and trust that God will do so much more with them than we could ever do on our own. It is where the sacred ordinance of marriage is performed, reminding us that a successful eternal marriage must include personal sacrifice and the putting to death of the natural man, the individual, and the ego. Only then will we be able to fully become one as a couple. Indeed, the altar is a most sacred place inside the holy temples.

The Veil

There are several veils in the temple: physical veils, the veil depicted in the film, even the veil which is not shown but is represented symbolically by the deep sleep into which Adam falls (see Genesis 2:21). In general, a veil symbolizes darkness, a pre-enlightened state, separation, and concealment. Passing the veil denotes degrees of initiation and gaining esoteric knowledge.[56] In terms of the temple, the most important symbols associated with the veil are those of separation, boundaries, and atonement.

The veil is an object of separation. "The veil keeps the first, second, and third estates separate."[57] This separation is both physical and intellectual. That means we, like Adam, have a veil of forgetfulness so that we don't remember our premortal existence. We don't remember our former home, the particulars of our relationships, or even what we agreed to do in this life. Just as the veil conceals our hindsight, it obscures our vision of the future as well. We can barely conceive of the future glories that await the faithful. Brigham Young said, "If that dissatisfied wife could behold the transcendent beauty of person, the godlike qualities of the resurrected husband that she now despises, her love for him would be unbounded and unutterable."[58] The veil also blurs our awareness of God's great love. As Paul Cox has said, "This 'mortal middle' is the only period in our entire existence in which we can live under the illusion that we are not surrounded by love."[59] However, this "partition is a veil rather than a wall, to show that it is not absolutely impenetrable and that messengers can pass through it, that dim sights and distant sounds might be detected, that we are not wholly cut off from our heavenly home unless we choose to be."[60] This is especially true of God's love, which can only be filtered, not occluded.

The veil is the boundary and divider between earth and heaven, time and eternity. It marks "the point or act of transition between man's sublunary [terrestrial] life and the vast open reaches of the immensity of space beyond, into which one passes by passing through that veil."[61] The

---

56 See Cooper, 184.

57 Neal A. Maxwell, *All These Things Shall Give Thee Experience* (Salt Lake City: Deseret Book Company, 1979), 11.

58 Brigham Young, *Discourse of Brigham Young,* October 8, 1861; quoted in Madsen and Covey, *Marriage and Family: Gospel Insights* (Salt Lake City: Bookcraft, 1983).

59 Paul Alan Cox, "Seeing with New Eyes," *Brigham Young University 1995–96 Speeches*, (Provo, Utah: Brigham Young University, 1996), 45.

60 Hugh Nibley, "On the Sacred and the Symbolic," 574.

61 Hugh Nibley, "The Early Christian Prayer Circle," *CWHN*, 4:73.

veil is a cosmic gate to the worlds beyond, a spirit door. As such, it is a place of testing. "All temples are marked by boundaries, stations, levels, doors, stairs, passages, gates, veils, etc. . . . At certain crucial passages one must identify oneself by an exchange of names and tokens and show oneself qualified by an exchange of words. This was characteristic of all ancient temples."[62] Hugh Nibley says that "the most sacred of the temple ceremonies were performed in front of this so-called spirit door"[63] and that the veil is "the place . . . to establish the identity and bona fides of one who wishes to pass."[64]

In the ancient temple in Jerusalem, a veil separated the Holy Place from the Holies of Holies.[65] This veil marked the point past which no man could go (except the high priest on the Day of Atonement). Since the ark within the Holy of Holies symbolized God's presence, the veil was the place where man and God met. The veil was made of a blend of blue, purple, and red wools and fine-twined white linen. According to Josephus, the four colors represented the four elements from which the earth was created: air (blue), fire (red or scarlet), water or the sea (purple, a color made from seashells), and earth (white, the color of the linen which had grown from the earth).[66] These colored threads were used to either embroider or weave designs of cherubim into the fabric of the veil. Cherubim are attested in the ANE as the "guardians of the sacred and of the threshold."[67] The Talmud says that this veil was sixty feet long, thirty feet high, and the thickness of the palm of the hand, making it extremely heavy.

In the book of Hebrews, we are told that the veil of the temple is the flesh of Christ (see Hebrews 10:20). This is significant for at least two reasons. First, "when in the endowment one ceremonially acts out his or her ascent back to God, at the final stages it is Christ who stands

62 Hugh Nibley, "A House of Glory," *Temples of the Ancient World*, 37–38.

63 Hugh Nibley, "On the Sacred and the Symbolic," 573.

64 Ibid., 574.

65 There was also a veil that hung between the porch of the temple and the Holy Place. It was made of the same material as the veil before the Holy of Holies except there were no angels upon it.

66 See Margaret Barker, *The Revelation of Jesus Christ* (London: T & T Clark, 2000), 20.

67 Cooper, 34.

between the patron and the Father."[68] Second, we need to remember that at the death of Christ, the veil of the temple was rent. The privilege to enter into the Holy of Holies was no longer restricted to the high priest of Israel or even to those who adhered to the Mosaic ordinances. Now believers of all nations could enter "into the highest and holiest of all places, that kingdom where eternal life is found."[69] Just as the veil of the temple was rent, even so Roman soldiers rent or pierced Christ's flesh with a spear. As a resurrected being, Christ retained these marks of violent death. They became tokens to prove to disciples on both hemispheres that He was the risen Christ. These marks evidence the immense cost of entering into God's presence.

Finally, the veil is a place of atonement. Hugh Nibley explains, "The Lord parted [the veil] to grant the people atonement after they had performed all the ordinances necessary on the Day of Atonement. . . . That was when He greeted them and claimed that He was one with them."[70]

Elsewhere Nibley explains:

> The basic word for atonement is *kaphar,* which has the same basic meaning in Hebrew, Aramaic, and Arabic, that being 'to bend, arch over, cover.' . . . The Arabic *kafara* puts the emphasis on a tight squeeze, such as tucking in the skirts, drawing a thing close to one's self. Closely related are Aramaic and Arabic *kafat,* meaning a close embrace, which are certainly related to the Egyptian *hpet*, the common ritual embrace written with the ideogram of embracing arms. It may be cognate with the Latin *capto*, and from it comes the Persian *kaftan*, a monk's robe and hood completely embracing the body. Most interesting is the Arabic *kafata*, as it is the key to a dramatic situation.
>
> It was the custom for one fleeing for his life in the desert to seek protection in the tent of a great sheik,

68 Alonzo L. Gaskill, *The Savior & the Serpent: Unlocking the Doctrine of the Fall* (Salt Lake City: Deseret Book Company, 2005), 90.

69 Bruce R. McConkie, *Doctrinal New Testament Commentary* (Salt Lake City: Bookcraft, 1974), 1:830.

70 Hugh W. Nibley, *Teachings of the Book of Mormon* (Provo, Utah: FARMS, 1993), 1:253.

> crying out, "Ana dakhiluka," meaning "I am thy suppliant," whereupon the Lord would place the hem of his robe over the guest's shoulder and declare him under his protection. . . . They embrace in a close hug, as Arab chiefs still do; the Lord makes a place for him and invites him to sit down beside him—they are at—*one.*[71]

That embrace also shows up in Greek drama, which "is bathed in religion."[72] In Greek recognition drama, "the embrace is the immediate seal of recognition and love when the identity of the tested party has been proved. . . . [It is] the outward token of the inward meshing of souls."[73] It is perhaps because of this close connection between the veil, atonement, and the embrace that "the Holy of Holies in the temple is called in Hebrew the *bet ha kapporet,* the house or room of the atonement, or the house or room of the embrace, the place where the presence of God is."[74]

Celestial Room

The pinnacle of the temple is the celestial room. Invariably, celestial rooms are beautiful and elegant. They have chandeliers that bathe the room in light. They are decorated with tasteful but understated elegance. They are places of rest and peace. The feeling in the celestial room is one of reverence and holy serenity, as well it should be, for this room "was created to represent the celestial kingdom."[75] First-time temple patrons and visitors at open houses are often awestruck by both the beauty and the spirit that is in the celestial room. As one four-year-old said at the open house of the Las Vegas temple, "Where is Heavenly Father? I felt Him there, but I couldn't see Him."[76] A woman from the highlands of Guatemala entered into the celestial room of the Guatemala temple, fell to her knees, bowed her head, and

71 Nibley, "The Meaning of the Atonement," *CWHN*, 9:558–559.

72 Todd M. Compton, "The Handclasp and Embrace as Tokens of Recognition," *By Study and Also By Faith*, eds. John M. Lundquist and Stephen D. Ricks (Salt Lake City and Provo, Utah: Deseret Book Company and FARMS, 1990), 1:611.

73 Ibid., 625.

74 M. Catherine Thomas, "Zion and the Spirit of At-one-ment," *FARMS Book of Mormon Lecture Series,* transcript (Provo, Utah: FARMS, 1994), 7.

75 Gordon B. Hinckley, "Closing Remarks," *Ensign*, November 2004, 105.

76 "Temple Open House Exceeds Hopes," *Church News*, December 2, 1989.

sobbed. For twenty minutes, she poured out her heart to her Father in Heaven. When she finally raised her head, a sensitive temple matron asked her if she could help. "She responded, 'Oh, would you? This is my problem: I've tried to tell Father in Heaven of my gratitude for all of my blessings, but I don't feel that I've communicated. Will you help me tell Him how grateful I am?'"[77]

In the 2004 October conference, President Hinckley remarked:

> When the Mesa Arizona Temple was extensively renovated some years ago and was opened for public tours, one visitor described the celestial room as God's living room. So it well might be. It is our privilege, unique and exclusive, while dressed in white, to sit at the conclusion of our ordinance work in the beautiful celestial room and ponder, meditate, and silently pray.[78]

In this statement, President Hinckley alludes to two important aspects of the celestial room. First, we enter the celestial room at the conclusion of our ordinance work. This evokes the image of the celestial room as a place of rest. It is the top of the mountain of the Lord, the place where we can rest after a grueling ascent and a long journey. But this rest is more than just a cessation of labor. We enter into "the rest of the Lord." This phrase has several meanings. From a temporal perspective, it means being at spiritual peace even while living in a troubled and turbulent world. In the eternal perspective, this phrase designates receiving the highest blessings of the priesthood and exaltation. It also means being justified or standing approved before God. Finally, "entering into the rest of the Lord" can mean being in the presence of the Lord even while we are still mortal.

A second aspect mentioned in President Hinckley's statement is the celestial room being the living room of God. This points to the sweet intimacy and fellowship that is possible for those who have done all that is required to enter into the celestial room. It is a sublime truth that "God desires to be as intimately present as possible" in the lives of His people.[79] This desire may be as much for God's sake as for ours.[80] He

77 Richard G. Scott, "Learning to Recognize Answers to Prayer," *Ensign*, November 1989, 32.

78 Hinckley, "Closing Remarks," 105.

79 Terence E. Fretheim, *The Suffering of God* (Philadelphia: Fortress Press, 1984), 65.

80 See ibid., 63.

is our loving Father and as such desires our association. Of course, too much association would interfere with the purpose of mortality. So that we might enjoy as much association as possible within the testing and training purposes of mortality, God has set aside times and places for intimate fellowship. Our regular Sunday worship with the sacred ordinance of the sacrament is one of those. Prayer is another. Our time in the temple is an especially concentrated time for us to experience intimate fellowship with God.

The ancient counterpart to the celestial room is the Holy of Holies. The name, the shape, and the symbolism of the Holy of Holies all affirmed its supreme holiness. In Hebrew, one of the ways to declare a superlative is to repeat a word. When Isaiah saw God sitting upon his heavenly throne, he heard the seraphim praise God with not two but three cries of holiness: "Holy, holy, holy, is the Lord of hosts" (Isaiah 6:3). This was the seraphim's way of saying the Lord of Hosts is the holiest of all, in all ways, to every degree. Another way to note a superlative is to juxtapose a singular noun with its plural form. Thus, *Holy of Holies* means the most holy of all places. The ancient Holy of Holies was a perfect cube. A cube symbolizes perfection, completion, stability, and eternal truth. The holiness and perfection of the Holy of Holies is magnified by the fact that it was the center of the concentric circles of holiness of the temple complex.[81] The center symbolized sacred space, absolute reality, pure being, and the origin of all existence. It was "the point containing the totality of all possibilities."[82] A journey to the center was a journey into sacred space and the point of reconciliation, a journey to God. The celestial rooms in our temples retain these associations.

The Holy of Holies was considered the throne room of God. In ancient Israel, as well as in most other ancient cultures, there was no separation of church and state. Therefore, it is not surprising that the

81 The concentric circles of holiness actually extended beyond the temple to Jerusalem then to the land of Israel. A Midrashic passage explains, "The land of Israel is found at the center of the world. Jerusalem is at the center of the land of Israel, and the Temple is at the center of Jerusalem, the Holy of Holies is at the center of the Temple, the Ark is at the center of the Holy of Holies." *Midrash Tanhuma, Kedoshim 10*, quoted in John Lundquist, "The Common Temple Ideology of the Ancient Near East," in *The Temple in Antiquity: Ancient Records and Modern Perspectives*, ed. Truman G. Madsen (Provo, Utah: Religious Studies Center Brigham Young University, 1984), 65.

82 Cooper, 32.

temple was considered the palace of God.[83] The Holy of Holies was the throne room within the palace, and the ark of the covenant that sat within was the throne of God, or more probably, the footstool beneath the invisible throne.[84]

Thinking of the celestial room as the throne room of God gives meaning to Doctrine and Covenants 93:1: "Verily, thus saith the Lord: It shall come to pass that every soul who forsaketh his sins and cometh unto me, and calleth on my name and obeyeth my voice and keepeth my commandments shall see my face and know that I am." The phrase "shall see my face" has royal overtones. Anciently, petitioners sought an audience with the king in order to present their cases or to seek his counsel, especially in times of danger or disaster. The technical expression for entering into the king's presence to obtain counsel, judgment, or succor was "to see the face of the king."[85] It was a sign of favor and privilege to be granted an interview with a king. Those who were privileged to see the face of the king on a regular basis were the members of his inner circle. Today, worthy members of the Church have unlimited access to the throne room of God. In the celestial room, we can listen for the Spirit to convey counsel from God, especially in times of trouble. We may present our cases, the troubles of our heart, to God. The more regularly we enter the celestial room, the more we can be said to be members of God's inner circle.

The celestial room is not only a throne room; it is a banquet room. In Isaiah 25:6 we read, "And in this mountain [the temple] shall the Lord of hosts make unto all people a feast of fat things, a feast of wine on the lees, of fat things full of marrow, of wine on the lees well refined." This is a description of a rich, lavish feast replete with all the best foods imaginable. "Wine on the lees" was the best wine. "Fat things full of marrow" is a picture of nourishment. To a people who did not have to worry about cholesterol, the fat portions of the meat were the best. These were the portions of the sacrifices reserved for God. But here God is giving His portion to the people who were in the temple, perhaps indicative of their new status.

---

83 In Hebrew, the word for *temple* is *hekal*, but it can just as well be translated as *palace*.

84 C. L. Seow, "Ark of the Covenant," *The Anchor Bible Dictionary*, 1:389.

85 Nahum Sarna, *On the Book of Psalms: Exploring the Prayers of Ancient Israel* (New York: Schocken Books, 1993), 125.

To enter into the celestial room is to be a guest at a covenant meal. As explained previously, the covenant meal was one way to seal or ratify a covenant. For ancient Israelites, this meal was tangible and literal. When an offerer brought a sacrifice to the altar, he returned with most of the meat and enjoyed a feast with his family. The sacrament seals the renewal of our baptismal covenants. The small piece of bread and tiny cup of water are tokens of the covenant meal. The feast in the celestial room seals the covenants just made in the endowment ceremony. There is no literal meal or even tokens of the meal. Here the feast is wholly spiritual.

Anciently, sharing a meal did more than seal a covenant. Eating together had important social significance. Even today, people go out to eat with friends to strengthen bonds of friendship. They eat with business associates to strengthen relationships in the business world or to close business deals, which are secular covenants. Families eat together not only for nourishment but to nourish feelings of familial love and belonging. So important is eating together that President Ezra Taft Benson included eating meals together as one of the ten points of counsel he gave to mothers in Zion in a Church-wide fireside for parents.[86] The act of eating together implies a close relationship of trust, a strong bond of affection, and enduring friendship. People who do not wish to be intimately related do not eat together. To enter into the celestial-banquet room is to feast with God and to strengthen the bonds of fellowship and love.

"Anciently to invite a person to a meal was to extend an honor. It was an offer of peace, trust, brotherhood, and forgiveness."[87] It also established a bond of protection. When a man takes refuge in another's house and shares a meal with the owner, the owner of that house must defend his guest at any cost, even with his life. One American who was entertained by an important Mideastern host was given a piece of roast mutton. The host asked the American if he understood the significance of this act. Answering his own question, the host stated, "By that act I have pledged you every drop of my blood, that while you are in my territory, no evil shall come to you. For that space of time we

86 See Ezra Taft Benson, *Come, Listen to a Prophet's Voice* (Salt Lake City: Deseret Book Company, 1990), 33.

87 Richard Neitzel Holzapfel, *A Lively Hope: The Suffering, Death, Resurrection, and Exaltation of Jesus Christ* (Salt Lake City: Bookcraft, 1999), 131.

are brothers."[88] Sharing a meal effected a change in status. It marked the transformation of an enemy into a friend, an ordinary person into a covenant partner, and a guest into a member of the family. That we are invited into the celestial room to share a feast with the Lord is no small thing. It is an honor of incalculable proportions.

Finally, the banquet is an image of the eschatological feast, or the feast of the end times. Jewish tradition has long held that the millennial kingdom of God would be ushered in by a great feast. This Messianic banquet is mentioned in Doctrine and Covenants 27, "For the hour cometh that I will drink of the fruit of the vine with you on the earth, and with Moroni" (v. 5). Also invited to this feast are John the Baptist, Elijah, Abraham, Isaac, Jacob, Joseph, Michael or Adam, Peter, James, John, and "all those whom my Father hath given me out of the world" (v. 14). The food served at this feast is the fruit of the tree of life, living water, and the bread of life—in other words, foods that grant eternal life. This banquet is sometimes represented as a wedding banquet or as a victory banquet where warriors gather to celebrate the victory of the Messiah, their new king. The noncanonical book of 1 Enoch states that those who are invited to this feast are "the righteous and elect ones. . . . [They] shall eat and rest and rise with that Son of Man forever and ever."[89] To enter into the celestial room of our temples is to claim a place or make a reservation at this glorious, future banquet. It is to participate in a preview of the victory celebration over the powers of darkness. It is to sup with the Lord and to declare our allegiance to Him as our king. It is to be a candidate for exaltation. It is to remind us of all these glorious possibilities.

---

88 H. Clay Trumbull, *Studies in Oriental Social Life Philadelphia: The Sunday School Times Co., 1984*; quoted in Fred H. Wight, *Manners and Customs of Bible Lands* (Chicago: Moody Press, 1979), 78.

89 1 Enoch 62:12–14. Dennis E. Smith, "Messianic Banquet," *The Anchor Bible Dictionary*, 4:789.

Understanding the Metaphorical and Symbolic Lessons of the Temple Drama

One of the great challenges of understanding the scriptures is discerning what is literal and what is figurative. Indeed, grave misunderstandings have occurred by erring in both directions. For instance, many in the Christian world accept the doctrine of the Trinity, believing that when Christ said, "I am in the Father, and the Father in me" (John 14:10), He was speaking literally. Catholics believe in a literal reading of Christ's words "Take, eat; this is my body" (Matthew 26:26), resulting in the doctrine of transubstantiation. On the other hand, many believe that the blood that oozed from the Savior's pores in Gethsemane was figurative, diminishing the suffering of Christ. Many in today's world believe that Satan and hell are mere figures of speech.

Discerning between literal and figurative is not a new challenge. Disciples at the time of Christ struggled with it. Nicodemus was baffled about how he could be literally, physically born again. When Christ offered the Samaritan woman living water, she thought of palpable water. When Jesus said, "Destroy this temple, and in three days I will raise it up" (John 2:19), people thought of the concrete temple in Jerusalem, Herod's temple. When Jesus declared He came from the Father, they could not understand how literal and true that was. The ambiguity regarding the literal and figurative is especially relevant to Genesis 1–3, the story of the Creation and the Fall.

The account of the Creation was never intended to be a scientific one that accords with the laws of astrophysics as we now understand them. Indeed, such an account would have been bizarre, totally incomprehensible, and even incorrect to ancient people who had very different paradigms for nature's laws. Rather, the Creation account is true in the sense that it teaches spiritual truths. It is like a poetic treatment of a sunset, which "is scientifically neither true nor untrue. It needs no harmonization with scientific theories and requires no scientific confirmation."[1] Insisting on a literal interpretation of the Creation not only sets up an irreconcilable discrepancy between science and religion, it also presupposes an "intention that is not there. In so doing, it misses the symbolic richness and spiritual power of what *is* there."[2]

The same is true of the Fall. How literal is the story of the Garden of Eden? We have prophetic statements that affirm certain aspects are definitely figurative. President Kimball stated emphatically, "The story of the rib, of course, is figurative."[3] Regarding Genesis 2:7, "And the Lord God formed man of the dust of the ground," Brigham Young asserted that Adam "was not fashioned from earth like an adobe, but begotten by his Father in Heaven."[4] Bruce R. McConkie declared: "The account [of the Fall] is speaking figuratively. What is meant by partaking of the fruit of the tree of the knowledge of good and evil is

1 Conrad Hyers, *The Meaning of Creation: Genesis and Modern Science* (Atlanta: John Knox Press, 1984), 28.

2 Ibid., 28–29.

3 Spencer W. Kimball, "The Blessings and Responsibilities of Womanhood," *Woman* (Salt Lake City: Deseret Book Company, 1988), 79.

4 Joseph Fielding Smith, *Man, His Origin and Destiny* (Salt Lake City: Deseret Book Company, 1954), 344. Some may wonder about Brigham Young's statement that Adam was begotten by his Father in Heaven when we speak of Jesus Christ as being the Only Begotten of the Father. Robert J. Matthews explains: "In the gospel of Jesus Christ the human family is at the pinnacle of dignity, because the first man and the first woman—Adam and Eve—were the direct and first-generation literal offspring of Heavenly Parents both in the spirit body and in the physical body. The human family is literally, in every sense, the offspring of God" (Robert J. Matthews, "The Origin of Man," in *Riches of Eternity: 12 Fundamental Doctrines from the Doctrine and Covenants,* eds. John K Challis and John G. Scott [Salt Lake City: Aspen Books, 1993], 23). Matthews quotes Elder Bruce R. McConkie commenting on Luke 3:38, which says that Adam is the son of God. Elder McConkie states, "Father Adam came, as indicated, to this sphere, gaining an immortal body, because death had not yet entered the world (2 Nephi 2:22). Jesus, on the other hand, was the Only Begotten in the flesh, meaning into a world of mortality where death already reigned" (Bruce R. McConkie, *Doctrinal New Testament Commentary*, 1:95, quoted in Matthews, 25).

that our first parents complied with whatever laws were involved so that their bodies would change from their state of paradisiacal immortality to a state of natural mortality."[5]

It may well be that the tree of knowledge of good and evil and the tree of life are also figurative. "Knowledge of good and evil" indicates moral autonomy and free agency. It is also a merism, a figure of speech in which the opposite ends of a spectrum are used to represent everything that is in between. For instance, "young and old" is a merism that means all people. "Heaven and earth" indicates all creation. "Night and day" denotes all the time, continually. Thus, "the knowledge of good and evil" means a knowledge of all things, or the totality of mortal experience. In addition, the word for knowledge in Hebrew is *yādaʿ*, which means to know by experience. This implies a kind of knowledge that is gained by firsthand experience. All this supports the idea that the tree of knowledge of good and evil is the tree of mortal experience or mortality.

Similarly, the tree of life is more than a tree. It is the symbolic representation of Jesus Christ. In 1 Nephi 11:4, the Spirit asks Nephi if he believes in the tree that his father saw. When Nephi says that he does, the Spirit cries out, "Blessed art thou, Nephi, because thou believest in the Son of the most high God" (1 Nephi 11:6), thus equating the tree with Jesus Christ. Robert Millet reflects:

> Why did the angel not ask Nephi if he believed that his father had seen a large and spacious building, or mists of darkness, or a strait and narrow path, or a rod of iron? The fact is, faith is not exercised in trees, and the Spirit of the Lord was not simply inquiring into Nephi's knowledge of a form of plant life. Indeed, it was not a belief in the tree which would qualify Nephi for the manifestation to follow; nor was this the concern of the Spirit. The tree was obviously a doctrinal symbol, a "sign" which pointed beyond itself to an even greater reality. Yet the tree was of marvelous importance, for it was the symbol, even from the time of the Edenic paradise, of the central and saving role of Jesus Christ

---

5 Bruce R. McConkie, "Christ and the Creation," *Ensign*, June 1982, 15.

> and the glorified immortality to be enjoyed by the faithful through his atoning sacrifice.[6]

It is unclear if some elements of the story of Eden are figurative or literal. Did a serpent actually tempt Eve, or is the serpent a personification of Satan and a symbolic warning of the life-threatening danger of sin? In this instance, the answer "matters little. Neither point of view changes or tampers with the integrity of the story."[7]

There are some points, however, that are absolute and unequivocal. Characterizing them as figurative would indeed tamper with the integrity of the story. Adam was real. Eve was real. The Fall was real. If not, the Atonement would not be necessary and the role of Jesus Christ is diminished. "What, then, do we conclude of the Eden story? Was it figurative or literal? We answer by way of comparison. It, like the temple ceremony, combines a rich blend of both."[8] The covenants we enter into in the temple are real. The blessings that accompany those covenants are real, "yet the teaching device may be metaphorical."[9] Alonso Gaskill said it this way:

> One major stumbling block in efforts to correctly understand this sacred and foreordained event is the tendency for many to interpret the story of Adam and Eve (as given in scripture and the temple) as a historical account. True, Adam and Eve existed as real people. There was indeed a garden in which they dwelt. They had interactions with God and Christ during their time there. . . . But the vast majority of what is related in scripture and ritual regarding these two is conveyed in metaphorical or symbolic language. . . . Inasmuch as the events surrounding the Fall are told in figurative language, the words in the scriptural and temple accounts

6 Robert L. Millet, "Another Testament of Jesus Christ," *The Book of Mormon: First Nephi, the Doctrinal Foundation*, eds. Monte S. Nyman and Charles D. Tate, Jr (Provo, Utah: Religious Studies Center Brigham Young University, 1988), 170.

7 Joseph Fielding McConkie, "The Mystery of Eden," *The Man Adam*, eds. Joseph Fielding McConkie and Robert L. Millet (Salt Lake City: Bookcraft, 1990), 29.

8 Ibid., 29.

9 Ibid., 29.

have been "deliberately chosen" to teach us "more than what is seen on the surface."[10]

Hugh Nibley expresses the same opinion. In *The Message of the Joseph Smith Papyri*, he writes, "The Mormon endowment . . . is frankly a model, a presentation in figurative terms. . . . It does not attempt to be a picture of reality, but only a model, . . . setting forth the pattern of man's life on earth with its fundamental whys and wherefores."[11]

As we contemplate the accounts of the Creation and the Fall, the essential issue is not what is real and what is metaphorical. Rather, what is at stake is discerning what these accounts teach us about the nature of God and the nature of man, about our mortal existence and our eternal destiny. The remainder of this chapter is dedicated to examining the accounts of the Creation and Fall in these terms. The interpretations are not exhaustive or definitive; they are a sampling. They are examples of what to look for and how to think. Their purpose is to be a springboard for your own discovery. We will limit our discussion to the accounts in Genesis and the Pearl of Great Price. There are some variations between these and the temple account, but since our purpose is to explore ways to think and learn, the differences are inconsequential.

The Creation of the Earth

If we were to designate a name for the origins of the earth in terms of the first verses of Genesis, "Big Splash" would be far more appropriate than "Big Bang."[12] According to Genesis 1:2, at the dawn of creation, the earth is a watery chaos shrouded in darkness. It is also "without form and void." This is an enigmatic translation of the Hebrew phrase *tōhû wābōhû*. *Tōhû* is used in the Old Testament to describe a desert or a wilderness but not just an ordinary wilderness. It is a grim desert waste that brings destruction (see Deuteronomy 32:10), the waste where man perishes (see Job 6:18), and a desolate waste where people wander (see Psalm 107:40). In some passages it denotes nothingness, but the idea is not that of nonbeing but of futility and the lack of

10 Gaskill, 21.

11 Hugh Nibley, *The Message of the Joseph Smith Papyri: An Egyptian Endowment*, eds. John Gee and Michael D. Rhodes (Salt Lake City and Provo, Utah: Deseret Book Company and FARMS, 2005), xxix.

12 Hyers, 39.

meaningful existence.[13] The *wā* in *tōhû wābōhû* is "and." *Bōhû* is used only three times in the Old Testament and always with *tōhû*. It means "emptiness." This phrase, along with the darkness that often represents whatever jeopardizes life, paints a picture of an earth that is incapable of sustaining life. Since the earth was created to sustain and support life, it was not yet capable of fulfilling its foreordained purpose. This parallels the condition of fallen man, the man who has not been spiritually awakened, who is spiritually dormant. The conditions that characterize fallen man are hunger or spiritual emptiness and "the feeling of darkness or spiritual twilight."[14] Fallen man is not necessarily bad or evil; he is simply in a natural state. Like sugarcane in its raw condition, he needs refining to be useful. He is not yet capable of fulfilling the purpose of his existence. But the earth and fallen man are both at the beginning of their creation. God is not yet finished.

Genesis 1:2 tells us that the Spirit of God "moved upon" the watery darkness. Instead of "moved upon," Abraham 4:2 says the Spirit was "brooding." Brooding describes the action of a bird as she sits upon her eggs in her nest. The bird is preparing to sustain life. It may be compared to the nesting instinct an expectant mother feels that compels her to prepare a nursery for her baby. Brooding also connotes the passage of a long time. Eggs do not hatch overnight. Day after day, a mother bird sits on her eggs, sustaining the perfect conditions for life to eventually flourish.[15] The mother bird in this instance is the Spirit of God (Genesis 1:2), which Elder Bruce R. McConkie identifies as the Light of Christ.[16] The light of Christ performs the same preparatory function with individuals as the mother bird does for her eggs. It effects the perfect conditions for spiritual life to eventually flourish. The light of Christ prepares people to receive the witness of the Holy Ghost, which is followed by the more constant gift of the Holy Ghost. The light of Christ can brood over individuals, nations, and even continents. When

---

13 See Claus Westermann, *Genesis 1–11: A Commentary*, trans. John J. Scullion (Minneapolis: Augsburg Publishing House, 1984), 102–103.

14 M. Catherine Thomas, "Alma the Younger," part 2, *FARMS Book of Mormon Lecture Series*, transcript (Provo, Utah: FARMS, 1994), 4.

15 See Hugh Nibley, "Before Adam," *CWHN*, 1:69.

16 See Bruce R. McConkie, *A New Witness for the Articles of Faith* (Salt Lake City: Deseret Book, 1985), 258.

President James Faust was visiting Africa in 1992, he stated, "The Spirit of the Lord is brooding over Africa."[17] Just over ten years later, in October conference of 2003, President Hinckley reviewed the growth of the Church and stated, "We are firmly established in Africa."[18]

Most missionaries have encountered dramatic examples of the Spirit preparing people to hear and receive the gospel. This brooding may show up in a variety of ways, from dreams to tragedies to a surprising series of "coincidences." Our son, Blake, while serving as a missionary in Argentina, shared this experience in a letter:

> We went to another apartment complex, and after getting rejected several times over a talk box, I "accidentally" slid my hand over all forty or so buttons in hopes that someone would be interested. At that very moment, two people who actually had a key to the building asked us to step aside so they could enter. I barely opened my mouth to talk to this couple before they rejected us in the most rude form, using words I dared not teach my companion. We just laughed it off, and I turned to talk to a family that had just walked by me while Elder Price attended the talk box. After the family declined my invitation to have the gospel bless their lives, I turned back around to Elder Price. He explained to me that as I was talking to the family, a voice came over the talk box and said "Elders?" Elder Price, in a stunned voice explained that he couldn't understand what the man was saying due to the extremely poor condition of the talk box. The voice in the talk box agreed to come down to the front door. It turns out that Miguel heard his intercom click on while he was sitting in his apartment. Before he could get up to answer it, he heard the whole conversation we had with those two people who so rudely rejected us. Due to the nature of the conversation, he realized that we were the missionaries.

---

17 James E. Faust, "Mission Presidents Conference," Nairobi, Kenya, November 10–11, 1992, quoted in Robert L. Mercer, "Pioneers in Ivory Coast," *Liahona*, March 1999, 16.

18 Gordon B. Hinckley, "The State of the Church," *Ensign*, November 2003, 5.

> Miguel has been inactive from the Church for more than four years but about a month ago decided to give the Book of Mormon another crack. As we taught Miguel, he really opened up to us. He told us that it was his birthday eight days ago, and as he was alone in his apartment, he made his birthday wish to God. He wanted to know if God really did listen to him and if He could really answer his prayers. In a sweet closing prayer, Miguel himself told God that he knew that God listens to him and that his prayer had been answered and that he will be returning to the Church.[19]

Such is the brooding of the Spirit in the lives of individuals.

After the Spirit has sufficiently brooded and prepared the earth, God introduces light. With light also comes its opposite, darkness. The existence of both light and darkness, day and night, is more than the pattern of the earth's twenty-four-hour period. It is the pattern for man. Light and darkness are mutually exclusive. We can have light or darkness but not both. How true this is in the case of spiritual light. We can't walk in darkness and in light. Whenever light is introduced, man must make a choice.

God's next action in Genesis is to place a firmament in the midst of the waters. A firmament is a vast expanse. In Hebrew, the word for *firmament* is *rāqīa'* and comes from the root *rq'*, meaning "to beat, stamp, beat out, to spread out." Literally, a firmament is "a pounded out thing." The idea is of a piece of metal that has been beaten out and formed into a bowl. In ancient thought, this bowl fit upside down over the rectangle called earth "like a cosmic version of a domed stadium."[20] This firmament has sluice gates, called windows of heaven, through which water, snow, hail, and even blessings may pour down onto the earth. These gates are necessary because the firmament is solid and substantial. The firmament manifests division and represents an uninterrupted area of considerable time and space. And so it is for us. When the light of the gospel begins to shine in our lives, a natural division takes place. A spiritual firmament separates us from the things the world honors and values.

19 Personal correspondence from Blake Hardison, June 23, 2007.

20 Hyers, 39.

After the creation of the firmament, God gathers the waters. Analogously, having chosen light, individuals are gathered to Israel through baptism. Next, the earth bursts forth with grass, seeds, and fruit of all kinds. Likewise, following conversion, one begins to produce spiritual fruit. Next, God designates the sun to rule the day and the moon and stars to rule the night. These heavenly bodies are also to be for signs and seasons. Herein is an important caution. As disciples of Christ, there will be times of profound light, joy, and revelation, but there will also be times of moonlight and even times of starlight. There will be times when the Spirit lights our hearts with a fire as strong as the noonday sun, a fire that feels almost consuming. There will be times when we yearn for a spiritual experience or personal revelation and it doesn't come. It appears that there is an ebb and flow of the Spirit that is part of life's tutorial and is unrelated to our worthiness. These are times of hanging on.[21] But even in these hanging-on times, when the light of the Spirit is like a faint and distant star, there is never complete darkness.

The ultimate stage in the Creation concerns man's relationship with others. Man is to care for the animals and is to exercise benevolent, righteous leadership, or dominion, over them. Even more importantly, Adam and Eve were to multiply and replenish the earth. Implied in this command is the obligation to exercise the same kind of loving, committed leadership over their family as they were commanded to exercise over the earth and the animals.

In the final stages of spiritual growth, our thoughts and our desires turn to others. Such was the case with the four sons of Mosiah. Having experienced the power of the Atonement and the joy of redemption, they could not restrain themselves from helping others receive these blessings. Catherine Thomas writes, "The thing that characterizes the Gods and those who aspire to godhood is the love of the work of redemption. . . . It may be that among the most enlightened beings, the power to bless is the most coveted power."[22]

The Creation account teaches so much more than the origins of the earth. It provides a keen parallel to the creation of a disciple of Christ. And there are other lessons. Genesis 1 is marked by the constant refrain,

---

21 See M. Catherine Thomas, "Alma the Younger," 2:7.

22 Ibid., 1:1,18.

"And God said." With these words, God transforms a chaotic universe into a cosmos, or ordered system. What is true for the elements is true for our lives. When God's word orders our lives, chaos disappears. It is also worth noting that in Genesis "everything is . . . assigned its proper region and allowed to have its own identity, place, and function in the overall scheme of created things."[23] That includes us. Each of us has a unique contribution to make in the kingdom of God. Each of us has a role to play and a work to perform. Each of us holds an essential place in the overall scheme of things. Finally, the phrase "each according to its kind" or "after his kind" is repeated ten times in Genesis 1. The creatures of the sea, the birds, the cattle, and all creeping things are all commanded to bring forth "after their kind" (Genesis 1:21–25). The pattern is set and prepares us for an astounding truth. God Himself brings forth "after His kind." He creates man "in his own image" (Genesis 1:27). The implications of this are profound. Being after God's kind means we have a genetic predisposition to be like our Heavenly Father—to love, to save, to nurture, to teach, and to create. It means that wickedness and immorality are foreign to our nature.[24] It means we can grow up to be like our Father.

The Nature of Man

Genesis 2:7 reads, "And the Lord God formed man of the dust of the ground, and breathed into his nostrils the breath of life; and man became a living soul." The word *formed* comes from the root *yṣr*. It is the word used when a potter forms vessels out of clay. With this word, God is depicted as a potter, shaping man from the dust or clay of the earth. This is an engaging image. It suggests that each of us, like raw clay, has limitless potential. We can be made into the most masterful of creations—but only if we are soft and pliable. However, raw clay must be worked and kneaded. If the clay were animated, it might consider this an uncomfortable and disagreeable process. However, without it, a lump of clay would never reach its potential. During the forming process, flaws are sometimes revealed. They need not, however, permanently disfigure the vessel. The clay can be re-kneaded

23 Hyers, 89.

24 See Richard G. Scott, "Do What Is Right," in *Brigham Young University 1995–96 Speeches* (Provo, Utah: Brigham Young University, 1996), 173.

and reshaped, leaving no evidence of the prior character. When the vessel has been thoroughly prepared and perfectly formed, it must be fired. All of this corresponds to the trials, challenges, and preparatory experiences we call life.

It is significant that man is said to be formed from the dust of the earth. Firstly, we are alerted to the fact that mankind was made from something already in existence. This resonates with the doctrine of our premortal existence.

Secondly, it ties us to the earth. "If the body of man be analyzed, the elements from which it is made are found to be those which exist in the air and in the soil, that is, the earth's crust."[25] The table in figure 3-1 shows just how literal this is. This connection between man and the earth is reflected in the phrase, "The Lord God formed *man* of the dust of *the ground*" (Genesis 2:7; italics added), though it is obscured in translation. The Hebrew says that man, *'ādām*, is made from the

Common Elements in the Human Body and the Earth

Element	Percent in the Human Body	Percent in the Earth
Oxygen	65	47
Carbon	18.5	0.03
Hydrogen	9.5	0.14
Nitrogen	3.2	Trace
Calcium	1.5	3.6
Phosphorus	1	0.07
Potassium	0.4	2.6
Sulfur	0.3	0.03
Sodium	0.2	2.8
Chlorine	0.2	0.01
Magnesium	0.1	2.1
Iron	Trace	5

Figure 3-1.

25 John A. Widtsoe and Leah D. Widtsoe, *Word of Wisdom: A Modern Interpretation* (Salt Lake City: Deseret Book Company, 1950), 111.

earth, the *ʾadāmâh*. A translation that better reflects this play on words would be, "The Lord God formed an earthling from the earth" or "The Lord God formed a human from clods of the humus." This play on words should not, however, be taken as mere punning. Names were not simply labels; they were indicators of the very essence of the thing designated. That we are *ʾādām* made from *ʾadāmâh* reminds us that our bodies are perishable, earthly, and temporary. We will die, and our bodies will return to dust.

Thirdly, in the scriptures dust is associated with humility.[26] Alma tells his son Corianton to let his sins bring him down "to the dust in humility" (Alma 42:30), and the subjected people of Limhi "did humble themselves even to the dust" (Mosiah 21:13). Dust, as the state of abasement, also represents a pre-royal status. God tells King Baasha, "I exalted thee out of the dust, and made thee prince over my people Israel" (1 Kings 16:2). To be raised or exalted from the dust means to be elevated to a royal office, to become a king or a queen. Thus, when Adam is lifted out of the dust, he is "being crowned king over the garden with all the power and authority which it implies."[27] "The operative vehicle that takes any man from the dust and installs him in a position of authority or favor is the power of covenant."[28] When a king or a people break their covenants, the Lord returns them to the dust. Prophetic calls to Israel to shake herself from the dust (see Isaiah 52:1–2) are calls for her to remember her covenants, leave her ignoble state, and return to the position of "high eminence she should occupy in the eternal scheme of things."[29] When we read of Adam, who typifies every man, being lifted up from the dust, we are being told of our regal destiny. We are created to become kings and queens. The promise of 1 Samuel 2:8—"He raiseth up the poor out of the dust, and lifteth up the beggar from the dunghill, to set them among princes, and to make them inherit the throne of glory"—is ours.

---

26 Dust is also associated with humiliation, extreme sorrow, and vast multitudes.

27 Walter Brueggemann, "From Dust to Kingship," *Zeitschrift für die alttestamentliche Wissenschaft* 84, 1; quoted in Stephen D. Ricks, "Kingship, Coronation, and Covenant in Mosiah 1–6," in *King Benjamin's Speech: 'That Ye May Learn Wisdom,'* eds. John W. Welch and Stephen D. Ricks (Provo, Utah: FARMS, 1998), 262.

28 Stephen D. Ricks, "Kingship, Coronation, and Covenant in Mosiah 1–6," 262.

29 Bruce R. McConkie, *Mormon Doctrine* (Salt Lake City: Bookcraft, 1966), 210.

After Adam is formed from the dust of the ground, God breathes the breath of life into his nostrils and man becomes a living soul (see Genesis 2:7). It is worth noting that life is God's gift; it is not man's possession. Not everyone today agrees with this. Life, they claim, is a choice, and many insist it is their right to determine when to end life, whether it be in utero or in advancing years. Such does not accord with scripture. God has mandated strict laws governing both our entrance into and exit from this world.

There are other implications of God breathing life into man. The word for *breath* used most frequently in the Old Testament is the word *rûaḥ*.[30] *Rûaḥ* can also be translated as *wind* or *spirit*. As mortal, living beings, the receipt of the Holy Spirit is what "makes us most fully 'alive.' Having that Spirit breathed into our lives makes us 'alive in Christ.'"[31] Also, we are reminded that "two ingredients constitute its [Adam's] life . . . dusty earth and divine breath. One comes from below, the other from above. One is visible; the other invisible."[32] In other words, we have a dual nature. We are both spirit and body, soul and flesh. One of the more complicated passages in the Book of Mormon is Mosiah 15:1–5, the passage that describes Christ as both the Father and the Son. A key to understanding these verses is seeing that one of the issues at the heart of this passage is Christ's dual nature. Christ was both human and divine and thus had two wills. As a mortal being, He desired to live and so He prayed, "Let this cup pass from me" (Matthew 26:39). As a divine being, He had the will of the Father and desired to work out salvation for mankind. In performing the Atonement, Christ submitted His mortal will to His divine will. Christ's divine breath was primary to his dusty earth. It is a pattern that, if followed, will endow us with spiritual life.

Adam was put into the Garden of Eden and given the assignment to "dress it and to keep it" (Genesis 2:15). We sometimes think of the Garden of Eden as the apogee of luxury and ease, but such was not the case. "The Garden of Eden was not the original couch potato life. It

30 This is not, however, the word used in Genesis 2:7. Here, the breath of life is *nišmat ḥayyim,* probably because it plays on "living soul," *nepeš ḥayyâ.*

31 Gaskill, 46.

32 Phyllis Trible, *God and the Rhetoric of Sexuality* (Philadelphia: Fortress Press, 1978), 80.

was the perfect garden, meaning when Adam worked it and tilled it, it yielded its fruit. But work he must."[33] Adam was told he could eat of every tree of the garden freely, meaning without consequences, except for one. If he ate of the tree of knowledge of good and evil, there would be consequences. He would become mortal. He would have to leave the garden. He would eventually die. Adam and Eve did eat of this tree, and God held them accountable for their actions. God's interview reveals much about the nature of man.

When God asks Adam if he has eaten from the tree of knowledge of good and evil, Adam says, "The woman whom thou gavest to be with me, she gave me of the tree, and I did eat" (Genesis 3:12). As we look at this passage, it is important to recognize that Adam and Eve represent all men and women. "The experience of Adam and Eve is an ideal prototype for our own mortal experience. Their story is our story."[34] Adam is "the archetype, prototype, and pattern for all subsequent human beings."[35] Even the name *Adam* in Hebrew is indistinguishable from the word *man* or *mankind*. They are one and the same. Context alone determines whether the word is translated as *Adam* or *man*. In addition, in Moses 6:9, we read that God "called *their* name Adam" (italics added). Thus their names are more accurately "Mr. and Mrs. Adam" or "Adam Adam and Eve Adam," again pointing to the more encompassing use of the word *Adam*. It is essential to understand that Adam represents all men and women. That is not to say that Adam and Eve were not real people, but it may well be that their portrayal in the accounts of the Fall is more metaphorical than literal. Their conversation as recorded in Genesis 3 may be less a literal quotation than a didactic discourse to teach us about the nature of man.[36]

Adam's explanation of why he partook of the fruit "is not a representation of Adam's actual response, but rather a symbolic reenactment

---

33 Amy-Jill Levine, *The Old Testament, Part 1*, CD-ROM (Great Courses, 2001).

34 Bruce C. Hafen, *The Broken Heart: Applying the Atonement to Life's Expereinces* (Salt Lake City: Deseret Book Company, 1989), 37.

35 Stephen R. Robinson, "The Book of Adam in Judaism and Early Christianity," *The Man Adam*, eds. Joseph Fielding McConkie and Robert L. Millet (Salt Lake City: Bookcraft, 1990), 128.

36 For an incisive treatment of the metaphorical nature of Adam and Eve, see Gaskill, 1–109.

of yours and mine. Adam is figuratively depicted as failing to confess his folly and casting blame on Eve. How common a practice this is."[37] We see in Adam's response the human tendency to blame others for our behavior. "*She* gave me of the tree," Adam declares, as if to say, "She's the one responsible for this fine mess. I never would have partaken of the fruit if it hadn't been for her." This response not only shifts responsibility, it slightly reworks the actual events in order to put Adam in a more favorable light. In Genesis 3:6 we read that Eve "took of the fruit thereof, and did eat, and gave also unto her husband *with her*; and he did eat" (italics added). The tiny prepositional phrase "with her" is significant. It reveals, particularly in the Hebrew, that Adam was by her side when Eve partook of the fruit. Indeed, he may not have been the instigator, but he was a willing partner. He did not object. Adam's response conveniently leaves out this detail.

Adam also justifies and defends his behavior. When Adam says, "The woman whom thou gavest to be with me" (Genesis 3:12), he is reminding God that he had been given a commandment to cleave to his wife. This had undeniably priority over not eating the fruit. In this, Adam is saying, "Yes, I ate of the fruit, but I was struggling with a complex issue. I wanted to be obedient. I made the best choice I could." Adam's statement, though accurate, still amounts to justification and defense. Some see Adam's statement as an attempt by Adam to blame God for his behavior. By emphasizing that God has given Eve to Adam as his wife, he is in essence saying, "God, this is your fault. You gave me this woman."

Next, God turns to Eve and asks, "What is this that thou hast done?" (Genesis 3:13). Eve responds, "The serpent beguiled me, and I did eat" (Genesis 3:13). Eve's answer differs from Adam's in three remarkable ways. "First, she does not blame God. She does not say, for example, 'The serpent you made to dwell in the garden with me.'. . . Second, she does not implicate her companion. . . . She speaks only for and about herself."[38] "The serpent beguiled *me*," (not us), she says, although Adam had been by her side. Third, Eve confesses more quickly than did Adam. In the Hebrew, Adam's response is ten words—and nine of them deflect his responsibility: "The woman whom thou gavest

37 Gaskill, 75–76.

38 Trible, 120.

to be with me, she gave me of the tree." Only in the last word, "and I did eat," does Adam accept responsibility. In Hebrew, Eve's rebuttal is only three words total. The first two blame the serpent, but she quickly acknowledges, "and I did eat." Adam uses almost five times as many words as Eve to explain his untoward action. This is not to say that men blame more than women. Adam represents all human beings, male and female. Eve represents a more mature human being, male or female, who is willing to take responsibility for his or her behavior.

The consequence of Adam and Eve's actions was mortality. Mortal life would be more rigorous than their existence in Eden. Work was not a new requirement, but now the work would be more intense, more demanding. The earth would not yield its fruit so easily. Man's labor would bring forth thorns and thistles as well as fruit. So it is with mortal life. Life is a mixed bag of joy and pain, success and failure, dreams and despair, fruit and thorns. Not everything we do is successful. Our best intentions can produce results we neither expect nor want. There is a lack of certainty. No stages of life are pure, unmitigated joy. Each brings difficulty as well as delight. The fact that man would have to work harder to produce bread also suggests that the things of the world will make greater demands on man—on his energy, thoughts, and time.

In Eden, man walked and talked with God. Outside Eden, in the fallen world, this contact would be limited and less direct yet still crucial. Man needed God more than ever, but to connect with Him, he would have to sacrifice some of the time and effort that would otherwise be spent on sustaining physical life. Man would have to balance the things of the sprit and the things of the world. It would not work to ignore the demands of the physical world; this would imperil physical life. The things of the world must be attended to. Yet, space must be made for the things of the Spirit. In working out this precarious balance, the things of the world must "never captivate our hearts . . . [or] become our principal concern."[39] This is the keen test of mortality.

God did not send Adam and Eve out of the Garden defenseless and naked. He made them coats of skins (see Genesis 3:21). Their protection was not just the protection of clothing. It is far more significant. The skins from which the clothing was made were the skins of an animal. The

39 Nibley, "Three Degrees of Righteousness from the Old Testament," *CWHN*, 9:336.

animal, perchance a lamb, was sacrificed to protect Adam and Eve. The sacrifice was a poignant lesson that in and through the blood of the Lamb they would be protected not only from cold and exposure but also from all the effects of the Fall. That promise was confirmed by a covenant. Adam and Eve went out into the world to experience all kinds of things they had not seen before, but they went with a covenant of protection.[40]

Adam and Eve are driven out of the garden, apprising us that "sin drives man from God's presence; and when man banishes God from his world, he dwells in a wilderness instead of a Garden of Eden."[41]

Marriage and Family

Metaphors are used in literature to draw us into a text. They invite a reader to slow down, ponder, and reflect. They paint a picture that is rich and multifaceted. This concentrated prose may elicit feelings as well as thoughts. The image will often linger longer than ordinary words. In short, metaphors transform words into an experience but only if we accept their invitation. Therefore, when we encounter metaphors in scripture, it is well to ask some questions: What is the literal meaning of the metaphor? What images are associated with the metaphor, and what do they say about the nature of the person, place, or thing being represented? Why *this* metaphor? What does this metaphor say that another would not? Adam was not, as we know, literally formed from the dust of the earth. This metaphor is used to teach us that man is perishable, earthy, and may be raised from a state of humility to royal status. What about Eve? What does the metaphor of her creation reveal about women and the relationship of husbands and wives?

In Genesis 2:21 we learn that God caused a deep sleep to fall upon Adam. While he was sleeping, God took one of Adam's ribs and from it made a woman. We know this is not a literal account of Eve's creation. The relevance of the account is in its imagery. Genesis 2:22 tells us that God made the woman. The word *made* is nondescript and fails to convey the nuances of the Hebrew word *bānâ*. *Bānâ* means "to build." It is used to describe the construction of buildings, temples, towers,

---

40 See Joseph Fielding McConkie, "Obedience and Sacrifice," *Pearl of Great Price Discussions*, BYU Television, August 31, 2006.

41 J. H. Hertz, *The Pentateuch and Haftorahs*, 2nd ed. (London: Soncino Press); quoted in Gaskill, 93.

and houses. The word *house* was used to describe not only a home but a family, clan, and dynasty, as in "the house of David." The phrase "to build a house" meant to perpetuate and establish a family. God "builds" Mother Eve just as "the mother of all living" (Moses 4:26) would build the human race. The house is also a sign of security, protection, and permanence. Often, a woman is a stabilizing effect in the lives of her family. Many were the times when my children came home from school calling, "Mom . . . Mom . . . Mom." As soon as I answered their call and asked what they needed, their response was, "Oh, nothing." They just wanted to know I was there. My presence meant security.

Bānâ is also associated with the building of a temple. In using this word to describe the creation of woman, God is declaring woman a temple and affirming the sanctity of birth. "You might say that children literally go through a temple when they are born. And that the birth of each child born in the covenant is building God's kingdom on earth."[42]

Eve is said to be taken from Adam's rib. This does not imply that Eve is subservient to Adam or of lesser importance. Adam was taken from the earth, but he is not subservient to the earth. He was given dominion over it. He is to be lord and master of the earth. This would not be the case if being created from something implied subservience to that thing. The salient point is that both the dust of the earth and the rib of man are just raw materials. The operative force is God, who shapes and builds and imbues with life. It is also symbolic that Adam and Eve are made from different materials, indicating that man and woman are different in their makeup and nature. In spite of the fact that over the years some have insisted that the differences are those of nurture not nature, science is now supporting what scripture told us long ago. "Women, it turns out, are very distinct from men—they have a distinct brain structure, hormones, even nerve fibers. 'Women are different from men in every organ system.'"[43] These differences are divinely ordained and complementary.

The word translated as *rib* also means *side*. It is from Adam's side that Eve is created, symbolizing not only that husband and wife are to

---

42 Donna Nielsen, *Beloved Bridegroom* (United States of America: Onyx Press, 1999), 9.

43 Marianne Legato, MD, "Why Men Never Remember and Women Never Forget" (Rodale Books, 2005); quoted in Michelle Stacey, "How the Sexes Differ," *Real Simple*, June 2006, 179.

walk through life side by side but also that they are to walk in equality. This is captured in the famous words of Matthew Henry: "Eve is not made out of his head to top him, not out of his feet to be trampled upon by him, but out of his side to be equal with him, under his arm to be protected, and near his heart to be beloved."[44] This same idea is expressed in "The Family: A Proclamation to the World," which states husbands and wives are to fulfill their sacred responsibilities as equal partners.[45] In addition, in Arabic, the rib is the expression for something that is as close to you as a thing can possibly be. It expresses the ultimate in proximity, intimacy, and unity. Woman is made from man's rib to reveal "the wholeness that is intended for them. From one they came and to eternal at-one-ment they are to return."[46] In the interim, it is the oneness of heart, mind, and purpose that often distinguishes a sweet marriage from a discordant one.

When Adam sees Eve, he responds in delight. After all, God had previously declared, "It is not good that man should be alone." In Hebrew, "not good" are the first words God speaks in this verse. A literal, word-for-word translation reads, "Not good it is the man to be alone." In Hebrew, placing something at the first of the sentence is a way to place emphasis on it. In addition, the usual way to express a less than ideal situation is *'ên ṭôb,* "it is lacking in goodness."[47] But that is not what is used here. The construction here is *lō' ṭôb,* "not good," meaning "not good in any way." Man's state of aloneness was not less than desirable or mediocre; it was the worst possible situation.[48]

To remedy this unfortunate situation, God announces that he will make man "an help meet" (Genesis 2:18). The word *helpmeet* is two words in Hebrew, *'ēzer kĕnegdô*. The first word, *'ēzer,* means "to help, succor." In English the word *helper* suggests an assistant, someone of lower status who helps a superior. This is not the case in Hebrew. In the Old Testament, *helper* is most frequently used of a superior, one who

44 Bruce K. Waltke with Cathi J. Fredricks, *Genesis: A Commentary* (Grand Rapids, Michigan: Zondervan, 2001), 89.

45 See "The Family: A Proclamation to the World," *Ensign*, November 1995, 102.

46 Thomas, *Spiritual Lightening*, 48.

47 Waltke, 88.

48 See Nielsen, 1.

is capable of providing help in times of distress.[49] Notably, it describes God, who helps and succors his people. Consider Psalm 121:1–2: "From whence cometh my help. My help cometh from the Lord." Occasionally, this term is used of human beings. In these instances, a helper is one of superior military strength or size that can come to the aid of the supplicant. Does this mean that Eve is superior to Adam? No, not any more than Genesis 1–3 makes a case for Adam being superior to Eve. Their relationship is defined by the second word in the phrase "help meet," *kĕnegdô. Kĕnegdô* means "opposite," "corresponding to," "parallel with," or "on par with." It establishes that the relationship between Adam and Eve is one of mutuality and equality.

The word *ʿēzer* is used twenty-one times throughout the scriptures. Twice it refers to Eve. Sixteen times it refers to God, who acts as Israel's mighty helper. Three times it refers to vital human assistance in times of extreme need. For example, it describes someone who gives water to a person dying of thirst or who places a tourniquet on the arm of a bleeding man, thereby saving his life. Putting all this together, God promises to provide Adam with a companion who is equal to him in all ways, "a good match," as we are likely to say of a well-suited couple. Adam's companion will save him from his solitude and, eventually, serve in a lifesaving or life-granting role.

We have been conditioned by the account of Genesis 1 that when God decrees something to happen, it happens immediately. "God said, Let there be light: and there was light" (Genesis 1:3). "And God said, Let the waters under the heaven be gathered together unto one place, and let the dry land appear: and it was so" (Genesis 1:9). So when God says, "I will make him an help meet" (Genesis 2:18), we expect a helpmeet to show up, at least by the next verse. But in the ensuing verses, God forms the beasts of the field and the fowl of the air. Could one of these be the promised *ʿēzer kĕnegdô*? God brings these animals to Adam for him to name. Adam names them, which places them under his protection and judgment, but he does not find in them a suitable companion. Indeed, "loneliness is not overcome by something other than humanity."[50] So Adam remains alone, in a state of isolation and

49 See Carol Meyers, *Discovering Eve: Ancient Israelite Women in Context* (New York: Oxford University Press, 1988), 85.

50 Trible, 103.

separation. He is a bachelor. This is a state that is antithetical to the plan of God. Marriage is ordained of God. So unacceptable was the idea of celibacy in the ancient Jewish world, there is not even a word in the Hebrew Bible for *bachelor*. Even in modern Hebrew, the word is *ravak*, which comes from a root meaning *empty*.[51] Moreover, in Jewish understanding, a man who didn't have a wife was not even considered a man. Nor could he have glory. "Glory was always associated with the ability to give life. . . . A woman was an important source of glory to her husband. Without her, he had no capacity to give life."[52] The biblical mindset was no wife, little glory. This perspective is congruent with the declarations of modern prophets who have unequivocally proclaimed that marriage is essential to God's eternal plan.[53]

When Adam awakens from his divinely induced sleep, he exclaims in delight at the sudden appearance of a creature unlike all the other living things heretofore created. God has finally given Adam the promised helpmeet. Adam exclaims, "This is now bone of my bones, and flesh of my flesh" (Genesis 2:23). "This is now" is equivalent to saying "at last." Finally, at last, Adam is not alone. "Bone of my bones and flesh of my flesh" is an interesting phrase. It is used five times in the Old Testament, and each time it refers to a permanent relationship. Some scholars suggest it is a covenant and pledge of loyalty. As such it serves as a biblical counterpart to the modern marriage ceremony. Since bones are a symbol of strength and flesh a symbol of weakness and frailty, this becomes a ritual pledge to be bound in the best of circumstances as well as in the worst—much like "for better or for worse; for richer, for poorer; in sickness and in health." Moreover, "bones and flesh" serves as a merism indicating the entire spectrum of human characteristics from strong to weak. Since both the man and the woman possess this fullness of traits, almost all couples will find there are things about their partner that they absolutely adore and things that drive them crazy. But when we marry, we marry the whole person, flesh and bone.

As mentioned, flesh is a symbol for an individual's weakness and frailty. Consider the Savior's assessment of his sleeping Apostles, "The spirit indeed is willing, but the flesh is weak" (Matthew 26:41). Nephi

51 See Nielsen, 3.

52 Nielsen, 154.

53 See *Ensign*, November 1995, 102.

attributes any error in his record to "the weakness which is in me, according to the flesh" (1 Nephi 19:6). Notably, it is the bones, not the flesh, that survive decay after death. Could it be that in the next life, the strengths in our relationships will endure and our differences and troubles will decompose? A dear friend shared with me a vivid dream wherein she saw her grandfather and his brother standing at the edge of her kitchen, just beyond the light of the room. She knew immediately, without anything being said, that she was to have her great-uncle's temple work done. Heavenly manifestations of this kind are not unprecedented among Latter-day Saints. What is more remarkable is my friend's experience with her grandfather. She had not cared much for her grandfather. He had been an alcoholic and had made life very difficult for her family when he lived in their home when she was a teenager. However, when she saw her grandfather, she was flooded with love for him. All the bitterness and dislike she had felt were immediately gone. My friend's experience accords with Brigham Young's statement:

> It has been taught by some . . . that if a wife does not love her husband in this state, she cannot love him in the next. This is not so. Those who attain to the blessing of the first or celestial resurrection will be pure and holy and perfect in body. Every man and woman that reaches to this unspeakable attainment [celestial glory] will be as beautiful as the angels that surround the throne of God.[54]

Genesis 2 ends with Adam's delight at having a helpmeet and a statement of their innocence and righteousness. Genesis 3 details the Fall. If we read Genesis 3 on the heels of Genesis 2, Adam and Eve's bliss is short-lived. However, many scholars believe that a long time passed as Adam and Eve carefully considered if and when they would partake of the tree of knowledge of good and evil. However, sooner or later, Eve does partake. When called to account for her actions, Eve claims that the serpent beguiled her. *Beguile* means to mislead or deceive. Once again, the traditional English connotation is misleading, even beguiling. Alonzo Gaskill writes:

> The traditional interpretation that Eve was somehow tricked is inaccurate. Such a reading stands in

54 Brigham Young, *JD*, 10:24, quoted in Madsen and Covey, 84.

> contradiction with the doctrine as taught by living prophets. In Eden, Eve was intellectually and spiritually mature, understood God's will, and then consciously made the informed decision to move the plan forward by eating the fruit that would bring mortality into the world. . . . Elder Jeffrey R. Holland wrote: "Adam and Eve made their choice for an even more generous reason than those of godly knowledge and personal progress. . . . They did it "that men might be."[55]

Clearly, the beguiling of Eve is another case of figurative language.

The word *beguiled* here is a rare verb that is almost impossible to translate. "It indicates an intense multilevel experience which evokes great emotional, psychological, and/or spiritual trauma."[56] In other words, this was not a split-second decision made in a moment of weakness but a decision that Eve grappled with, thoughtfully evaluated, and surely prayed about. Inasmuch as this decision was made "that men might be," it is possible that a mothering instinct and the desire for children were pressing upon Eve. But why does Adam partake? God had commanded Adam to cleave, or cling, unto his wife, and this commandment had undeniable priority over not partaking of the fruit. Hebrew legend tells us that Adam's decision was not only governed by wisdom and obedience but also by love. When faced with the decision of partaking of the fruit and being cast out of Eden or not partaking of the fruit and losing Eve, Adam said, at least according to legend, "'Eve, I would rather die than outlive you. If Death were to claim your spirit, God could never console me with another woman equaling your loveliness.' So saying, he tasted the fruit."[57]

When God details the consequences of Eve's action, He tells her, "I will greatly multiply thy sorrow and thy conception; in sorrow thou shalt bring forth children; and thy desire shall be to thy husband, and he shall rule over thee" (Genesis 3:16). God is not cursing Eve

---

55 Gaskill, 20.

56 Dr. Nehama Aschkenasy, personal conversation; quoted in Beverly Campbell, *Eve and the Choice Made in Eden* (Salt Lake City: Bookcraft, 2003), 71.

57 Robert Graves and Raphael Patai, *The Hebrew Myths: The Book of Genesis* (New York: McGraw-Hill, 1964), 77–78; quoted in Stephen D. Ricks, "The Garment of Adam in Jewish, Muslim, and Christian Tradition," *Temples of the Ancient World*, 723.

or punishing her with pain. He is making her aware that her newly mortal body will experience pain in the process of childbirth. "Sorrow and conception" is actually a hendiadys, the expression of two words that work together as a compound word, in this case for childbearing. Thus, to have her sorrow and conception multiplied means Eve will bear children over and over. God is blessing Eve with fertility, one of the greatest blessings of the ancient world.

The second part of God's statement, "in sorrow you shall bring forth children," sounds at first to be a rephrasing of "I will greatly multiply thy sorrow and thy conception." This is parallelism, a common feature of Hebrew poetry. However, the second phrase of a parallelism is not meant to merely repeat or restate; it usually expands or develops the idea in the first clause. The emphasis in the second clause is not on labor or childbirth but on parenting.[58] The "sorrow" includes the mental labor, the anguish, and the heartbreak that so often accompany the joy of parenting and are often more intense than the physical labor.

In spite of the difficulties of pregnancy, childbirth, and parenting, Eve is promised "she shall be saved in childbearing." This phrase is not in Genesis, Abraham, or Moses, but it is in 1 Timothy 2:15. The promise that a woman's life would be spared would have been a valuable assurance in times when the mortality rate of birthing mothers was high. However, the promise of spiritual salvation is even greater. Bearing children is an act of extreme selflessness and love. Many expectant mothers experience unremitting nausea for months on end. A woman watches her body morph into a bulbous shape prone to backaches and heartburn and with a diminutive bladder. As a crowning experience, there is labor and delivery. But this is only the beginning. What follow are months of sleep deprivation, changing diapers, and worry. There are years of homework, Eagle projects, music lessons, late nights, and early mornings. The physical, emotional, and spiritual demands on mothers are incredible. Yet, as a mother labors and sacrifices in the cause of love, she becomes more like the Savior. She is saved and sanctified by her love and sacrifice.

When God explains the conditions of mortality to Eve, He also tells her, "Thy desire shall be to thy husband" (Genesis 3:16). This phrase has been interpreted variously by different commentators. *Desire* may

---

58 See Carol Meyers, *Discovering Eve: Ancient Israelite Women in Context,* 107–109.

be a reference to a woman's sexual desire for her husband—something good and divinely sanctioned inside of marriage. This phrase may mean that because of childbearing, a woman will desire her husband's protection against the dangers of a fallen world. Alternatively, this phrase may be a "reference to the prevalent female longing for the male social status and position. Although Latter-day Saint women have not been as susceptible to this temptation as have been others, the world does shout the familiar sophistry that success in the corporation is to be valued above success in the clan."[59]

God also tells Eve, "Thy husband . . . shall rule over thee" (Genesis 3:16). Unfortunately, this phrase has been grossly misunderstood. "The Lord was telling Eve that as she had entered the fallen world to bear and rear children . . . she would be watched over, cared for, and protected by the righteous love of a noble husband. How ironic that men would use this verse as license to exercise unrighteous dominion over their wives."[60] President Kimball suggested that *preside* is a better word than *rule*.[61] This change would make this passage correspond to the Family Proclamation, which tells us that fathers are "to preside over their families in love and righteousness and are responsible to provide the necessities of life and protection for their families."[62]

Giving Adam the presiding and leadership role in the family placed Eve in a counseling role. She was well suited for this task. She had proven wise and courageous in taking the fruit of the tree of knowledge of good and evil. But even such meritorious virtues as wisdom and courage must not be exercised without restraint. Eve had taken the fruit without consulting Adam (at least according to the reading in Genesis). "Far from being a punishment, [it] was a sacred tutorial designed to sanctify both of them. . . . [Eve's] divine developmental need is to act within a relationship."[63] Adam's developmental need was to have dominion without domination. We are still learning these lessons today.

---

59 Gaskill, 84.

60 S. Michael Wilcox, *Daughters of God: Scriptural Portraits* (Salt Lake City: Deseret Book Company, 1998), 18.

61 See Spencer W. Kimball, *The Teachings of Spencer W. Kimball*, ed. Edward L. Kimball (Salt Lake City: Bookcraft, 1982), 316.

62 *Ensign,* November 1995, 102.

63 Thomas, *Spiritual Lightening*, 53–54.

I have many times heard wives complain that their husbands do not take the leadership in spiritual things, from family scriptures to family prayer—yet it is men's role to preside. What is a woman to do? Just like Eve, she must learn to act within a relationship.

Adam is also held accountable for his actions because he "hearkened unto the voice of thy wife" (3:17). This does not mean that husbands should not listen to and counsel with their wives. Rather, this refers to "the tendency to hearken to the counsel of other humans, over and above the counsel and commands of God."[64] Adam's consequences for his choice are nearly identical to Eve's consequences. He will have to labor and toil to bring forth the bread that will sustain life, and he will have to do it over and over.[65] In other words, both Adam and Eve receive the same consequence—mortality. Their consequences are also a reminder that "the fulfillment of God's charge does not automatically entitle one to bliss and joy, that anguish is inevitably an accompaniment to the carrying out of life's tasks."[66] As President Hinckley was fond of saying:

> Most putts don't drop. Most beef is tough. Most children grow up to be just people. Most successful marriages require a high degree of mutual toleration. Most jobs are more often dull than otherwise. Life is like an old-time rail journey—delays, sidetracks, smoke, dust, cinders, and jolts, interspersed only occasionally by beautiful vistas and thrilling bursts of speed. The trick is to thank the Lord for letting you have the ride.[67]

As part of the consequence for their actions, Adam and Eve are driven from the Garden of Eden. Many couples experience a Garden of Eden in their marriage, a honeymoon period or time of innocence and bliss. However, there comes a moment when they realize that living with a person of the opposite sex, someone who in many ways is incomprehensible, and building their life together is not as simple and idyllic as anticipated. Like Adam and Eve, they have eaten of

---

64 Gaskill, 86.

65 See Nibley, "Patriarchy and Matriarchy," *CWHN*, 1:89–90.

66 Meyers, *Discovering Eve*, 109.

67 Jenkins Lloyd Jones, *Deseret News*, June 12, 1973; quoted in Hinckley, *Teachings*, 254.

the fruit and their eyes are now open. They must leave the garden of innocence and step into the wilderness, probably with a good amount of sorrow and disappointment. But in the wilderness they will mature and grow in capacity, knowledge, and experience. At times, they may be overwhelmed at how difficult life is in the wilderness and may be sorely tempted to flee from the current difficulties and return to the bliss and simplicity of Eden. Our first parents may have entertained the same desire. God, seeing this eventuality, wisely closed the way and barred the gate. He stationed cherubim with flaming swords to guard the entrance to Eden. Today, many disillusioned couples seek to return to Eden through divorce. Our temple sealings serve as a kind of cherubim and flaming sword, standing guard over our covenants, encouraging us to work our way through the wilderness.

Before leaving our discussion of Adam and Eve and the Fall and its implications for marriage, one final point should be considered. While in the garden, Adam and Eve were commanded to multiply and replenish the earth. At the same time, they were commanded to not eat of the fruit of the tree of knowledge of good and evil, which would bring about mortality and procreation. Many are confused that Adam and Eve received what seem to be contradictory commandments. However, herein is an important lesson. As we go through life, we find there are times when we have to grapple with how to live the commandments of God in everyday life. We learn that not everything is cut and dried, black and white. We find there are times when we have to choose between two good things and even conflicting commandments. For instance, President Hinckley encouraged young adults to get all the education they can.[68] Other prophets have cautioned young adults not to put off marriage and having children.[69] Several prophets have encouraged mothers to stay at home with their children.[70] It is not easy to do all these things. Determining how to fulfill such prophetic counsel will demand prayerful thought, careful consideration, and personal revelation. Grappling with such issues is an important part of spiritual maturation.

---

68 See Hinckley, *Teachings*, 172.

69 See Benson, *Come Listen to a Prophet's Voice*, 27.

70 See Kimball, *Teachings*, 318; Benson, *Come Listen to a Prophet's Voice*, 31; Hinckley, *Teachings*, 389–393, 416.

The Problem of Evil

In the First Presidency message in the January 2007 *Ensign*, Elder James E. Faust wrote, "I feel impressed to sound a warning voice against the devil and his angels—the source and mainspring of all evil. I approach it prayerfully, because Satan is not an enlightening subject."[71] The first chapters of Genesis are also a warning voice against Satan. They expose Satan for what he is: cunning, crafty, and relentless. We learn from the temple account that he is insolent, calculating, and vindictive. In the book of Moses, we see that he works through intimidation and bullying; he rants and raves when Moses repeatedly rejects his advances (see Moses 1:12–22). But his preferred mode of operation is more discreet. He usually conducts himself with the veneer of sophistication and reason. He entices men with persuasive and seductive arguments. This is how he approached Eve in the garden, and it is how he still entices us. Satan's strength lies in his cunning, and his cunning shows up in his lies. Recognizing his lies for what they are is essential for disarming Satan.

When Satan sets foot in Genesis, he does so as a serpent. It is unclear whether this is metaphorical or literal. A case could be made for both. It could be that there was never a serpent in the garden, at least not one that talked and tempted. Rather, a serpent could have been used in the account because of its associated images. For most people, a snake generates fear. Several years ago, I heard my son, who was then twelve years old, shouting. My first thought was he and his brother were roughhousing and his brother was prevailing. But his shouts had an intensity about them that suggested something more serious was going on. I hurried down to his room to find him standing on his bed, shrieking, "There's a snake in Clint's room! There's a snake in Clint's room!" Incredulous, I looked into Clint's room in time to see a snake slithering through the long pile of the carpet. Within seconds, I was standing next to my son on his bed, and we were both shouting, "There's a snake in Clint's room!"

Often, snakes incite fear and for good reasons. Snakes can be dangerous, even deadly. This in and of itself is sufficient reason for a snake to symbolize Satan. However, it is also worth noting that fear is the opposite of faith. Where there is fear, there is no faith. Satan continually seeks to undermine our faith. It is also interesting that

71 James E. Faust, "The Forces That Will Save Us," *Ensign*, January 2007, 4.

snakes slither in S-shaped movements. Their path is the antithesis of the strait and narrow way. Genesis 3:1 tells us that the outstanding characteristic of the serpent is its subtlety. The association with subtly and craftiness may be because a snake is not usually found out in the open but hiding in the grass or among rocks. In addition, "many cultures believe that snakes hypnotize their prey, because the victim often appears mesmerized during a snake's slow but visible approach, watching until it is too late to escape."[72] Finally, snakebites can be deadly, but there is an antivenom that is administered in a series of shots. However, it is not cheap, costing as much as $20,000. The Savior has provided an antivenom to counter the effect of Satan's bites, but it too came at a price, an inordinate price.

It is possible that the serpent in Genesis 3 was actually a serpent and that Satan worked through a snake to entice Eve. Such would require a talking snake, but legends that animals were able to speak prior to the Fall are widespread. It was believed they lost their voice at the time of the Fall. When God punishes the serpent for its role in the Fall, He says, "Upon thy belly shalt thou go, and dust shalt thou eat all the days of thy life" (Genesis 3:14). "Does this suggest that snakes once stood upright, having legs and arms, as they are so commonly depicted in ancient Egyptian drawings?"[73] Perhaps. But whether it is metaphorical or literal, losing its arms and legs suggests a limitation of power (arms) and sphere of influence (legs, the symbol of mobility). The snake is at a decided disadvantage against man, who has both limbs. This corresponds with Joseph Smith's statements that wicked spirits, which would include Satan, "have their bounds, limits, and laws by which they are governed"[74] and "all beings who have bodies have power over those who have not. The devil has no power over us only as we permit him."[75] Without arms and legs, the serpent is cast down into the dust, the symbol of humiliation, and consigned to the lowliest existence. He has descended in station and status. Slithering through the dust, the snake could easily be trod upon, the symbol of conquest.

---

72 Ryken, Wilhoit, Longman, 773.

73 Joseph Fielding McConkie, "The Mystery of Eden," 28.

74 *History of the Church*, 4:576; quoted in Faust, "The Forces That Will Save Us," 8.

75 Joseph Smith, *Teachings of the Prophet Joseph Smith*, ed. Joseph Fielding Smith (Salt Lake City: Deseret Book Company, 1976), 181.

The serpentine tempter of Genesis may be metaphorical or literal—or it could also be a mistranslation. The Hebrew word for serpent is *nāḥāš*. It comes from the root *nḥš*. From this same root also comes the word for *copper* or *bronze—n^{e}ḥōšet,* indicating a shining or luminous object. In Hebrew legend, the tempter is not a snake but an angel of light who says he is authorized of God to do this thing. 2 Nephi 9 supports this idea. Jacob calls Satan "that being who beguiled our first parents, who transformeth himself nigh unto an angel of light" (2 Nephi 9:9). Joseph Smith records in Doctrine and Covenants 128:20, "What do we hear? . . . the voice of Michael on the banks of the Susquehanna, detecting the devil when he appeared as an angel of light!" (D&C 128:20). In the next section, Joseph gives counsel on what to do if the "devil as an angel of light" appears and tries to deceive you (D&C 129:8). "As the great imitator, Lucifer has marvelous powers of deception,"[76] but his powers are not perfect. Jacob notes that he transformed himself "*nigh unto* an angel of light" (2 Nephi 9:9; italics added). When Satan appeared to Moses, he tried to deceive him, apparently by appearing as an angel of light. But Moses could discern between Satan and God because Satan's glory did not compare to God's (see Moses 1:13–14).

Whether Satan shows up as a serpent or an angel of light, he almost always shows up in disguise. In our world, he cloaks his dark doctrines in sophistry and enlightenment. He obscures his evil with familiarity. He pushes his program under the guise of tolerance and diversity. The scriptures and the temple alert us of his artifice and help us detect his methods.

Genesis 3:1–7 describes Eve's encounter with Satan and the subsequent partaking of the fruit by Adam and Eve.[77] These verses are the perfect test case on the subject of temptation, setting forth many of the ways in which Satan tries to deceive us. In Genesis 3:1 we read that the serpent "said unto the woman, Yea, hath God said, Ye shall not

76 Faust, "The Forces That Will Save Us," 6.

77 Of these verses, Allen P. Ross says, "The unit provides a perfect test case for the subject of temptation, for the disobedience cannot be blamed on the environment, and certainly not on heredity. . . . On the archetypical level the story describes the process of temptation that occurs repeatedly in human experience." Allen P. Ross, *Creation & Blessing: A Guide to the Study and Exposition of Genesis* (Grand Rapids, Michigan: Baker Books, 1998), 130.

eat of every tree of the garden?" This is like the question, "Have you stopped beating your wife?" It is difficult to answer such a question with a simple yes or no. The answer requires an explanation. The serpent has deliberately misquoted God. Eve cannot answer with a simple, one-word response. She is drawn into a conversation. Her exposure to evil is prolonged, and the silver-tongued serpent is granted valuable time to exercise his considerable powers of persuasion. The serpent has also grossly exaggerated God's prohibition. God did not deny Adam and Eve access to every tree of the garden. Indeed, every tree was available to Adam and Eve except one. The serpent perniciously inflates God's prohibition, insinuating that God's commandments are overly restrictive and that obedience to such a commandment is unreasonable. Moreover, by this one statement, the serpent has called into question the character of God. "God has moved from beneficent provider to cruel oppressor."[78] Distorting the nature of God has always been one of Satan's best techniques.

In response to the serpent's question, Eve explains, "We may eat of the fruit of the trees of the garden: But of the fruit of the tree which is in the midst of the garden, God hath said, Ye shall not eat of it, neither shall ye touch it, lest ye die" (Genesis 3:2–3). Actually, God's command did not include the prohibition against touching the tree. In her response, she does the same thing the serpent had done. She exaggerates. Eve may only have done so out of a desire to honor the word of God, but still, she was out of line with God's commandment. We can veer off the strait and narrow path on the right or the left—it doesn't much matter to Satan.

Following Eve's explanation that touching the tree results in death, the serpent retorts, "Ye shall not surely die" (Genesis 3:4). Here, Lucifer denies that there is any danger in breaking God's commandments. He insists there is no punishment for disobedience. This same argument is noted many years later by Nephi, who tells us that many will say we need not worry about breaking God's commandments. "If it so be that we are guilty, God will beat us with a few stripes, and at last we shall be saved in the kingdom of God" (2 Nephi 28:8). Later, Nehor taught God would redeem all men, regardless of their behavior. All would

78 Victor P. Hamilton, *The Book of Genesis: Chapter 1–17* (Grand Rapids, Michigan: William B. Eerdmans Publishing Company, 1990), 189.

have eternal life (see Alma 1:4). Today's versions of Satan's lie, "ye shall not surely die," are many. Some people insist there are no absolute truths. Everything is relative. Consequently, things that used to be considered violations of God's law are now simply personal choices. Other people deny the justice of God by affirming that God is love but in a kind of ethereal, nondemanding way. Many people deny the reality of sin and Satan. Hell is simply too barbaric of an idea to be seriously entertained. Satan is dismissed as a superstition or an excuse for not taking responsibility for one's choices. However, "we Latter-day Saints need not be, and we must not be, deceived by the sophistries of men concerning the reality of Satan. There is a personal devil, and we had better believe it. He and a countless host of followers, seen and unseen, are exercising a controlling influence upon men and their affairs in our world today."[79]

The serpent continues, "For God doth know that in the day ye eat thereof, then your eyes shall be opened, and ye shall be as gods, knowing good and evil" (Genesis 3:5). The serpent suggests that there are great advantages to be had by eating the fruit—which is true. However, just because the fruit is good, it does not necessarily follow that it was right to take the fruit at the behest of the serpent. The serpent did not have the authority to offer the fruit, and in God's kingdom, authority is essential. The serpent states that if Eve eats of the fruit, she will be as the gods. Yet, God has prohibited her from partaking of the fruit. The implication is that God is holding Adam and Eve back. Some people buy into this idea today. They see God's commandments as limitations and restrictions. For instance, some see God's ordained role for woman as mother and keeper of the hearth as a limitation of her power rather than an acknowledgment of it. This idea is simply false. Another insidious implication is the idea that Eve needs something other than what she has to be happy. Additionally, the serpent implies that life after taking of the fruit will be glorious not difficult. Such is contrary to the plan of salvation. President Spencer W. Kimball said, "We knew before we were born that we were coming to the earth for bodies and experience and that we would have joys and sorrows, pains and comforts, ease and hardships, health and sickness,

---

79 Marion G. Romney, "Satan—The Great Deceiver," *Ensign*, June 1971, 35.

successes and disappointment."[80] To expect otherwise is to set ourselves up for disappointment and disillusionment. A final distortion of truth comes not from the serpent but from an erroneous assumption held by some non-Latter-day Saint theologians that desiring to "be as gods" is arrogant and sinful, a reaching beyond the limits set for man by God.[81] Nothing could be further from the truth. Implanted in our hearts is the righteous desire to be like our Father, a desire to have godly power to do godly works. The only sin "is in attempting to do so without God . . . and in attempting to do so aside from the path He has laid out for us through entrance into covenants and obedience to commandments."[82]

While the interchange between Eve and the serpent teaches us much about sin and temptation, there are other ways to view this interaction. Don C. Benjamin advances an interpretation that stands apart from most traditional Christian interpretations but accords with the LDS perspective of the nobility, greatness, and courage of our first parents. Based on the euphemisms in Semitic languages, Benjamin believes that when the serpent said to Eve, "Hath God said, Ye shall not eat of every tree of the garden?" (Genesis 3:1), he was really saying, "Are you fertile?" The serpent's statement, "Your eyes shall be opened . . . knowing good and evil" (Genesis 3:5) means "you will become fertile." When the serpent insists that Eve "shall not surely die" (Genesis 3:4), he is saying "the woman will not be summarily executed for eating of the fruit of the tree. Instead the woman will labor and eventually die in exchange for the ability to bear children."[83] In Benjamin's view, the essence of this passage is not sin or temptation but mortality and families. He writes:

> The snake and the woman discuss whether humans should be mortal or immortal, fertile or infertile. The snake does not offer immortality to the man and the woman; they are already immortal when the story begins. The snake does not steal immortality from them;

---

80 Spencer W. Kimball, *Faith Precedes the Miracle* (Salt Lake City: Deseret Book Company, 1972), 106.

81 See Hamilton, *Genesis 1–17*, 190.

82 Gaskill, 68–69.

83 Don C. Benjamin, *Old Testament Story—An Introduction* (Tempe, AZ: Scholargy Custom Publishing, 2003), 31.

> it simply convinces them to exchange their immortality for fertility by pointing out that the wise know that human life, which is good, requires suffering, which is bad. . . . The snake chooses to speak with the woman, not because she is gullible, but because women play a more important role than men in human reproduction, which is the subject of the conversation.[84]

If Eve's decision to partake of the tree of knowledge of good and evil is at least partially driven by her desire to become a mother, as suggested previously, then Benjamin's point of view makes sense. It also drastically alters the traditional view of Eve as weak, proud, and sinful. Indeed, she is quite the opposite. "On the basis of her discussion with the snake about the quality of their life primeval, she decides to lay down her life in order to create life. The woman is willing to create and to die, and so, by implication, is the man."[85] Undoubtedly, Adam and Eve are courageous, noble, and magnanimous.

God does not curse Adam or Eve for partaking of the fruit. It's questionable if He even punishes them. Perhaps He simply announces their consequences. With the serpent, it is different. The serpent is "cursed above all cattle and above every beast of the field" (Genesis 3:14). He also receives a more enigmatic punishment. God says, "I will put enmity between thee and the woman" (Genesis 3:15). Enmity is a feeling of bitter hatred and ill will. It is a natural revulsion, the same thing most people feel when they see a snake. This is indeed a cursing of Satan, for it thwarts his purposes. When we first encounter sin, it is repulsive to us. We retreat because it's offensive to our souls. This enmity is, as Hugh Nibley says, "our first line of defense"[86] against sin. It is a powerful protection, but it is not invincible. We can neutralize this aversion just as people overcome the natural horror of snakes and even take them for pets. *Enmity*, as it is used in the Old Testament, also conveys a sense of fervid hostility, the kind that exists among nations that are at war. It implies the kind of intense animosity that results in murder. The implication here is that the continuing war between man

84 Ibid., 31–32.

85 Ibid., 32.

86 Nibley, "Law of Consecration," *CWHN*, 9:435.

and the serpent is a life-and-death struggle. It demands our best defense and constant vigilance. George Q. Cannon stated:

> I have come to the conclusion that if our eyes were open to see the spirit world around us . . . we would not be so unguarded and careless and so indifferent whether we had the spirit and power of God with us or not; but we would be continually watchful and prayerful to our Heavenly Father for His Holy Spirit and His holy angels to be around about us to strengthen us to overcome every evil influence.[87]

Satan is indeed a formidable enemy. He is cunning, calculating, and ruthless. The scriptures and the temple raise a warning voice and give us keys of detection and the power to overcome. It is yet another reason why we need the temple more than anything else.

87 George Q. Cannon, 1:82.

Understanding Covenants and Ordinances

The temple endowment includes a series of covenants and ordinances. Covenants and ordinances are standard features of Latter-day Saint vocabulary and an integral part of Latter-day Saint life. However just because we speak of and participate in covenants and ordinances, it does not necessarily follow that we thoroughly understand them. Consequently, it is worth taking a closer look. "Ordinances and covenants can hardly be understood apart from each other. By ordinances we enter into covenants, and by covenants we receive the ordinances. . . . There is no eternal covenant that is not connected to an ordinance."[1] Covenants and ordinances are a source of protection[2] and the means by which godly power is channeled to men and women. "They give us access to spiritual gifts necessary to bring about perfection."[3] It is hard to overstate the essential role of covenants and ordinances in the gospel of Jesus Christ.

Not all religions place equal value on covenants and ordinances. Elder Dennis B. Neuenschwander explains:

> In Protestant denominations, grace and faith have gained ascendancy as the primary, or sole, requirements of salvation. The more singular the role of grace in the process of salvation, the less important is the role of ordinances in that process. . . . As personal participation in ordinances loses significance, the importance of

1 Dennis B. Neuenschwander, "Ordinances & Covenants," *Ensign*, August 2001, 24.

2 See Howard W. Hunter, 154.

3 Glenn L. Pace, *Spiritual Plateaus* (Salt Lake City: Deseret Book Company, 1991), 72.

> divine authority also becomes less significant. . . . [On the other hand,] the more claim a church has on antiquity and apostolic authority, the more prominent the emphasis on sacred ordinances and upon divine authority to perform them. The Catholic Church in the Western development of Christianity and the Orthodox Church in the East both assume this position. Each claims divine authority and teaches the importance of sacred ordinances. . . . The Church of Jesus Christ of Latter-day Saints also claims an ancient origin and thereby places exceptional importance both on the role of ordinances and covenants and on the necessity of divine authority to administer them.[4]

Indeed, so vital are covenants and ordinances to The Church of Jesus Christ of Latter-day Saints that the threefold mission of the Church essentially revolves around them. Proclaiming the gospel is to offer the people of the world the ordinance of baptism and the covenants of the gospel. Perfecting the Saints is helping members of the Church receive the ordinances of exaltation and to sustain them in living all the covenants they have entered into. Redeeming the dead is performing vicarious ordinances for those who have passed on. Truly, covenants and ordinances are what the gospel is all about.

Covenants

As Latter-day Saints, we are steeped in covenants. We make covenants at baptism, covenants which we renew weekly with the sacrament. When a man receives the Melchizedek Priesthood, he does so with an "oath and covenant," wherein he promises to be faithful and magnify his calling.[5] The temple endowment contains a series of sacred covenants. When we marry in the temple, we make covenants with God and our spouse. Our children are then privileged to be "born in the covenant." We are a covenant people. We are heirs of the Abrahamic covenant. We read the Old Testament and the New Testament and Another Testament of Jesus Christ. Since *testament* and *covenant* are basically

4 Neuenschwander, 22.

5 See Leaun G. Otten and C. Max Caldwell, *Sacred Truths of the Doctrine and Covenants* (Salt Lake City: Deseret Book Company, 1983), 2:73.

synonymous, our scriptures are books about covenants—the old, the new, and the everlasting. Covenants mark the significant transitions of our lives and even preceded this life—our first covenants being made in the premortal existence. Even the gospel itself is The New and Everlasting Covenant, a title used to encompass all its covenants.[6]

If asked to define *covenant*, most Latter-day Saints could quickly respond with something like, "a two-way promise" or "a binding, solemn agreement between God and man." Yet, our covenants are so much more. "They are vehicles the Lord has provided to conduct us into eternal life."[7] On a more immediate level, covenants grant us vital strength to help us spiritually survive in a world that is hostile to the ways of God. "Covenants actually provide us with immunity from Satan's power."[8] It is not surprising that Russell M. Nelson, the physician-Apostle, also sees covenants in medical terms—as a means of producing a strain of souls resistant to sin.[9] The source of this protection is the Holy Ghost, which is given to us in added measure with each covenant we make and keep. Covenants give us stability and direction in a world of shifting values and spiritual turmoil. "The covenants we make on this earth are designed to lead us through our complexities and help us decide what to do when we do not understand, or when demands press upon us, or when we feel as if we cannot hold on one second longer. . . . They are sure sources of guidance and strength."[10] Yet, the power of covenants is not merely defensive. Every covenant we make creates a bond between us and the Savior. I believe that the more covenants we enter into, the greater the bond. The greater the bond, the greater the flow of enabling power, healing, light, and especially love from the Savior to us.

6 See Henry B. Eyring, "Covenants and Sacrifice," General Authority Address, Old Testament Symposium 1995, *The Nineteenth Annual Church Educational System Religious Educators' Symposium* (Salt Lake City: The Church of Jesus Christ of Latter-day Saints, 1995), 6.

7 James E. Faust, "Search Me, O God, and Know My Heart," *Ensign*, May 1998, 20.

8 Steven R. Covey, "The Abundant Life in Christ," *The Redeemer: Reflections on the Life and Teachings of Jesus the Christ* (Salt Lake City: Deseret Book Company, 2000), 115.

9 See Russell M. Nelson, "Children of the Covenant," *Ensign*, May 1995, 33.

10 Cheryl Brown, "Complexities, Covenants, and Christ," *To Rejoice as Women: Talks from the 1994 Women's Conference*, eds. Susette Fletcher Green and Dawn Hall Anderson (Salt Lake City: Deseret Book, 1995), 148.

Covenants are eternal. Our baptismal and temple covenants will be efficacious throughout eternity. However, eternity stretches behind us as well as before. Elder Bruce R. McConkie states, "Israel is an eternal people. She came into being as a chosen and separate congregation before the foundations of the earth were laid."[11] If Israel is an eternal people set apart in the premortal existence, that which set Israel apart then must surely be that which sets Israel apart now: the entering into covenants, particularly covenants pertaining to salvation and exaltation. In addition to this, we made covenants and pledges regarding how we would conduct our lives. President Spencer W. Kimball says:

> We made vows, solemn vows, in the heavens before we came to this mortal life. . . . We have made covenants. We made them before we accepted our position here on earth. . . . We committed ourselves to our Heavenly Father, that if He would send us to the earth and give us bodies and give to us the priceless opportunities that earth life afforded, we would keep our lives clean and would marry in the holy temple and would rear a family and teach them righteousness. This was a solemn oath, a solemn promise.[12]

It seems we also entered into covenants regarding our missions in life—unique, tailor-made covenants based on our talents and abilities. Elder Neal A. Maxwell reflects, "The degree of detail involved in the covenants and promises participated in at that time may be a more highly customized thing than many of us surmise."[13] Since every covenant, even premortal ones, comes with guaranteed grace to help us keep that covenant,[14] we can rest assured that everything—everything—we need to fulfill our premortal covenants will be given to us. Of course, the things we *need* are not always the things we *want*. No matter how

---

11 Bruce R. McConkie, *New Witness for the Articles of Faith*, 510.

12 Spencer W. Kimball, quoted in Barbara W. Winder, "Enjoy Your Journey," *Brigham Young University 1989–1990 Speeches* (Provo, Utah: Brigham Young University, 1990), 105.

13 Neal A. Maxwell, *But for a Small Moment* (Salt Lake City: Bookcraft, 1986), 99.

14 See Henry B. Eyring, "Covenants and Sacrifice," General Authority Address Old Testament Symposium 1995, *The Nineteenth Annual Church Educational System Religious Educators' Symposium* (Salt Lake City: The Church of Jesus Christ of Latter-day Saints, 1995), 4.

difficult our challenges, we can know that "all things work together for good to them that love God, to them who are the called according to his purpose" (Romans 8:28). That means we can quit worrying about this or that eventuality. "We can go about our business . . . and not fear that some random event will arrest our forward progress to our spiritual destiny."[15] This is one of the great gifts of being in covenant with God.

Covenants have a binding power. Covenants "bind us to a course of righteous living."[16] They bind us to our promised blessings. Doctrine and Covenants 82:10 states, "I, the Lord, am bound when ye do what I say." Doing what God says is tantamount to faithfully keeping our covenants. When we do so, promised blessings are assured. Covenants bind us to each other, creating sacred relationships of belonging. As members of the Church, we are not simply members of a common organization. Because of our baptismal covenants, we belong to each other. We are bound by covenant to care and to love. We are to be deeply affected by each other's sorrows and to delight in each other's joys and successes. We are to matter to each other. As C. Terry Warner put it, "We are not oysters or abalones, existing in shells. . . . We are members one of another connected to each other and especially to God by spiritual sensitivities and obligations as profound as eternity."[17]

Temple covenants bind husbands and wives, parents and children. Death will not disrupt these tender relationships or our familial responsibilities. Just before he passed away, Oscar McConkie gathered his family together. At this poignant moment, he said, "I am going to die. When I die, I shall not cease to love you. I shall not cease to pray for you. I shall not cease to labor in your behalf."[18]

Covenants also bind us to God. An evocative image of being in covenant with God is captured in Matthew 11:28–30, wherein Christ enjoins His disciples to "come unto me . . . and take my yoke upon you."[19]

15 Thomas, *Spiritual Lightening*, 45; see also 26–27, 39–45.

16 Delbert L. Stapley, Conference Report, October 1964, 64.

17 C. Terry Warner, "Honest, Simple, Solid, True," *BYU Speeches 1995–1996*, 133.

18 Robert L. Millet, *When a Child Wanders* (Salt Lake City: Deseret Book Company, 1996), 133.

19 The Jews who personally heard the Savior's invitation would not have thought of the yoke in positive terms, as a means of sharing burdens with and drawing strength from their yoke mates. Rather, the yoke was a heavy, oppressive burden and represented the onerous demands of the law of Moses.

A yoke connects two animals and harnesses their collective strength. If the two animals aren't evenly matched, the stronger animal shares its strength with the weaker animal. A burden that is overwhelming or perhaps impossible for one can be equitably and comfortably borne by two bound by a yoke. By analogy, the yoke is our covenants that bind us to Christ. In this union, we are unquestionably the weaker animal. But Christ shares His strength with us. Yoked with Him, we can do things that are impossible for us to do by ourselves. Though we must labor, the grace and power of Christ assure our eternal success.

I recently discovered a nonscriptural allegory of what it means to be in covenant with Christ and thereby profit from His grace. My husband and I took ballroom dance lessons for a couple of years. Most of the time, my husband and I danced with each other, but occasionally we each danced with an instructor. On one of these occasions, I was dancing with our instructor while my husband was sitting on the side, watching. Our instructor led me through all kinds of dance steps, including some I had never done before, with his characteristic grace and aplomb. When I sat down, my husband said, "Wow. You were incredible!" I am not a natural dancer, and I certainly wasn't incredible. However, *we* were incredible. With the instructor's superior skill and knowledge, I had no choice but to follow. He made me look good. He made me much better than I am. So it is being in covenant with Christ.

The blessings that flow from our covenants are almost beyond comprehension. Our baptismal covenants open the door to the kingdom of God on the earth and the celestial kingdom in heaven. They also include an extraordinary promise described by George Q. Cannon:

> When we went forth into the waters of baptism and covenanted with our Father in heaven to serve him and keep His commandments, He bound Himself also by covenant to us that he would never desert us, never leave us to ourselves, never forget us, that in the midst of trials and hardships, when everything was arrayed against us, He would be near unto us and would sustain us. That was his covenant.[20]

The covenants of baptism bless us individually with supernal blessings; the blessings of the covenants of the temple surpass the

20 Cannon, 1:170.

baptismal covenants in both nature and scope. Our temple covenants open the door to the highest degree of the celestial kingdom and a fulness of blessings and glory. They also reach beyond our individual lives and bless us as families. Through the temple covenants, "a faithful man and woman, by means of their diligence and faith, can secure blessings for their children."[21]

A scriptural type for this is found in the story of David and Jonathan, the son of Saul and the crown prince of Israel. David and Jonathan entered into a covenant of loyalty, protection, and peace. They were true and faithful to this covenant in the face of great opposition. In time, Jonathan is killed in battle, and soon thereafter David rules over all Israel. Jonathan left a son, Mephibosheth. Being a direct heir to the previous king can be a dangerous position, so Mephibosheth was justifiably concerned when David summoned him. As soon as Mephibosheth appeared before David, he fell to the ground in submission and deference. David assuages his fears by pledging covenant loyalty, protection, and peace to Mephibosheth "for Jonathan thy father's sake" (2 Samuel 9:7). God blesses the posterity of those who honor their covenants, particularly their temple covenants. President George Q. Cannon stated, "Be it known unto you that God makes covenants with men and He blesses men and He will bless their posterity. This ought to be an incentive to every man to live as he should do, not only for his own sake, but for the sake of his posterity."[22] At another time, President Cannon said that when he sent his sons out on missions he told them, "'Boys, God is your father's friend. . . . You can trust Him and can call upon Him with confidence; for I tell you that while I live and keep his commandments, God will watch over my children and will preserve them and bless them.' And he has done it. So it will be with every faithful man and woman."[23]

More recently, Boyd K. Packer taught in conference:

> It is a great challenge to raise a family in the darkening mists of our moral environment. . . . It is not uncommon for responsible parents to lose one of their children, for a time, to influences over which they have no control.

21 Ibid., 2:86.

22 Ibid., 2:85.

23 Ibid., 2:88.

> They agonize over rebellious sons or daughters. They are puzzled over why they are so helpless when they have tried so hard to do what they should. It is my conviction that those wicked influences one day will be overruled. . . . We cannot overemphasize the value of temple marriage, the binding ties of the sealing ordinance, and the standards of worthiness required of them. When parents keep the covenants they have made at the altar of the temple, their children will be forever bound to them.[24]

When we break our covenants, we cut our ties with the Lord, and we lose His protective power. Jeremiah likens erring Israel who has broken her covenants to oxen that have "altogether broken the yoke, and burst the bonds" (Jeremiah 5:5). The oxen's newfound freedom has placed them in grave peril. A lion from the forest will slay them, a wolf shall spoil them, and a leopard shall lurk about, suggestive of the constant threat of danger (see Jeremiah 5:6). We once had a dog that exemplified this scripture. This dog loved to escape out the front door every chance she had. Had she been able to talk, she most surely would have shouted, "I'm free! I'm free!" as she dashed out the door. However, more than once, when we chased her down, we found her sitting in the middle of a busy city street in mortal danger. Such is the freedom of being outside the covenant.

Spiritual peril is not the only consequence of breaking our covenants. If our covenants draw us closer to Christ, the breaking of covenants moves us away from Him. The greater the distance, the less we experience the love of our Savior. That is not to say that Christ ceases to love us. His love is constant and eternal. It is like a bonfire on a cold night. We can stand close to the fire, enjoying its warmth and light. We can step back into the shadows where the heat and light are less intense. Or we can withdraw so far from the fire that the light is but a glimmer. To be so far from Christ is lonely indeed. Spiritual loneliness and self-alienation from the love of God is a formidable cost for violating our covenants.

Ordinances

The word *ordinance* has both a general and a specific definition. In general, an ordinance is a law, a statute, or a commandment. This is

24 Boyd K. Packer, "Our Moral Environment," *Ensign*, May 1992, 68.

the meaning of the word *ordinance* in Exodus 18:20: "And thou shalt teach them ordinances and laws and shalt shew them the way wherein they must walk, and the work that they must do." The more specific definition and the one that concerns us here is "an established rite or ceremony." More specifically, "an ordinance is a sacred ceremony that has a spiritual meaning and effect."[25] It is "an outward manifestation or symbol of a principle."[26] For instance, the ordinance of baptism symbolizes the putting to death of the natural man and the raising to life the new man of Christ. The ordinance of "laying hands on the head of the sick symbolically suggests the invocation and transmission of power from on high."[27] In order to be valid, "an ordinance must always be performed by one who is ordained—or in other words, an ordinance requires the action of the priesthood."[28]

There are ordinances that are essential to salvation and exaltation—such as baptism and sealing—and ordinances that are nonessential to salvation but are for comfort and encouragement, such as the blessing of children and the dedication of graves. The most frequently repeated ordinance in the Church is the sacrament. Because we do it so often, we may lose sight of the great spiritual power available in the sacrament, as in all ordinances. However, it is well to remember that "the ordinances represent channels of divine power, the means whereby the power of the Almighty is brought into our individual and congregational lives."[29]

The saving ordinances of the gospel were "instituted from before the foundation of the world" (D&C 124:33). They have always been "an immutable part of the gospel."[30] However, they have not always made their appearance in sacred literature under the word *ordinance*. According to Hugh Nibley, "The ancient saints always designated a

---

25 *Endowed From on High: Temple Preparation Seminar, Teacher's Manual* (Salt Lake City: The Church of Jesus Christ of Latter-day Saints, 2003), 16.

26 Daniel H. Ludlow, *Selected Writings of Daniel H. Ludlow: Gospel Scholars Series* (Salt Lake City: Deseret Book Company, 2000), 354.

27 Immo Luschin, "Ordinances," *Encyclopedia of Mormonism,* ed. Daniel H. Ludlow (New York: Macmillan Publishing Company, 1992), 1032.

28 Ludlow, 354.

29 Robert L. Millet, *Alive in Christ: The Miracle of Spiritual Rebirth* (Salt Lake City: Deseret Book Company, 1997), 141.

30 Neuenschwander, 22.

mystery as an ordinance, and vice versa."[31] For instance, Nephi desired to know the mysteries of God (see 1 Nephi 2:16). He later states, "And I, Nephi, did go into the mount oft, and I did pray oft unto the Lord; wherefore the Lord showed unto me great things" (1 Nephi 18:3). Elder Neal A. Maxwell reflects, "It seems likely that some of the things taught to him when he was on such mountains pertained to temple ordinances. In any case, Nephi was 'bidden that [he] should not write them.'"[32] In Matthew 13:11, we read, "It is given unto you to know the mysteries of the kingdom of heaven, but to them [the unbelieving] it is not given." Elder Maxwell also illuminates this passage. "Jesus was able to teach his Apostles things that were kept from the world, including information about sacred ordinances."[33] During His forty-day ministry, the period of time between Christ's Resurrection and His Ascension to heaven in Acts 1, Christ continued to teach His Apostles about sacred ordinances. In fact, "the major purpose of the forty-day ministry [was] to teach the nature of vicarious ordinances and to instruct the Apostles in the fulness of the temple ceremony."[34] The connection between ordinances and mysteries is clear when we remember that sacred ordinances are not spoken of openly. It is a small step for ordinances to become "mysteries." In 1973, a scholar by the name of Morton Smith published a book in which he made an extensive argument showing that the word *mystery* as used by early Jews and Christians "was nothing else than a series of initiatory ordinances for achieving the highest salvation which today are lost and unknown to the Christian world. . . . We don't know what they are; but that is what Christ meant by the mysteries of the kingdom. He meant ordinances."[35]

Washing and Anointings

Washing and anointings are the first ordinances performed in the temple for a living endowment and are therefore preparatory or

---

31 Nibley, "Return to the Temple," *CWHN*, 12:56.

32 Neal A. Maxwell, *Not My Will, But Thine* (Salt Lake City: Bookcraft, 1988), 131.

33 Ibid., 130.

34 Joseph Fielding McConkie and Robert Millet, *Life Beyond* (Salt Lake City: Bookcraft, 1986), 158.

35 Nibley, "The Meaning of the Temple," 12:28.

initiatory ordinances. Ritual washings are not new. In Exodus, the people were to wash their clothes preparatory to seeing God at Sinai (see Exodus 19:10–11). Lavers stood in the courtyards of the temple and the tabernacle for the priests to wash their hands and feet before officiating at the temple. Jesus washed the feet of His Apostles at the Last Supper. Many non–Latter-day Saint scholars sense that this action is significant and something more than an example of humility, but they aren't sure exactly what it means. They postulate it is connected with baptism, the sacrament, penance, and apostolic ordination. Some scholars think it may have been a symbol of Jesus's death.[36] The confusion over the meaning of this ritual action can be attributed to the fact that the washing of the feet was a mystery, or a sacred ordinance, not spoken of openly. Apostles and prophets of this dispensation have enlightened our understanding. Bruce R. McConkie explains that by washing the feet of His Apostles, Jesus "instituted a sacred ordinance which should be performed by legal administrators among His true disciples from that day forward. As part of the restoration of all things, the ordinance of washing of feet has been restored in the dispensation of the fulness of times."[37]

Not only Israel, but virtually all religions of the Ancient Near East incorporated purification rituals into their worship. Because of water's obvious use in cleansing, it was a natural medium to symbolize attaining ritual purity. In Egypt, the priest had to purify himself before he could enter the temple. Even the pharaoh himself was ritually washed every day at dawn.[38] Ritual washings are attested among the Mandaeans in the sixth century AD:

> He washes his hands in order to be freed from all the prohibited things to which he has stretched his hands before; he rinses his mouth in order to cleanse it from all falsehood and fault that may have issued from it; he rinses his nose to cleanse it from whatever forbidden things he has smelt; he washes his face in order to be absolved from every shameful thing; his feet in order

---

36 For a summary of the varying theories, see Raymond E. Brown, *The Gospel According to John XIII–XXI*, Anchor Bible (New York: Doubleday, 1970), 558–559.

37 Bruce R. McConkie, *Mormon Doctrine*, 829.

38 See Nibley, *Message of the Joseph Smith Papyri*, 135, 138.

> to be cleansed from every instance of having walked in rebellious and mistaken paths; while he wipes his head and ears he wishes to be absolved from every unreasonable thing which is counter to the religious law, and further, while wiping his face from all the acts of disobedience which he has committed.[39]

Purification was not the only purpose of ritual washings. They also "represented the symbolic bestowal of other attributes and blessings as well. In the Ancient Near East, ceremonial washings, or ablutions, were believed to purify the initiate, avert evil, give life and strength, and at times, symbolize a rebirth."[40] In addition, "in the minds of the ancients there was a close connection between the notion of purity or cleanness and the notion of being consecrated to God."[41] Hugh Nibley remarks, "Purification rather than being an end in itself, always prepares the way for things to follow, being part of a larger sequence of ordinances."[42] To be effective, ritual washings had to be followed by an anointing.[43]

"The rite of anointing . . . is the most sacred moment of all the royal ceremonies."[44] Understanding the significance of this rite begins with understanding the oil itself. Anointing oil is consecrated olive oil. "To the ancient Hebrews, olive oil was one of the necessities of life."[45] It was the staple of the Near Eastern diet and was present at every meal.

---

39 E. S. Drower, *The Mandaeans of Iraq and Iran* (Oxford: Clarendon Press, 1937), 104; quoted in J. Lyman Redd, "Aaron's Consecration: Its Nature, Purpose and Meaning," *Thy People Shall Be My People and Thy God My God: The 22nd Annual Sidney B. Sperry Symposium* (Salt Lake City: Deseret Book Company, 1994), 121.

40 Redd, 122.

41 Charles F. Pfeiffer, Howard F. Vos, and John Rea, eds., *Wycliffe Bible Dictionary* (Chicago: Moody Press, 1976), 1:7; quoted in Joseph Fielding McConkie, *Gospel Symbolism* (Salt Lake City: Bookcraft, 1988), 201.

42 Nibley, *Message of the Joseph Smith Papyri*, 143.

43 See ibid., 148.

44 S. Mayassis, *Mysteres et initiations dans la prehistoire et protohistoire de l'ante'-diluvien a Sumer-Babylone: La familiarite divine originelle.* 381. BAOA 3. Athens: BAOA, 1961; quoted in Nibley, *Message of the Joseph Smith Papyri*, 149.

45 John Gee and Daniel C. Peterson, "Graft and Corruption: On Olives and Olive Culture in the Pre-Modern Mediterranean," *The Allegory of the Olive Tree*, eds. Stephen D. Ricks and John W. Welch (Salt Lake City and Provo, Utah: Deseret Book Company and FARMS, 1994), 214.

It was the chief source of edible fat and was used as a condiment for salads, breads, and meats. Olive oil was just as valuable for medicinal purposes. It was an almost universal antidote. It was used in poultices to drain infection or sickness and as an ointment to soothe bruises, wounds, and open sores.[46] It was used as an emollient to soften wounds. People believed that it actually soaked deep into the bones.[47] It was also thought to lower fevers when applied to the head, to cure hemorrhoids, and to ease the pangs of childbirth.[48] It was used on the skin to prevent dryness and windburn and to cleanse the skin. In addition to these uses, olive oil was used in lamps to provide light, as in the parable of the ten virgins. Symbolically, olive oil represents the Holy Ghost. Just like oil, the Holy Ghost nourishes our soul, heals our spiritual wounds, softens our "skins," cleanses our sins, and is a source of spiritual light.

Ritual anointing was performed in ancient Israel for three groups of persons: prophets, priests, and kings. Anointing was also used on objects that were to be associated with the temple (i.e., the lampstand, the altars, the shovels, and other appurtenances) and on the temple itself. The primary purpose of this anointing was to set apart an object or individual for divine service. Once anointed with oil, the object or person was considered to be in a state of holiness and thus worthy to stand before God in a sacred setting.[49] When persons were anointed, the anointing served to formalize an elevation in official status. At the same time, it was believed to impart something of the holiness of God to the person.[50] In 1 Samuel 10:1, we read that Samuel took a vial of oil and poured it on Saul's head. This is particularly significant because Saul was the first king of Israel. Previous to this, anointing was a religious rite, performed on priests. By anointing Saul, the monarchy was inaugurated as a divine institution. Moreover, Samuel told Saul that having been anointed, the Spirit of the Lord would "rush upon

46 See Truman G. Madsen, "The Olive Press: A Symbol of Christ," *The Allegory of the Olive Tree*, eds. Stephen D. Ricks and John W. Welch (Salt Lake City and Provo, Utah: Deseret Book Company and FARMS, 1994), 3–4.

47 See Gee and Peterson, 222.

48 See ibid.

49 See Donald W. Parry, "Ritual Anointing with Olive Oil in Ancient Israelite Religion," *The Allegory of the Olive Tree*, 274.

50 See P. Kyle McCarter Jr., *I Samuel*, Anchor Bible, 178.

him."[51] Roland De Vaux explains, "Anointing is a religious rite. It is accompanied by a coming of the Spirit: we would say that it confers a grace."[52] The endowment of grace, power, and Spirit that came with this anointing was not for Saul alone. It was to enable him, and all kings of Israel, to bless God's people.

The anointing of oil was also a gesture of approach. In the ancient world, the sacred and the profane were antithetical powers and were to be kept separate and distinct. Not even the profane dust on the shoes was to be taken into holy space. Therefore, those priesthood holders who were to enter into holy space were required to remove any profane items (such as their shoes) from their persons, to ritually wash their hands and feet to further remove any traces of the profane world, to be sanctified through the anointing with oil, and finally to be clothed in the vestments of the priesthood. Only after these gestures were completed could they approach God.[53]

Anointing oil was also a part of secular gestures of approach. In a world where streets weren't paved, travel was dusty and dirty. When a guest arrived, it was customary to provide him with water in which to wash his feet. If the guest was an honored one, the host might also provide anointing oil. "In Homeric Greece . . . newly arrived guests at the house of a great king or Lord are washed, anointed with olive oil, and clothed before they sit down to the banquet table."[54] It seems this is but a type and shadow for the ultimate homecoming of righteous Saints. In an early Christian document, *Recognitiones,* Christ anoints "every one of the pious when they come to His kingdom, for their refreshment after their labours, as having got over the difficulties of the way; so that their light may shine, and being filled with the Holy Spirit, they may be endowed with immortality."[55]

One anointing rite that is found throughout the ancient world is the Opening of the Mouth. It was important in Babylonia, India, and

---

51 1 Samuel 10:6 and P. Kyle McCarter Jr., 166.

52 Roland de Vaux, *Ancient Israel: Its Life and Institutions*, trans. John McHugh (Grand Rapids, Michigan: William B. Eerdmans Publishing Company, 1961), 104.

53 See Parry, "Ritual Anointing with Olive Oil," 275–278.

54 Gee and Peterson, 219.

55 Stephen D. Ricks, "Olive Culture in the Second Temple Era and Early Rabbinic Period," *The Allegory of the Olive Tree*, 465.

especially in Egypt.[56] In this rite, the mouth was anointed to breathe, speak, and eat; the eyes were anointed to see; and the ears were anointed to hear. The purpose of the Opening of the Mouth rite was to assure a person's rebirth to a higher existence. It was an act of purification, exaltation, and deification.[57] It was the last rite performed on a person and was to immediately precede death. It ensured that each part of the body would once again perform its function, and thus the rite served to reverse the blows of death. In this, it fulfilled the same purpose as mummification—to prepare the dead to arise refreshed in the next world.[58]

The Opening of the Mouth rite was used on other occasions besides death. It was also part of the rites in which a king participated before receiving "the oils, the garments, and the simple ritual meal."[59] A corresponding rite was performed in Babylonia on priests at the time of their consecration and whenever they desired a renewal of their spiritual power.[60] The parts of the body that were touched in this rite vary. Hugh Nibley explains:

> Typical of one of the fuller lists is the anointing of Re himself, who receives the oil on head, cranium, brow, eyes, nose, mouth, tongue, teeth, lips, chin, back, arms, heart, belly, buttocks, thighs, legs, feet, and toes, in that order. The specific function of each part is usually named, as in the tomb of Tutankhamen: "I open thy mouth that thou mightest speak with it, thine eyes that thou mightest behold Re, thine ears that thou mayest hear the words of glorification (or exaltation), thy legs to walk with, thy breast and thine arms to drive off thine enemies."[61]

The Opening of the Mouth rite has Jewish and early Christian parallels. In an ancient apocryphal record called the Apocalypse of Moses, when Adam felt his death was imminent, he sent Eve and Seth "near to paradise" to ask God to send an angel to give them oil

56 See Nibley, *The Message of the Joseph Smith Papyri*, 168.

57 See ibid.

58 See ibid., 13.

59 Ibid., 168.

60 See ibid., 168–169.

61 Ibid., 179.

from the tree of life that Adam might be anointed preparatory to his death.[62] In another early Christian document, the Psalm of Thomas, "the gatekeeper asks of the candidate, 'Do his eyes see well? Does his mouth speak the truth? Are his hands pure? Is his heart firm? Do his feet run in the path of truth?'"[63] These questions seem to be another way of asking if the anointing rites had been performed.

Mesopotamian sources suggest "the washing of the mouth or purifying of the mouth grants or symbolizes special divine or quasi-divine status to the person or object so designated. The pure mouth enables the person or object to stand before the gods or to enter the divine realm, or symbolizes a divine status."[64] So it was for Isaiah. When he ascended into heaven to receive his prophetic call, he cried out, "Woe is me! for I am undone; because I am a man of unclean lips" (Isaiah 6:5). To be undone is to be cut off, ruined, or destroyed. In response, a seraph took one of the coals from the heavenly altar, placed this coal in Isaiah's mouth, and declared, "Thine iniquity is taken away, and thy sin purged" (Isaiah 6:7). Like water, fire, as represented by the coal, is another cleansing agent. Purified, Isaiah can "now fully participate with the heavenly host in offering praises to the Lord. He had become a member of the heavenly court."[65]

Following the rites of washing and anointing comes the rite of clothing in a sacred garment. Washing and anointing must precede this rite, for "no unclean person can be clothed in the garments of glory."[66]

Together, all three rites played an important role in the ancient world. They were part of coronation ceremonies and the investiture of priests. In Latter-day Saint temples today, they still "represent a call to the royal priesthood in the kingdom of God."[67] Anciently they were often done in preparation for marriage. In Ezekiel 16, Jerusalem (a

---

62 See ibid., 174.

63 Ibid., 175.

64 David E. Bokovoy, "The Calling of Isaiah," *Covenants, Prophecies, and Hymns of the Old Testament: The 30th Annual Sidney B. Sperry Symposium* (Salt Lake City: Deseret Book Company, 2001), 134.

65 Ibid.

66 Nibley, "Sacred Vestments," *CWHN*, 12:120.

67 John A. Tvedtnes, "Olive Oil: Symbol of the Holy Ghost," *The Allegory of the Olive Tree*, 434.

synecdoche for Israel) is personified as an abandoned baby girl whom Yahweh rescues from the wilderness, raises to maturity, and marries. Unfortunately, the bride does not stay faithful but becomes wildly promiscuous. For our purposes, the significant point is that before Yahweh marries his bride, she is washed with water, anointed with oil, and clothed in broidered work, fine linen, and silk (see Ezekiel 16:9–10). Similarly, before Ruth goes to Boaz with her proposal of marriage, Naomi tells her to "wash thyself therefore, and anoint thee, and put thy raiment upon thee" (Ruth 3:3). In ascension literature, before a visionary can enter into the celestial Holy of Holies, where he is transformed and becomes a member of the heavenly angelic host, he must be washed, anointed, and clothed. We see this in the ascension of Enoch. "God said to his angels, 'extract Enoch from [his] earthly clothing, and anoint him with my delightful oil, and put him into the clothes of my glory.'"[68] In the Epic of Gilgamesh, the Babylonian creation epic, the coming of age is signified by washing, anointing, and clothing. There, "Enkidu eats breads, drinks wine, anoints himself with oil, and puts on a garment 'and is like a man.'"[69] We may draw the correlation that washing, anointing, and clothing in special garments signifies a spiritual coming of age.

As we contemplate these rites and ordinances, it is intriguing to keep in mind that "ordinances are more than just symbols—they go beyond that. . . . They always have a double nature: they are or mean something that is real."[70] Heber C. Kimball said it this way, "All ordinances . . . are signs of things in the heavens. Everything we see here is typical of what will be hereafter."[71]

Prayer Circle

The *Encyclopedia of Mormonism* states, "The prayer circle is part of Latter-day Saint temple worship, usually associated with the endowment

68 2 Enoch 22:9, quoted in William J. Hamblin, "Temple Motifs in Jewish Mysticism," in *Temples of the Ancient World*, 453.

69 Stephen D. Ricks, "The Garment of Adam," 733.

70 Hugh Nibley, *Of All Things! Classic Quotations from Hugh Nibley*, ed. Gary P. Gillum (Salt Lake City and Provo, Utah: Deseret Book Company and FARMS, 1993), 42.

71 Heber C. Kimball, quoted in Linda Aukschun, "The Ordinances and Performances That Pertain to Salvation," *Riches of Eternity: 12 Fundamental Doctrines from the Doctrine and Covenants* (Salt Lake City: Aspen Books, 1900), 135.

ceremony. Participants, an equal number of men and women dressed in temple clothing, surround an altar in a circle formation to participate unitedly in prayer."[72] While most temple-attending Latter-day Saints would associate the prayer circle primarily with the temple endowment, the prayer circle is used in other contexts as well. It is part of the weekly meetings of the First Presidency and Quorum of the Twelve and the monthly meeting of all General Authorities in the Salt Lake Temple. In the history of the Church, it was used at times when there was a dire need to implore God, as when someone was critically ill. However, "on May 3, 1978, the First Presidency announced that all prayer circles outside the temple were to be discontinued."[73]

The prayer circle as we know it was introduced by Joseph Smith in 1843; however, praying in a circle had been going on for many years. It was inaugurated in the School of the Prophets at Kirtland, Ohio, in 1833.[74] Praying in circles would have been familiar to Joseph Smith and many of the early brethren, for it was part of many Protestant revivals in the early 1800s in America. "In the Methodist Episcopal revivals of the 1820s and 1830s, 'when the invitation was given, there was a general rush, the large 'prayer ring' was filled, and for at least two hours prayer ardent went up to God.'"[75] However, prayer circles did not originate in America in the 1800s. They have been around for a long time in many cultures.

We see allusions to prayer circles among the Plains Indians, who gather in a great circle, put their arms around each other, and then "begin to dance toward the flowing Tree."[76] "According to the Moslem commentators, all creatures form in circles around God to be taught."[77] As early as the fourth century BC, a man named Heliodorus was traveling in Egypt and saw a council of twelve holy

72 George S. Tate, "Prayer Circle," *Encyclopedia of Mormonism*, 1120.

73 Ibid., 121.

74 See D. Michael Quinn, "Latter-day Saint Prayer Circles," *BYU Studies* 19, no. 1 (Fall 1979): 83–84.

75 Rev. James Erwin, *Reminiscences of Early Circuit Life Toledo* (Ohio: Spear, Johnson & Co., 1884), 68; quoted in Quinn, 81.

76 Hyemeyohsts Storm, *Seven Arrows* (New York: Harper & Row, 1979), 20; quoted in Nibley, "The Early Christian Prayer Circle," *CWHN*, 4:65.

77 Nibley, "The Early Christian Prayer Circle," 4:65.

men sitting in a circle. In the midst of the circle were three altars.[78] More explicit references fill early Christian documents. Hugh Nibley discusses many of these in his article, "The Early Christian Prayer Circle." Two of his many examples will suffice here. "In 2 Jeu the apostles and their wives form a circle around Jesus specifically 'so that he can *teach* them the ordinances of the treasury of light, they being conducted by him through all the ordinances and thereby learning to progress in the hereafter."[79] Nibley comments, "The whole situation centers around the Last Supper and belongs to the church from the beginning."[80] A very old text attributed to Clement of Rome and preserved in a seventh-century Syriac translation describes in great detail one prayer circle: "As leader the bishop stands in the middle . . . all give each other the sign of peace. Next, when absolute silence is established, the deacon says: 'Let your hearts be to heaven. If anyone has any ill feeling towards his neighbor, let him be reconciled. If anyone has any hesitation or mental reservations [doubts] let him make it known.'"[81] Nibley further explains, "A sort of antiphonal follows with the people on the ring responding to the words of the bishop. Then the bishop begins the prayer proper, the people repeating these same things, praying."[82]

According to the early documents, the prayers offered in the prayer circle are not set prayers. Each prayer is unique and determined by the one leading the circle. The leader speaks as the Spirit directs him, and those in the circle repeat each line after him. One feature that is fairly standard was to pray for others, both the living and the dead. "As Cyril of Jerusalem explains it, 'In the circle we pray for those who are sick and afflicted; in short, we pray for whoever is in need of help.'"[83] Since the list of names could be quite long and some names could inadvertently be left off, it became common to write these names down. "At first the list of names was read aloud before being placed on the altar, but as that took up too much time (one of the surviving lists has more

78 See ibid., 4:66.

79 Ibid., 4:63.

80 Ibid., 4:64.

81 Ibid., 4:47–48.

82 Ibid., 4:48.

83 Ibid., 4:79.

than 350 names), the reading was phased out; 'the list could be placed on the altar without any vocal reading of the names.'"[84] Interestingly, today, many Jews write prayers on pieces of papers and slip them into the crannies of the Western Wall, a place of supreme holiness to the Jews because it is the only remaining structure from the ancient temple complex (see figure 4-1). Instead of prayers, the Orthodox Jews used to write lists of names on the pieces of paper.[85]

For the first-time temple patron, a prayer circle may initially seem quite unfamiliar. However, with a moment's reflection, we see that we are actually quite accustomed to the idea. We frequently see a circle of priesthood holders gather to pray over and bless a baby or to confer the Holy Ghost upon one who has just been baptized. There are also some scriptures with which we are well acquainted that may be tacit references to prayer circles. For instance, in 3 Nephi we read of "angels descending out of heaven as it were in the midst of fire; and they came down and encircled those little ones about, and they were encircled about with fire; and the angels did minister unto them" (3 Nephi 17:24). The text is silent at this point, shrouding in sacredness the details of the angelic ministration, but the image of children encircled by angels (probably heavenly priesthood holders) evokes images of a prayer circle. It may not be immaterial that angels encircle little children. "The prayer circle is the nearest approach to the Lord that men make on earth—and they can approach him only 'as little children.'"[86] Luke 11:1–2 may also be a reference to prayer circles: "As he was praying in a certain place, when he ceased, one of his disciples said unto him, Lord, teach us to pray" (Luke 11:1). Christ responds with what is known as

Figure 4-1. Prayer papers at the Western Wall.

84 Ibid., 4:76.

85 Orthodox Jews would likely find prayer circles familiar. Jewish law stated that ten was the minimum number required to form a minyan, or quorum, for group prayers. These prayers were typically offered while the group stood in a circle.

86 Nibley, "The Early Christian Prayer Circle," 4:56.

the Lord's Prayer. We can almost imagine Christ teaching His disciples just as we teach children, by repetition.

Prayer circles are not limited to mortality. Lehi sees "God sitting upon his throne, surrounded with numerous concourses of angels in the attitude of singing and praising their God" (1 Nephi 1:8). Nibley explains that "surrounding concourses are concentric circles."[87] It appears that Lehi sees a celestial prayer circle. We know that in the premortal councils God "stood in the midst" of the noble and great ones and said, "These I will make my rulers; for he stood among those that were spirits, and he saw that they were good" (Abraham 3:23). It may well be that God was standing in a celestial prayer circle and that "Abraham was standing in that circle."[88] Nibley suggests "each [earthly] prayer circle is a faithful reproduction of the celestial pattern."[89]

In contemplating the significance of the prayer circle, it is well to remember that in forming a prayer circle, one turns his back on the outer world and turns toward God, as represented by the altar. But facing God with heart and soul is not enough. We must draw close to God not as lone individuals but collectively as Saints who live in unity and harmony, bearing no ill will or negative feelings toward others. Why this emphasis on unity and collective righteousness? According to Joseph Smith, "The greatest temporal and spiritual blessings . . . always come from faithfulness and concerted effort . . . [rather than through] individual exertion or enterprise."[90] But there is more than that. The temple endowment presents a series of covenants that are increasingly more demanding. Even above chastity, even above losing our attachment for the things of the world, the pinnacle of Christian life is living in complete harmony with our families, wards, societies, and world. It is this that typified the Zion societies of Enoch and 4 Nephi. Unity of heart and mind is enjoined not only to eliminate the effect of contention but because it is sanctifying. We simply cannot become like Christ by ourselves. As Marcus Barth has written:

> Love needs the neighbor and is dependent upon him.
> The neighbor—even the one who is a burden and

87 Ibid., 4:53.

88 Nibley, "Unrolling the Scrolls—Some Forgotten Witnesses," *CWHN*, 1:162.

89 Nibley, "The Early Christian Prayer Circle," 4:69.

90 Smith, *TPJS*, 183.

> whose character and behavior prove cumbersome—is much more than an occasion or test of love. He is the very material. Love . . . does not exist in a vacuum, *in abstracto*, in detachment from involvement in other men's lives. . . . [It] takes place exclusively when one lives with specific men, women, children, old people, relatives, and strangers.[91]

The prayer circle symbolizes the Zion-like unity of those who are about to enter into the presence of God. It is the goal and the ideal of Saints who might experience slightly less unity in their everyday relationships. However, this is the purpose of all the temple covenants and ordinances, to help us become like Christ, to learn to love as He loves, to achieve "that divine nature that will return us into his presence again."[92]

---

91 Markus Barth, *Ephesians 4–6*, Anchor Bible, 460.

92 Howard W. Hunter, *Teachings*, 218.

Understanding the Symbolism of Clothing

Since earliest times, clothing has been highly symbolic. Only language surpasses clothing in its ability to convey important information about power, authority, status, and identity.[1] This is true in both the ancient world and in our world today. For instance, in our world a policeman's uniform and a judge's robes symbolize power and authority. Labels like Christian Dior and Versace say things that less expensive labels do not. Clothing conveys information about identity. A kilt, a kimono, and wooden shoes identify specific countries. The plaids of a kilt and the pattern of an Arab headdress define a clan and a tribe, respectively. Hassidic Jewish men are identified by their dark coats and brimmed hats. Catholic clergy are distinguished by their clerical collars and nuns by their habits. The *color* of clothing also conveys information. Schools have specific colors that students and alumni wear when they want to declare their allegiance to that school. In the fashion world, red is bold; black is chic. Black and white have traditionally represented good and evil. White represents purity, as in the case of a wedding dress. Light blue is associated with baby boys and pink with baby girls. Clothing also provides protection. Coats and sweaters protect us from the cold. A firefighter's uniform protects against fire. A football uniform, with its pads and helmet, protects a football player from pounding tackles. Certain clothing is associated with rites of passage. At a graduation the "cap and gown announced that the wearer had accepted certain rules of living and been tested in special kinds of knowledge."[2]

---

1 See Carol Meyers, *Exodus* (Cambridge: Cambridge University Press, 2005), 244.

2 Hugh Nibley, "Leaders to Managers: The Fatal Shift," *CWHN*, 494.

In the biblical world, clothing was even more significant, largely because this world was predominantly a subsistence economy. Procuring clothing was not as simple as going to the local department store and picking out the latest fashion. It diverted valuable resources from the all-consuming task of sustaining life. Therefore, garments were scarce and consequently valuable. Only the rich could afford multiple garments. For rich and poor alike, the wearing out of a garment was a distressing event. Clothing was so valuable it was taken as a plunder of war and was given as surety for one's pledge. Another indicator of the preciousness of clothing shows up in the realm of covenants. In the ancient world, covenants were accompanied by curses and blessings for breaking and keeping one's word. The curses were meant to be forceful deterrents to breaking a covenant and were therefore graphic and horrifying. They included devouring beasts, parents eating their own children because of famine, men eating their own dung, wives being ravished, warriors being turned into women, warriors being left unburied as food for vultures and moths. Moths? In our world, moths rarely strike terror to our souls. They seem out of place on this rather grim list. But the fact that moths make their way into covenant curses reveals how valuable clothing was. [3] On the other end of the spectrum, clothing is listed as one of the rewards and blessings for keeping one's covenants. We read in 1 Enoch that when the righteous and elect are resurrected they shall be given garments of glory that shall never wear out.[4]

Clothing in the Bible had a variety of symbolic associations. Tearing one's clothing was a powerful statement of intense grief, rage, or fear. For instance, in Matthew 26:64, Christ declared that in the future He would be "sitting on the right hand of power and coming in the clouds of heaven." Sitting on the right hand of a deity implies ruling alongside God and sharing in His authority by His invitation and with His support. It signifies equality with God and was an extraordinary claim for a man to make. To Caiaphas, it was nothing less than outrageous blasphemy. It warranted a gesture of shock and horror. And so the high priest rent his clothes.

In the book of Ruth, we see a different symbolic use of clothing. In the middle of the night, Ruth approached Boaz and uncovered his

3 See Isaiah 51:8.

4 See Darrell L. Bock and Gregory J. Herrick, *Jesus in Context: Background Readings for Gospel Study* (Grand Rapids, Michigan: Baker Academic, 2005), 118.

feet. Shortly thereafter, she asked Boaz to cover her with the corner of his robe. With this request, Ruth was asking him to protect her and more specifically to marry her. We see clothing as a status marker when Jacob gave Joseph the "coat of many colors." This garment signified that Joseph was the birthright son and heir to the spiritual leadership of the family. Since clothing was an identity marker, appropriating another's clothing was an act of deceit, as when Jacob donned Esau's clothing to receive his father's deathbed blessing.

Most interesting is the act of putting on clothing. When Esther put on her royal robes to come into the presence of the king, she was asserting her rights as a queen. When Elijah gave his mantle to Elisha, he was issuing a call to Elisha to be the next prophet. Taking the symbolism to the next level, Paul admonished the Saints to put off the old man and to "put on Christ" (see Colossians 3:9; Galatians 3:27). Paul is enjoining the Saints to put on Christ's identity, protection, and authority as they would put on a garment. "To put on Christ" means being completely enwrapped by Christ and being completely transformed.

It may be that in the next world, clothing will also be significant. We know from the parable of the wedding feast in Matthew 22 that those who are invited to the eschatological wedding banquet will need to wear a wedding garment. Several times in Revelation, inhabitants of this earth who become exalted beings are said to be "clothed in white" (Revelation 3:5, 4:4, 7:9). Angels who have great power and authority are dressed not only in white but with special golden girdles or sashes like those worn by Christ (see Revelation 15:6). The importance of clothing in the next world is also found in apocryphal writings. In the Manual of Discipline, found among the Dead Sea Scrolls, we read that all who walk in truth shall be crowned with "a crown of glory and a garment of majesty in unending light."[5] In 1 Enoch, it says, "My spirit passed out of sight and ascended into the heavens. And I saw the sons of the holy angels walking upon the flame of fire; their garments were white—and their overcoats—and the light of their faces was like snow."[6] In the *Pistis Sophia*, a glorious garment "is a means to pass by the angels

5 Geza Vermes, ed. and trans., *The Dead Sea Scrolls in English* (Baltimore, MD: Penguin Books, 1962), 76; quoted in Blake Ostler, "Clothed Upon: A Unique Aspect of Christian Antiquity," *BYU Studies* 22, no. 1 (Winter 1982): 38.

6 Bock and Herrick, 191.

stationed to block the way to the gate of heaven."[7] In the Gospel of Philip, "The (demonic) powers do not see those who are clothed in the perfect light, and consequently are not able to detain them."[8] According to apocryphal literature, the righteous are ultimately "received into the presence of God and are allowed to wear the special clothing."[9]

In this dispensation, some have had experiences that have confirmed the importance of clothing in the next world. One such person was Sister J. W. Crosby. When Sister Crosby was eighty years old and had been working for some years in the temple, she decided she had done enough and did not need to tax her strength any longer. She, in effect, announced her retirement from temple work. A short time later, she was back in the temple, serving as always. When asked what happened, she recounted a dream she had. She had finished her work and passed to the other side. There, she saw a procession of women with white robes coming to meet her with banners of welcome. She did not recognize any of the women and asked why they were honoring her. They explained it was because she "honored them by giving them their white robes."[10] She also saw some women dressed in common clothes. When she asked why they had not joined the others in the joyful procession, she learned they had not yet had their white robes given to them. Consequent to her vision, Sister Crosby recommitted to temple work for as long as she lived.[11]

Aprons of Fig Leaves

In Genesis, the newly formed Adam and the newly built Eve were "naked . . . and were not ashamed" (Genesis 2:25). It is not clear whether this nakedness was literal or figurative. If the nakedness was literal, Adam and Eve, like newborn babies, were simply too innocent to be bothered by their lack of clothing. On the other hand, their nakedness may have been figurative. Nakedness is frequently symbolic of judgment and humiliation, but it also represents its opposite—innocence. Because Adam and Eve were innocent, they were not

7 Ostler, "Clothed Upon," 41.

8 William J. Hamblin, "Aspects of an Early Christian Initiation Ritual," *BSAABF*, 1:213.

9 John A. Tvedtnes, "Priestly Clothing in Bible Times," *Temples of the Ancient World*, 685.

10 Joseph Heinerman, *Spirit World Manifestations* (Salt Lake City: Joseph Lyon & Associates, 1978), 83.

11 See ibid.

ashamed, independent of what they were or were not wearing. But there is also a third possibility. It may be that Adam and Eve were not ashamed because they were clothed with glory. "The Book of the Rolls informs us that when Adam was created, 'his body was bright and brilliant like the well-known stars in the crystal.' When Adam and Eve were placed on earth, 'God clothed them with glory and splendour.'"[12] The glory with which they were clothed could be considered a garment of light. This they wore until they partook of the fruit. At this time they lost their garments of light, symbolizing their premortal glory,[13] and they became truly naked. Satan pointed out their nakedness as if it were something new, and Adam and Eve made aprons of fig leaves to cover up. God upgraded their makeshift aprons to garments of skins.

There is an interesting wordplay between garments of light and garments of skin. In Hebrew, the word for *light* is אוֹר *'ôr*. The word for *skins* is עוֹר *'ôr.* It is the same word except the first, silent letter is different.[14] Indeed, it is even pronounced the same. Thus, God exchanges one garment of *'ôr* for another garment of *'ôr*. According to many ancient documents, the first garment of *'ôr*, the garment of light, is laid up in heaven and will be restored to Adam and Eve when they return to God. The second garment of *'ôr*, the garment of skin, is an interim garment, a reminder of the glory and light that await them. Even though this second garment is inferior to the first, it was still "of extraordinary brilliance and splendor and possessed of supernatural qualities."[15] These powers include protecting the wearer's body and imparting wisdom.[16] This garment was also a sign of authority, one that even the animals recognized.[17]

12 Tvedtnes, "Priestly Clothing," 653.

13 See Nibley, *Message of the Joseph Smith Papyri*, 489.

14 Hebrew reads from right to left. Therefore, the first letter in the word אוֹר is א.

15 Ricks, "Garment of Adam," 710.

16 See Tvedtnes, "Priestly Clothing," 661.

17 "The coats which the Holy One . . . made for Adam and his wife were with Noah in the ark . . . . When they went forth from the ark, Ham, the son of Noah, brought them forth with him, and gave them as an inheritance to Nimrod. When he put them on, all the beasts, . . . came and prostrated themselves before him [because this was the garment which Adam wore in the garden, and the beasts all reverenced him because he had dominion over them as long as he acted as God would act]." Gerald Friedlander, *Pirke de Rabbi Eliezer* (New York: Hermon, 1965), 175; quoted in Nibley, "Sacred Vestments," 12:129–130.

When Adam and Eve discovered their nakedness, their immediate response was to make aprons of fig leaves. An apron of fig leaves is one of those rich symbols that can be interpreted on several levels. First and foremost, the aprons represent Adam's and Eve's efforts to cover their sins. Having one's sins exposed is an uncomfortable, humiliating, vulnerable experience. The natural desire is to cover them up. There are two ways to do so. First, sins can be covered up by hiding them. We can hide them by lying about them or by trying to conceal their consequences, particularly the public, visible consequences. Abortion is an example of this. We may also try to hide our sins more subtly by simply ignoring them and pretending they don't exist or minimizing them with rationalization and excuses.

The second way to cover our sins is through the Atonement of Christ.[18] When sins are covered through the Atonement, they are not simply concealed; they are deleted. They are covered because they are no more. When Adam and Eve made aprons of fig leaves, they attempted to hide their transgression. Their efforts were flawed, not only because hiding is inferior to atoning, but also because they attempted to take care of their transgression through their own efforts. This denies the Savior's role. Moreover, when God covered their nakedness, he did so through the sacrifice of an animal, teaching them that the true cost of covering one's sins is the blood of the Lamb. Leaves can be plucked off a tree without hurting the tree. This is not so with animal sacrifice, which requires the total surrender of the animal's life. The implications of this are sobering. Salvation is not casual or cheap—not for Christ and not for us. It is soul trembling and knee bending. No half measures will do.

The covering of sins is probably the most evident meaning associated with the fig leaf apron, but it is not the only one. Aprons symbolize fertility and reproduction. "Apparently, in ancient Semitic custom, young children ran about with a loose shirt or cloak. As they reached sexual maturity, they began to wear an 'apron' or loincloth."[19] Not

18 In Hebrew, the word for "atonement," *kipper,* means "to cover over." Yom Kippur is the Day (*yom*) of Atonement, or the Day of Covering. We might say that the Sabbath Day with the sacred ordinance of the sacrament is, at its ideal, our Day of Covering.

19 Carol Meyers, "Apron," *The Anchor Bible Dictionary*, 1:319.

only the apron, but the fig also represents fertility. The fig, along with wheat, barley, vines, pomegranates, olive oil, and honey, represented the fertility of the promised land (see Deuteronomy 8:8). Figs also have a lot of seeds. Adam and Eve put on aprons of fig leaves because they could now bear seed.

To make aprons from the leaves of fig trees, one has to pull the leaves off the tree.[20] Detached from the branches and deprived of nourishment, the leaves won't live long. Thus, fig-leaf aprons represent death and mortality. In addition, when Adam and Eve covered themselves with leaves, they became, in a sense, trees. Trees frequently represent mankind. Proud men are the tall cedars of Lebanon. Israel is an olive tree. A tree that does not bear fruit represents a person who does not perform good works. But Adam and Eve aren't to be just any trees. They are to be trees planted by a river, the trees described in Ezekiel 47 and which show up again in the book of Revelation. These trees bear fruit continuously and have leaves that never fade and have the power to heal. They represent righteous men and women whose roots are deep and who drink in the divine knowledge, power, and attributes of Living Water. So nourished, they bear the fruit of righteous works, and they heal themselves and others (see Revelation 22:2). These are they who have eternal life, as represented by the leaves that never fade. It may also be that in becoming like trees, Adam and Eve are also expressing their spiritual destiny of becoming like Christ, the Tree of Life. The temple is a series of ordinances that help us become more like Christ.

Finally, the aprons of fig leaves reveal something about the identity and origin of the wearer. While traveling in Guatemala, Milton R. Hunter noticed as they passed through one village after another that "all the men in each village wore identical clothing, and each woman was dressed like all the other women in her particular village. We observed also that the clothing worn in one village was entirely different from that of other villages."[21] Similarly, the pattern of Scottish kilts varies

---

20 According to the *Genesis Rabbah*, the tree of knowledge of good and evil is the fig tree. It was with great difficulty that Adam and Eve sewed these leaves together to "make girdles, shirts, robes, and linen cloaks." Ricks, "Garment of Adam," 709.

21 Milton R. Hunter, *Archaeology and the Book of Mormon* (Salt Lake City: Deseret Book Company, 1956), 66.

from clan to clan and serves as an identity marker. The *Encyclopedia of World Costume* shows various aprons worn in Egypt by kings, priests, and initiates. One of these aprons was made to look like the "lily and papyrus plants, which were, respectively, the sacred symbols of Upper and Lower Egypt. The foliage on this apron thus served to identify the nationality of the wearer."[22] To wear aprons of fig leaves, plucked from a tree of the earth, is to identify oneself as an earthling, or a human being.

The color of an apron, as well as the material from which it is made, may also convey specific things about the identity of the wearer. For instance, in ancient Israel, the mixture of the colors blue, purple, and scarlet was sacred. The high priest wore three articles of clothing (the ephod, breastplate, and belt) that contained this sacred combination of colors. The priests could only use these colors in a belt, and the ordinary Israelite was permitted only a single blue thread of wool in his linen tassels.[23] Green, the color of the fig-leaf aprons, symbolizes life. When Adam and Eve don green aprons, they are signifying they have become living, mortal beings; they have begun their journey through mortal life. A black apron could signify the wearer comes from a place of darkness or that his power and authority come from darkness and evil.

Garments of Skins

God exchanged the aprons of figs leaves for "coats of skins" (Genesis 3:21). The word used for *coat* is *kuttōnet* and could also be translated as *tunic* or *garment*. A *kuttōnet* is a garment that is worn next to one's skin. Both men and women wore it. It is also the word used for the garments worn by the priests of Israel, indicating that these garments were ones designating priesthood authority. The garment of skins given to Adam and Eve were to be garments of protection. They would protect Adam and Eve from the harsh elements of nature and from the even harsher onslaughts of Satan. The garments that faithful, endowed members of the Church wear today serve the same purpose. The temple garment is endowed with the power to protect us from the dangers of the physical world that would threaten our lives. But the spiritual risks of the world

22 Matthew B. Brown, "Girded about with a Lambskin," *Journal of Book of Mormon Studies* 6, no. 2 (1997): 139.

23 See Jacob Milgrom, *Leviticus 17–22*, Anchor Bible, 1660, 1662.

in which we live are far greater. The garment insulates us from the dangers of the fallen world—pride, immorality, and assimilation into the ways of the world. The garment gives "protection from Satan by continually reminding the person of his or her true identity."[24]

Our garments are a reminder of the sacred covenants we make with God. Thus, our relationship to the garment is tantamount to our relationship to our covenants. As the First Presidency said, how we wear the garment is an "outward expression of an inward commitment to follow the Savior."[25] But the relationship between the garment and the Savior is even more poignant. The ordinance that provided Adam and Eve with their garment of skin was the sacrifice of an animal, probably a lamb. Christ is the Lamb of God. He was slain to cover our sins. Thus, it "is also Christ who is symbolized by the clothing Adam and Eve received as they left Eden. This clothing represents the crucified flesh of Christ."[26]

The early Christian saints were admonished by Paul to "put on Christ" (Galatians 3:27), which they did when they were baptized. It appears this was not merely figurative. Baptism into the early Christian church "presupposes the [literal] removal of clothing as one enters the water, signifying separation from 'the old man with his deeds' (Colossians 3:9). The new robe, put on as one comes out of the water, signifies Christ himself."[27] The early Saints saw putting on this garment as putting on Christ. It meant taking on the character and authority of Christ. It is also an image of being enwrapped in Christ's protection and love. Latter-day Saints put on Christ with the temple garment. When our eyes are open to the connection between the garment and Christ, wearing the garment can be a constant expression of being "encircled about eternally in the arms of his love" (2 Nephi 1:15). It is no small thing that our "garments bear several simple marks,"[28] for Christ's flesh also bears the marks of His sacrifice. In his heavenly vision, John

---

24 Tvedtnes, "Olive Oil," 436.

25 First Presidency Letter, October 10, 1988; quoted in Carlos E. Asay, "The Temple Garment: 'An Outward Expression of an Inward Commitment,'" *Ensign*, August 1997, 22.

26 Gaskill, 90.

27 J. Louis Martyn, *Galatians*, Anchor Bible, 375–376.

28 Asay, 20.

sees "a Lamb as it had been slain" (Revelation 5:6) near the throne of God. The Lamb bears "the marks of a violent death."[29] It is an image that should give us pause as we consider both the Atonement and the garment. Among other things, these marks should serve as a reminder of just how costly the temple garments are. Indeed, they are one of the costliest garments we can wear.

CLOTHING IN ANCIENT ISRAEL

In the Biblical world, men typically wore an undergarment that was either a skirt that wrapped around the waist and hung to the knee or a short-sleeved, tunic-like garment (the *kuttōnet*). This would usually be belted with a leather or cloth strip. On top of this, they wore an outer garment or robe that was draped around the body and pinned, belted, or fastened. This garment was ultimately practical, providing warmth, a convenient way to carry things, and a cover for sleeping. But it was also symbolic. "Typically, the greater the ornamentation on the outer garment, the greater the importance of the individual in society."[30] A king's outer robe would be decidedly different from that of an ordinary Israelite. A priest's "special outerwear depicted power, prestige, and identity."[31] Robes are standard symbols for the power of heaven, or priesthood, and the wearer is to be viewed as the earthly representative of God. Hugh Nibley notes, "The classic robe of the initiate through the East has always been and still is the pure white . . . wrap thrown over the shoulder, which also represents an embrace."[32] This statement points out three important ideas associated with the outer garment: the white robe, the robe over the shoulder, and the robe as an embrace.

THE WHITE ROBE

White is not the color of everyday wear, especially in the ancient world, where the physical demands of daily life were rigorous. It was, however, the color of the linen garments the Jewish priests wore as they officiated in the temple. It was also the color of garments regularly worn by the

29 Richard D. Draper, *Opening the Seven Seals: The Visions of John the Revelator* (Salt Lake City: Deseret Book Company, 1991), 55.

30 Douglas R. Edwards, "Dress and Ornamentation," *The Anchor Bible Dictionary*, 2:234.

31 Ibid., 2:233.

32 Ricks, "The Garment of Adam," 723.

Romans and Greeks when they worshipped their heavenly deities and on ceremonial occasions in general.[33] In addition, it was the color of the robes given to newly baptized members of the early Christian Church.[34] In other words, white is the color of the sacred and the celestial.

The symbols associated with white garments are many and varied. White garments are symbolic of heavenly splendor and salvation. White is also the color of victory and triumph, which is another reason celestial beings are clothed in white—they have triumphed over their enemies and have put them under their feet.[35] For human beings, white garments represent a state of innocence, purity, and righteousness. Walking in white (see Revelation 3:4) is a way of describing those who are justified. The white clothes that a priest in Israel wore, called the garments of salvation or the garments of righteousness, "show[ed] that his sins had been forgiven and he was fit to serve before the throne of Elohim."[36] The "white robe, along with the anointing, symbolized the Holy Ghost's protection against Satan."[37]

As Latter-day Saints, we could say that white is the color of the covenant, for it is the color of the clothing we wear when we are baptized and when in the temple. From this perspective, Rabbi Levi Nydle's observation is particularly interesting. "According to the mystics, the color white is symbolic of the divine attribute of mercy or Chesed."[38] In scripture, *ḥesed* (or *chesed*) is usually translated as "loving kindness," "unfailing love," and "faithfulness." It describes a tender love expressed in acts of kindness. However, it is not random kindness or universal love. It is the love that exists between people in a covenant relationship. Indeed, it exists *because* of the covenant relationship. It is no small thing that when God is seen He is always dressed in white, the color of *ḥesed*, for God is the embodiment of covenant faithfulness. From His *ḥesed*, rich blessings flow. "Both forgiveness for the penitent and assistance for the obedient are regarded as expressions of God's faithfulness [His *ḥesed*]

33 See ibid., 724.

34 Stephen D. Ricks, "The Garment of Adam," 715–716.

35 See Smith, *TPJS*, 297.

36 Rabbi Edward Levi Nydle/Levi bar Ido, "White Garments: Significant of Wearing White Garments on the Shabbat," February 26, 2007, http://www.bnaiavraham.net/teaching_articles/english_teachings/RabbiEd/WHITE_GARMENTS.htm.

37 Tvedtnes, "Priestly Clothing," 672.

38 Rabbi Edward Levi Nydle/Levi bar Ido.

to his covenanted people, his willingness to meet fully his responsibility for the people with whom he initiated a relationship."[39]

The opposite of white garments are defiled garments, garments that bear the blood and stains of sin. We defile our garments by breaking or ignoring our covenants. "Inscriptions found in Asia Minor . . . announced that soiled garments disqualified the worshiper and dishonored the god."[40]

The Robe Draped over the Shoulder

Images of priests, kings, and heroes wearing special robes made from animals skins draped over one shoulder have survived from the ancient world. For instance, an Egyptian votive bronze statue of a man with a leopard skin draped over his left shoulder was found in the Greek city of Ephesus. Paintings of couples walking into eternity with the man wearing a leopard skin robe on one shoulder can be seen inside of tombs located in Heliopolis and Thebes.[41] A picture of Jehu, an Israelite king, on the Black Obelisk of Shalmaneser III, an Assyrian king, can be seen in the British Museum. In this depiction, Jehu has a robe with tassels thrown over his shoulder. His attendants also have fringed mantles upon their left shoulders.[42] The image of a robe draped over one shoulder can also be found in the Old Testament. Isaiah 9:6 reads, "For unto us a child is born, unto us a son is given and the government shall be upon his shoulder." This verse describes "the vesting right of a king as part of the coronation and enthronement ceremony wherein the king places or has placed upon his shoulders the robe of legal authority."[43] It is noteworthy that Isaiah uses the singular *shoulder*, not the plural. What is the significance of this image that shows up in so many places

---

39 Katharine Doob Sakenfeld, *The Meaning of Hesed in the Hebrew Bible: A New Inquiry* (Eugene, Oregon: Wipf and Stock Publishers, 1978), 237.

40 Ford, 409.

41 See Nibley, "Sacred Vestments," 12:101. Hugh Nibley points out that while the early Egyptian priests wore real leopard skins, in later times they wore a "close-fitting coat of fine linen in the form of a leopard-skin." (H. R. Hall, "The Bronze Statuette of Khonserdaisu in the British Museum," *Journal of Egyptian Archaeology* 16 (1930); quoted in Hugh Nibley, "Notes to 'The World of the Jaredites,'" *CWHN*, 5:267.

42 See Edwards, 2:233.

43 Donald W. Parry, Jay A. Parry, and Tina M. Peterson, *Understanding Isaiah* (Salt Lake City: Deseret Book Company, 1998), 96.

and so many cultures? (For example, see figure 5-1.) In all these cases, a robe draped over one shoulder represents kingly or priestly power. However, there are other associations as well.

The pseudepigraphic work entitled "The Shepherd of Hermas" describes a vision of twelve virgins, four of whom were standing at the gate of a tower. The tower represents the Church. The virgins are "clothed with linen tunics, and gracefully girded, having their right shoulders exposed, as if about to bear some burden."[44] The exposed right shoulders imply that the robe was draped over the left shoulder.[45] That they are about to bear a burden implies that the women are in the exalted role of service and bearing others' burdens. Hermas is told by an angel that all those who were to be found in the kingdom of God would need to have received clothing from these virgins. The clear implication is that in the kingdom of God, kingly and priestly power is inextricably connected with service and bearing one another's burdens.

Figure 5-1. Coat worn on one shoulder.

The Robe as An Embrace

The robe over the shoulder also represents an embrace. In an embrace, one arm goes up over the shoulder while the other encircles the waist, just like a robe draped on a shoulder. The embrace symbolizes atonement. Hugh Nibley writes, "How do you become one? Well, the ultimate becoming one is a fusion in an embrace. . . . *Kippur* means atonement, and it also means embrace, the literal act of hugging."[46] Elder Bruce Hafen adds, "Being clasped in the arms of Jesus Christ symbolizes the fulfillment of His Atonement in our personal lives, here as well as in heaven, becoming literally 'at one' with Him, belonging to Him, as He will belong to us."[47]

44 Pastor of Hermas, Similitude 9:2 in Coxe, *Fathers of the Second Century*, 43; quoted in Tvedtnes, "Priestly Clothing," 674.

45 See Tvedtnes, "Priestly Clothing," 700.

46 Hugh Nibley, *Teachings of the Book of Mormon*, 2:270.

47 Bruce C. Hafen and Marie K. Hafen, *The Belonging Heart: The Atonement and Relationships with God and Family* (Salt Lake City: Deseret Book Company, 1994), 102.

Sashes, Bows, and Knots

Not only robes, but sashes, bows, and knots also had symbolic meaning. The sash "is a typical ceremonial accouterment of high officials."[48] In the Old Testament period, the Mosaic priests wore a sash or girdle around their waist when working in the tabernacle. In the book of Revelation, John sees Christ "clothed with a garment down to the foot, and girt about the paps with a golden girdle" (Revelation 1:13). The New International Version uses the word *sash* instead of *girdle*. Robert Mounce says, "The sash that gathered together the long robe of the exalted Christ ([the robe] probably came down diagonally from one shoulder to the waist) was gold."[49] The "high girding ('around his chest') denotes the dignity of an important office."[50]

Sashes and belts were tied with bows and knots. These too are symbolic. In some Eastern cultures, the tying of a bowknot was a marriage custom that symbolized the binding of two people. This was also a British and Irish marriage tradition called "handfastening." In this custom, the couple's hands were joined and then wrapped and tied with ribbon. From this comes the old cliché "tying the knot." In many cultures, a knot represents a covenant, something that binds and fastens. A knot can also represent security and safety because with a knot, you tie a thing and make it safe. If you look carefully at Facsimile 3 in the Pearl of Great Price, you can see two knots (see figure 5-2). Matthew B. Brown explains:

> Figures 5 and 6 are both dressed in pleated and fringed aprons secured by knotted sashes. "The apron was generally fastened by a girdle, or by a sort of sash, tied in front in a bow or knot." . . . This sounds very much like the Israelite priest's sash which was "wound under the breast, twice around the body, was tied in an ample bow or loop, and the ends reached to the ankles. It was thrown over the left shoulder while the priest was officiating."[51]

48 Meyers, *Exodus*, 243.

49 Robert H. Mounce, *The Book of Revelation* (Grand Rapids, Michigan: William B. Eerdmans Publishing Company, 1998), 58.

50 Mounce, 58.

51 Brown, "Girded about with a Lambskin," 138, 139.

Figure 5-2. Facsimile 3, book of Abraham.

Figure 5-3. The Ankh.
Image courtesy of Alexi Helligar

The Egyptian symbol of life, the *ankh*, closely resembles a sash tied around the waist with a knot in the sash and the ends of the tie extended instead of hanging down,[52] which "is similar in many ways to the knot in the girdle worn by gods."[53] (See figure 5-3.)

Marks

One interesting peculiarity of clothing in ancient Israel is the presence of certain marks on the garments. John Welch writes:

> Among the textile fragments excavated at Masada were the remains of pieces of fabric with L-shaped cloth markings affixed to them. Dating to before AD 73, these are among the very earliest known examples of such marked garments. Scholars refer to these markings as *gammadia,* some of them being shaped like the Greek letter gamma (G). Though similar patterns have been found in several locations, the significance of these markings remains unknown to archaeologists and art historians. . . . These markings seem to appear artistically in conjunction with some hope for life or glory after death.[54]

Though much is not known about these marks, Erwin Goodenough notes that sometimes the *gammadia* on the garment and robe appear not L-shaped but "simply with a straight bar with prongs."[55] He also notes that these marks are "usually placed in consistent locations on the clothing—they are not just random decorations"[56] and that they only "appear on characters of especial sanctity."[57] It appears that "the purpose of the marks on the garment and the veil was to initiate the recipient into the divine secrets of the universe."[58]

---

52 See Allen J. Fletcher, *A Study Guide to the Facsimiles of the Book of Abraham* (Springville, Utah: CFI, 2006), 102.

53 Brown, "Girded about with a Lambskin," 139.

54 John W. Welch and Claire Foley, "Gammadia on Early Jewish and Christian Garments," *BYU Studies* 36, no. 3 (1996–97): 253.

55 Ostler, "Clothed Upon," 35.

56 Welch and Foley, "Gammadia," 256.

57 Ibid., 256.

58 Ostler, "Clothed Upon," 36.

Putting On Clothes

Not only is clothing symbolic, but the *act* of putting on clothes is laden with meaning. The changing of robes represents a change of condition or roles. The coronation of a king generally entailed dressing the person in a regal robe and placing a crown on his head and a scepter in his hand. The royal garment was believed to have special powers.[59] An Israelite priest donned special white robes to officiate in the temple, and the high priest put on clothing reserved for him and him alone before acting in his high priestly role.

The ritual action of putting on a sacred garment is properly termed an endowment.[60] The first step of this endowment, or vesting rite, is washing, purifying, and anointing, "for no unclean person can be clothed in the garments of glory."[61] Once ritually purified, a white garment is placed on the initiate. This vesting rite is only the first of many. Each step in the process of initiation is marked by some change of the garment or robes. At each step "the symbolism of the garment implied increased glory, moving from one existence to another,"[62] from one state to a higher one. "An added robe represented the added righteousness procured for entrance into the kingdom of God and for passing by the angels posted there."[63]

The Clothing of the High Priest

As human beings, we are often able to see a part and know the whole. This means that when we hear the words, "Do you solemnly swear to tell the truth, the whole truth . . . ," we can not only finish the statement but conjure up the context as well. We see the judge, the witness stand, and the witness with his hand raised to the square. This principle is operative in the scriptures. In Jewish thought, you don't have to quote a whole scripture. You can merely quote part of it, or just allude to it, and the whole passage should come to mind. Since the Jews were well versed in their scriptures, this was an effective technique. We still do it.

59 See Stephen D. Ricks and John J. Sroka, "King, Coronation, and Temple: Enthronement Ceremonies in History," *Temples of the Ancient World*, 261.

60 See Ostler, "Clothed Upon," 31.

61 Nibley, "Sacred Vesetments," 12:120.

62 Ostler, "Clothed Upon," 36.

63 Ibid., 45.

By quoting "And it came to pass in those days, that there went out a decree from Caesar Augustus, that all the world should be taxed" (Luke 2:1), the whole Nativity story is evoked—Mary, Joseph, the Wise Men, the angels, all of it. It may even evoke some of the cherished and joyful feelings we have at Christmastime. The book of Revelation is filled with allusions to scriptures in the Old Testament. If you don't recognize the allusion or understand the scripture in its Old Testament context, your understanding of the passage in Revelation is seriously limited. Sometimes, what *isn't* said is as important as what is said. For a full understanding, you have to consider the larger context and source.[64] This principle applies to the sacred clothing we wear in the temple. Our temple robes have similarities to the clothing worn by the high priest of ancient Israel, enough to evoke the whole. If we are to truly understand the significance of our temple robes, we must go to the source.

The high priest of ancient Israel "was described as the priest who 'wears many garments,' a reference to the eight garments worn by him on Yom Kippur."[65] (See figure 5-4.) The first garment the high priest wore was the white fine-linen tunic—the undergarment. It is the garment, the *kuttōnet,* that is worn next to the skin and represents the garment given to Adam and Eve in the garden. As we have discussed this garment extensively, a few comments regarding its history and its appearance will suffice.

The garment given to Adam was handed down from Adam to his descendants, passing to the righteous firstborn sons, who wore the garment while officiating in the priestly ordinance of sacrifice. According to Jewish legend, it is this sacred and prized garment that is at the heart of the enigmatic story in Genesis 9, where Ham sees his father's nakedness while Noah is sleeping (see Genesis 9:20–25). According to Rabbi Eliezer, Ham did not see the *nakedness* of his father but his "skin covering" or "skin garment."[66] In other words, he saw

64 See S. Michael Wilcox, *Who Shall Be Able to Stand? Finding Personal Meaning in the Book of Revelation* (Salt Lake City: Deseret Book Company, 2003), 5, 184.

65 Margaret Barker, *The Great Angel* (Louisville, Kentucky: Westminster John Knox Press, 1992),15; quoted in Kevin Christensen, "The Temple, the Monarchy, and Wisdom," *Glimpses of Lehi's Jerusalem*, eds. John W. Welch, David Rolph Seely, and Jo Ann H. Seely (Salt Lake City: FARMS, 2004), 462.

66 "Skin covering" or "skin garment" is a secondary meaning for the word translated as "nakedness." See Nibley, "Sacred Vestments," 12:129.

Redrawn and modified from Nibley, "Temple and Cosmos," *CWHN* 12:98–99 from Moshe Levine, *Melekhet ha-Mishkan: Tabnit ha-Mishkan ve-Kelav* (Tel Aviv: Melekhet haMishkan, 1968), 124–41.

Figure 5-4. The clothing of the high priest.

the garment of skin. Ham steals this garment in an attempt to illegally seize priesthood power. It is for this reason that Noah curses Ham.[67] The garment eventually passes into the hands of Nimrod and then Esau. Jacob buys the birthright from Esau because he desires to offer sacrifices to the Lord but cannot because he does not possess either the birthright or Adam's garment. Jacob later gives this garment of honor to Joseph.[68] It is the bestowal of this garment and all the privileges and powers it represents that engenders so much jealousy. While its history may be more legendary than literal, it stands as a witness of the priestly power and authority associated with this garment and the supreme privilege it was to possess it.

Regarding the appearance of the fine-linen undergarment, the Hebrew word that is translated as "fine linen" is *šēš*. According to the

67 See Nibley, "Sacred Vestments," 129.

68 See Tvedtnes, "Priestly Clothing," 658.

Brown-Driver-Briggs lexicon, it is a loan word from Egypt, and it refers to fine Egyptian linen. The Egyptians were famous for their skilled manufacture of linen and other cloth. One piece of fine linen found near Memphis provides evidence of that fine craftsmanship. It is, to the touch, comparable to silk.[69] The fine linen undergarment of the high priest was to be embroidered (see Exodus 28:39). Though the nature of this embroidery, or "checkerwork,"[70] is not clear, the undergarments of regular priests did not bear this special marking, indicating the embroidery made the high priest's garments holier than those of the other priests.

The high priest and the priests also wore breeches under their undergarments. This was not part of the usual attire for Israelite men. However, because the priests would be ascending the great altar of sacrifice, which according to 2 Chronicles 4:1 was fifteen feet high, breeches were necessary to preserve the priests' modesty.

On top of the undergarment of fine linen, the high priest wore a robe "all of blue" (Exodus 28:31). Contrary to the undergarment, whose purpose was to cover, the outer robe was a symbol of office and authority. The high priest was the highest spiritual leader in Israel. At times he was also the political head of state. His robe was equal to his office and authority. First, it was "all of blue." Blue was the dominant color of the cloth furnishings in the temple. When the holy combination of three colors—blue, purple, and scarlet—is mentioned, blue is always first, indicating its preeminence. The color blue is significant symbolically, for it is the color of heaven and suggests that the high priest's authority comes from God.[71] But even more than the symbolism of the color, blue is significant because of

> the extraordinary cost of coloring the material. Blue dye, for example, was obtained from the hypobranchial gland of the murex snail. The snails were plentiful, but the amount of dye each yielded was infinitesimal, requiring twelve thousand snails to provide 1.4 grams

69 See Charles W. Slemming, *These Are the Garments: A Study of the Garments of the High Priest of Israel* (Fort Washington, Pennsylvania: Christian Literature Crusade, 1998), 34.

70 Edwards, 2:234.

71 See Redd, 124.

> of dye. Milgrom fixes the cost of one pound of dye in 200 BC at $36,660. Thus, the garment described in the Pentateuch would not only have had a "royal price tag" but would also have commanded respect; certainly it could have been afforded only by the affluent or those in positions of power and authority.[72]

Anciently, the hem of a garment made an important social statement. "The more ornate the hem, the greater the social status and wealth of a person."[73] An ornate hem "was worn by those who counted; it was the 'ID' of nobility."[74] "Extrabiblical texts teach us that an ornate hem was a symbolic extension of the owner himself and, more specifically, of his rank and authority."[75] When Isaiah sees "the Lord sitting upon a throne, high and lifted up, and his train filled the temple" (Isaiah 6:1), he is seeing the hem of the Lord's robe, which in its amplitude fills the temple. This profuse hem symbolizes the power, authority, and glory of the Lord. With this understanding of the hem of the garment, the story of David cutting off the skirt (the corner of the Israelite garment) of Saul's robe takes on additional meaning. At the time, David is a fugitive in the wilderness, and Saul is the reigning king. David and his men are sitting in the inner recesses of a cave when Saul enters the cave to relieve himself. David's men encourage David to kill Saul, who has relentlessly pursued David and sought his death. Surely, they argue, this is the deliverance of the Lord. David refuses to kill the Lord's anointed, but he does cut off the hem of Saul's garment. Afterward, David is guilt ridden. Had David's action been a simple attempt to show Saul how close he had come to death or to reveal David's mercy and forbearance, it is unlikely David would have felt any guilt. But David's act was tantamount to invalidating the king's authority, and for this, David was grieved.

The hem of the high priest's robe was decorated with an ornate border of bells and tassels made to resemble pomegranates. This border extended the hem and thus extended the prestige and authority of the high priest.

---

72 Ibid., 123–124.

73 Edwards, 2:233.

74 Jacob Milgrom, "Of Hems and Tassels," *Biblical Archaeology Review* 9 (May/June 1983), 61–62; quoted in Redd, 124.

75 Redd, 123.

Additionally, the pomegranates and the bells were in and of themselves significant. A pomegranate symbolizes immortality. Because of its many seeds, it represents perennial fertility and abundance.[76] As a sweet, refreshing fruit, it also represents "the refreshing nature of Jehovah's word in a dry, barren, and desolate world."[77] The calyx of the pomegranate (the outer cluster of sepals) has the appearance of a crown. Kingship is an important aspect of temple worship. The bells were also significant. Bells symbolize consecration. They represent protection against the powers of destruction. The sounding of small bells in the breeze symbolizes the sweet sounds of paradise. All three of these associations are apropos for the high priest. First, the high priest was consecrated and dedicated to God. Second, in the ancient world, entering into the presence of God was considered life-threatening. The bells may have been thought to protect the high priest from the mighty, awesome, and dangerous power of God (see Exodus 28:35). Third, nowhere on earth was there a place closer to paradise than the Holy of Holies, for both paradise (Eden) and the Holy of Holies were places where God walked and talked with man. It may also be that the bells served to invite the attention of God, to signify the sounding of revelation from God, and to enable those outside the tabernacle or temple to participate vicariously with the high priest as he served inside the holy temple, a place the ordinary Israelite would never see. It may be there is no correlation to bells in our modern temple robes because there is no need for us to experience the temple vicariously. All worthy Latter-day Saints can enter these most holy precincts for themselves. The pomegranates interspersed between the bells prevented the bells from clanging together and producing harsh discord. Together, bells and pomegranates produced the sweet sounds of paradise, or the sweet music of being close to God. Interestingly, in Hebrew the words *bells* and *pomegranates*, *pa'amon ve rimmon,* themselves are a sweet sound, pleasing to the ears.

The most important article of the high priest's vestments was "a curious piece of clothing called the *ephod*, a Hebrew word left untranslated in the King James Bible and in numerous other Bibles because of the uncertainty among scholars regarding its identity, form,

76 See Cooper, 134.

77 Redd, 124.

and function."[78] The LDS edition offers some clarity. In Exodus 39:2, the footnote to *ephod* says, "IE a special apron." The ephod was indeed special, for it was believed to grant oracular and divinatory power. In the Testaments of the Twelve Patriarchs, a second-century BC text, we read, "And I saw seven men in white clothing, who were saying to me, 'Arise, put on the vestments of the priesthood, the crown of righteousness, the oracle of understanding, the robe of truth, the breastplate of faith, the miter for the head and the *apron for prophetic power*.'"[79]

The exact appearance of this sacred apron is uncertain in spite of the vast amount of detail provided in Exodus 28 and 39. One scholar believes that the word *ephod* is derived from the Egyptian word *ifd*, and he "concludes that the Israelite ephod may have been similar to the Egyptian linen apron. This apron . . . was generally of precious cloth, of gold and gilded leather, until the Nineteenth Dynasty, when it was changed to a pleated and decorated apron."[80] It seems that "this priestly apron covered only the lower front part of the body, 'extending from the loins to the thighs,' and was secured by the priest at his waist by tying together the ends of an attached white linen belt behind his back."[81] The apron was made of fine white linen and was embroidered (or perhaps woven) with the sacred blend of blue, purple, and scarlet threads. Along with these three colored threads, golden threads were used. These gold threads were not simply a golden color. Gold was actually pounded into thin sheets from which thin "wires" were cut (see Exodus 39:2–3). A gold thread was combined with each blue, purple, and scarlet thread, making gold the main element in this garment and the dominant color. "Fabrics treated in this manner [were] fit only for deities or humans of the highest rank."[82]

The ephod consisted of four elements: the main body of the garment (i.e., the "apron" that covered the lower body); a richly decorated waistband or belt, called a "curious girdle" in Exodus 28:8; and two embroidered shoulder straps which were permanently attached to the

78 Brown, "Girded about with a Lambskin," 132.

79 *Testament of Levi 8:2–10*, in OTP, 1:791; quoted in Tvedtnes, "Priestly Clothing," 666; italics added.

80 Redd, 125.

81 Brown, "Girded about with a Lambskin," 133.

82 Meyers, *Exodus*, 242.

waistband.[83] (In form, the shoulder straps are roughly analogous to the suspenders of bib overalls.) At the top of the shoulders were two onyx stones on which the names of the tribes of Israel were engraved, six on each stone. When the high priest entered the temple attired in his priestly robes, with the onyx stones on his shoulders, he symbolically carried the twelve tribes into the presence of God. In this, the high priest is a type of Christ, the Great High Priest, who brings us to God.

The high priest also wore a breastplate, the top of which was attached to the shoulder straps, and the bottom of which was attached to the ephod with gold chains. (The breastplate is analogous to the "bib" of bib overalls.) Today, a breastplate evokes the image of armor and has military associations. However, this breastplate was not used for war but for judgment. In Exodus 28:15, it is called "the breastplate of judgment," and in the Tanakh it is rendered "the breastpiece of decision."[84] "All available sources indicate that it was a device for determining divine will."[85] It was made of the same sacred material and colors as the ephod. The breastplate was a rectangle, twice as long as it was wide, which was folded in half so that it became a nine-inch square and formed a pocket into which the Urim and Thummim were placed. *Urim* in Hebrew means *lights*, and *thummim* means *perfections*. The LXX renders *thummim* as *truth*, giving "Urim and Thummim" the English translation of "light and truth."[86] Indeed, the Urim and Thummim is an instrument for receiving light and truth, an instrument of revelation. The breastpiece had twelve precious stones on it. Each stone had the name of a tribe of Israel etched upon it. Just as a woman wears a locket with a picture of her beloved in order to keep him next to her heart, so the Great High Priest wears Israel next to His heart.

Finally, the high priest had a special headdress that consisted of a miter and the golden plate. Regular priests had a decorated turban instead

83 See Nahum M. Sarna, *The JPS Torah Commentary: Exodus* (Philadelphia: The Jewish Publication Society, 1991), 178.

84 Ibid., 180.

85 Ibid.

86 "The Dead Sea Scrolls have disclosed a new Hebrew word *'wrtwm*, which, according to context, means "perfect illumination." Jacob Milgrom, *Leviticus 1–16*, 511. It may well be that this word was formed by combining light (*'wr*) and truth (*twm*). Thus, the Urim and Thummim (or light and truth) is a means for perfect illumination.

of a miter. "The decorated turban of the other priests was considered an accoutrement of beauty and distinction, but the more imposing miter is considered a synonym for a crown."[87] Josephus describes the miter as a nonconical cap—in other words a "flattish-cap"[88] "over which was stitched another cap embroidered in blue, encircled by a three-tiered golden crown, and topped by a golden calyx."[89] While Josephus's description does not draw a crystal-clear picture of the miter, it does reveal that the flat cap was a kind of foundation or support for the crown. Hugh Nibley adds this insight: "The round linen cap was to act as a cushion for a metal crown during a long ceremony."[90] Over time, the cap alone came to symbolize the whole. The cap indicated that "the owner was qualified to wear the 'crown of justification.'"[91] From this miter hung a gold plate inscribed with the words "Holiness to the Lord." The plate was to rest upon the high priest's forehead, that he "may bear the iniquity of the holy things . . . that they may be accepted before the Lord" (Exodus 28:38). In other words, any inadvertent iniquity or imperfection in the offerings and even in the offerers would be removed by this plate.[92] It may also be that this plate described the character of the one who wore it. The high priest was "holiness to the Lord," or dedicated and consecrated to God. In addition, he was one who had obtained a degree of holiness like unto the Lord. The gold plate is one of the definitive markers for the high priest. Crowns are symbolic of kings and queens. Together, the crown (miter) and the gold plate represent eternal kingship and priesthood, or in other words, godhood.

The vestments for the high priest clearly are more than coverings for the body. Exodus tells us they are to be "for glory and for beauty" (Exodus 28:2). Truly, they were astoundingly beautiful, made of the finest workmanship and the most exquisite material. Truly, they elicited honor, awe, and respect—glory. Aristeas described the experience of seeing the high priest arrayed in his holy robes:

87 Redd, 126.

88 Sarna, *JPS Exodus,* 185.

89 Ibid., 184.

90 Nibley, "Return to the Temple," 12:55.

91 Ibid.

92 See Milgrom, *Leviticus 1–16*, 512.

> It was an occasion of great amazement to us when we saw Eleazar engaged on his ministry, and all the glorious vestments. . . . Their appearance makes one awe-struck and dumbfounded: A man would think he had come out of this world into another one. I emphatically assert that every man who comes near the spectacle of what I have described will experience astonishment and amazement beyond words, his very being transformed by the hallowed arrangement on every single detail.[93]

It is no wonder these garments conferred dignity and authority. They were believed to confer spiritual gifts, particularly the gift of revelation. The ephod, breastplate, and Urim and Thummim together became known as the principle vehicle for inquiring of God.[94] The apron (prophetic power), the pomegranates (the sweet and refreshing word of the Lord), the bells (the sounding of God's word), and the Urim and Thummim (light and truth) all represent revelation from God, our special privilege in the House of the Lord. Moreover, "communication between deity and human was effected, in part, by having the human arrayed in unique and splendid clothing similar to that of the deity. Godlike in their priestly garments, they were positioned to receive the divine will."[95]

The unique and splendid clothing of the high priest "was intended to represent the garb of God and of the angels."[96] This was a visual declaration that the high priest had authority to act as God's representative among men.[97] Dressed like God, he also shared in some of God's power. Little wonder that this extraordinary attire "is reserved for the righteous who will enter God's presence."[98] To wear the robes of the high priest during mortality is an unsurpassed honor and privilege. To wear them on the other side of the veil is to become divine.

---

93 Tvedtnes, "Priestly Clothing," 664–665.

94 See Redd, 134.

95 Meyers, *Exodus*, 244.

96 Tvedtnes, "Priestly Clothing," 665.

97 See Tvedtnes, "Priestly Clothing," 694.

98 Tvedtnes, "Priestly Clothing," 694.

Understanding Names

At this very moment, as I write, our daughter Lindsey is expecting twins, a girl and a boy. We anticipate their arrival in a few short weeks. Over the past several months, our family has enjoyed many an hour discussing possible names. My husband, Steve, has been lobbying for the girl to be named Stevie and the boy to be named Forbes, after his middle name. Our son who is on his mission suggested Elder Hardison and Elder Clinger. Hundreds of names have been suggested and evaluated under the criteria of how the names sound with their last name, what initials the names will make, and if the name is too strange—or too common. Names have been considered because of family ties and eliminated because of unfavorable associations with someone else. Of course, the most important determinant is simply if the parents like the name. Few of these considerations would have occurred to a person in the ancient world.

In the ancient world, children's names often recorded the parents' experience. Several of the names of Jacob's twelve sons reflect the rivalry between Leah and Rachel. In Egypt, Joseph names his first son Manasseh, which means "he who causes to forget," suggesting that the joy of fatherhood has swallowed up the pain of past injustices and being cut off from his home and family. Hannah, who "was in bitterness of soul" (1 Samuel 1:10) over her infertility, weeps, prays, and petitions God fervently for a child. When God answers her prayer, she names her son Samuel, which means "heard of God." The prophet Hosea gives his daughter the name Lo-ruhamah. In Hebrew, *lō'* is a particle of negation, meaning "no" or "not." *Ruḥāmâ* comes from a root word that means "pity, compassion, mercy." It refers to the deep feelings of love a mother has for her children. Hosea gives his daughter the name of "no mercy" or "not loved," not to describe his feelings about his daughter but to describe the experience of her parents: Hosea is not loved by his unfaithful wife (a type of Israel), who has forfeited the mercy of God.[1]

It was common in ancient Israel for parents to give their child a name that expressed their testimony and devotion to God. For instance, Elimelech is made from the name for God, *'ēl*, (*'elî* means "my God") and the word for *king*, *melek*. Thus, Elimelech means "my God is king." "Elijah" is created from two divine names: *'ēl*, God, and the divine name *Yahweh*, shortened to "*Yah*/*Yâ*." Thus, Elijah means "my God is Yahweh." The name Ezekiel is the combination of *ḥāzaq* "to be strong" or "to be victorious" with the name of God, *'ēl*, resulting in "God will be victorious." These names are called theophoric names because they are a compound name created with a name of God. Such names expressed devotion but were also used in both Egypt and Israel to petition a deity to place a person under His protection. "A man named Ramoses might expect the sun god Ra to protect and guide him for life. When in the Bible, Hannah names her son Samuel, she is inviting the Israelite deity El to watch over the child."[2]

Parents might also choose a particular name because of its associations with others who bore that name. Helaman, the son of Helaman, named his sons Nephi and Lehi, hoping they would remember and emulate their righteous forebears. Father Lehi named the first son born to him in the wilderness Jacob, which means "supplanter" or "successor, replacement." This name evokes images of an earlier Jacob, the brother of Esau, who was a younger son but who supplanted his older brother as the birthright son and spiritual leader of the family. The fact that Lehi chooses this name with its etymology and associations and also calls Jacob "my firstborn in the days of my tribulation in the wilderness" (2 Nephi 2:1) suggests "Lehi may have considered Jacob to be a replacement for his eldest son, Laman, with his younger son, Joseph, being a replacement for the second son Lemuel."[3]

---

1 See Francis I. Andersen and David Noel Freedman, *Hosea*, Anchor Bible, 228.

2 Ogden Goelet, "Moses' Egyptian Name," *Bible Review*, June 2003, 15.

3 John A. Tvedtnes, "My First-Born in the Wilderness," *Journal of Book of Mormon Studies* 3, no. 1 (Spring 1994): 207.

More than anything else, names were to reflect the essence of a person, one's very nature. "The name and the personality were so closely associated in Hebrew thought that they were considered almost identical."[4] "According to Philo of Alexandria, the name 'is like a shadow which accompanies the body.'"[5] In many instances, the names we find in the scriptures are telling. For instance, the name Abel (*Habel* in Hebrew) comes from the word *hebel*, meaning "vapor, breath, nothingness." "*Hevel* [*hebel*] is often used to express the fleeting nature of life."[6] It is an appropriate name for Abel, whose life was relatively brief and whose breath was cut short by his brother Cain.[7] It must be noted that unless Eve knew by revelation that Abel would not live a long life, naming a child "breath, nothingness" is unintelligible. It may be that the name was given after his death or that the name is a title, added to his given name.[8] The name Cain, on the other hand, is related to the word *qānâ,* "to get, acquire." When Eve bares this son, she says, "I have gotten a man from the Lord" and names her son Cain.[9] In time, Cain displays an acquiring, grasping nature, coveting the flocks of his brother (see Moses 5:32–33). He even enters into a covenant with Satan that he might "murder and get gain" (Moses 5:31). Sadly, Cain lives up to the negative connotations of his name.

In order to understand how powerful a name was in the ancient world, we must understand that this was an age that "tended to identify words and realities."[10] God spoke, and the world came into existence.

---

4 E. Cashdan, *The Twelve Prophets: The Soncino Books of the Bible*, ed. A. Cohen (Bournemouth: Soncino, 1948), 339; quoted in Andrew E. Hill, *Malachi*, Anchor Bible, 189.

5 Bruce H. Porter and Stephen D. Ricks, "Names in Antiquity: Old, New, and Hidden," *By Study and Also By Faith*, 1:501.

6 Nahum M. Sarna, *The JPS Torah Commentary: Genesis* (Philadelphia: The Jewish Publication Society, 1989), 32.

7 Alternatively, it may be related to the Syriac word for herdsman. Both meanings are appropriate for Abel, who was also a keeper of the sheep.

8 See Westermann, *Genesis 1–11*, 285.

9 The actual etymology of Cain is disputed. It may come from *Nyq qayan*, "to fit together, to forge." However, it is at least related by sound to *qanah,* "to acquire." Many of the wordplays in Hebrew are not exact. If two of the three tri-literal roots agree, that is enough.

10 Ryken, Wilhoit, Longman, 583.

However, words didn't even have to be spoken to be effectual; they could be acted out. Isaiah, Jeremiah, and Ezekiel are all commanded by God to perform certain actions: to walk barefoot and naked (probably dressed in only a loincloth) for three years; to smash an earthen bottle; to bury a belt in the ground until it decayed; and to shave off a beard and to burn, smite, and throw into the wind equal parts of the hair. When such acts were commanded by God, they were called "prophetic action." Prophetic action was not playacting or merely an object lesson—it was God's word made visible. Even more than that, it was viewed as actually setting in motion the judgment of God. Little wonder prophets' denunciations were met with such hostility. Whether spoken or acted out, prophetic words had the power to create reality.[11] Names had a similar power. "Names in Hebrew society had to be either lived up to or lived down."[12] This is true not only of people but of places. In Jeremiah 33:16 we read, "In those days shall Judah be saved and Jerusalem shall dwell safely: and this is the name wherewith she shall be called, The Lord is our Righteousness." "The inference is that Jerusalem would so manifest the qualities of justice and righteousness (in contrast to her past bad record) that she would be worthy of such a name and exemplify the divine order for all the cities and all the people in Israel."[13]

Bestowing a name is a great honor. It signifies dominion and places the one being named under the protection and judgment of the one who names. When God brings the beasts and fowls to Adam to name them, He is by implication declaring Adam's dominion and authority over the animals (see Genesis 2:19). It is important to note that Adam does not name his wife, Eve; rather he calls her by the title God conferred upon her. Thus, it is God who has dominion over Eve, not Adam. Earlier Adam calls Eve by a different title. He calls her woman, *'issah,* because she was taken out of man, *'ish* (see Moses 3:23; Genesis 2:23).

---

11 See John Bright, *Jeremiah*, Anchor Bible, 133 and Moshe Greenberg, *Ezekiel 1–20*, Anchor Bible, 122. The efficacy of words depended on the power and authority of the one who uttered them. God's assent or God's authority is the sine qua non.

12 Ryken, Wilhoit, Longman, 583.

13 J. A. Thompson, *The Book of Jeremiah* (Grand Rapids, Michigan: William B. Eerdmans Publishing Company, 1980), 601.

The title Adam chooses emphasizes their mutuality.[14] When Ishmael is born to Abraham and Hagar, Abraham names him. By the act of naming, Abraham announces that Ishmael is to be fully reckoned as his son. When Joseph names Mary's baby Jesus, Joseph "acknowledges him as his own."[15] What is true for people is true for places. When Enoch builds a city and names it, he is assuming "ownership over and responsibility for the city that bears his name."[16] When Isaac re-digs wells that his father Abraham had dug, wells which had been filled in by the Philistines after the death of Abraham, he names the wells using the names his father had used. In doing so, he is claiming incontestable ownership.

Being called by one's name is a special privilege and "means divine selection for a task."[17] It is significant that when God the Father and Jesus Christ appear to Joseph Smith in the Sacred Grove, they call him by name (see Joseph Smith—History 1:17). Moses, Samuel, Martha, and Mary Magdalene are all called by name. When the Savior calls Lazarus to come forth from his tomb, He does so by calling his name. Each of these is either a call to a special mission or a call to discipleship. As such, being called by name also suggests a special relationship and intimacy. Therefore, it is not surprising that God says to the whole house of Israel, "I have called thee by thy name; thou art mine" (Isaiah 43:1).

New Names

When Elder John Groberg was serving in Tonga, one of the challenges he ran into was the frequency with which the Tongans changed their names. He writes:

> I used to get after them for changing their names, and they would always come back to me and say, "Do you *palangis* die with the same name you are born with?"
>
> "Yes," I said. Then I explained how for the records of the Church that is the best thing. They looked at me

14 See Trible, 101.

15 Raymond E. Brown, *The Birth of the Messiah,* Anchor Bible Reference Library (New York: Doubleday, 1993), 139.

16 Hamilton, *Genesis 1–17*, 237.

17 Ryken, Wilhoit, Longman, 582.

> in disbelief and said, "Then you don't progress at all through life?"
>
> At first I did not understand, but they explained that in their culture, when they changed their attitude or position or proved themselves in life, they changed their name as a sign of their new situation. . . . According to their custom, if you die with the same name you were given at birth, it is a sign of failure in life.[18]

In societies where names change throughout life, taking on a new name signals a new status or a new phase. It is a mark of progression. When Gordon C. Thomasson worked among the Kpelle of West Africa, a tribe with a high infant mortality rate, he discovered that infant boys were given names such as "good for nothing" or "dirt" so the powers of death would overlook them. "Upon reaching the age where they are initiated into the secret men's Poro society, these boys will be given 'manly' names such as *Leopard*, that reflect their real worth to society."[19]

The changing of names as a mark of progression is a common occurrence in the scriptures. Abram is changed to Abraham, Sarai to Sarah, Jacob to Israel, Oshea to Joshua, and Simon to Peter. With reflection, we can recognize that even in our society, where names are relatively static, we take on new names or titles to mark progression. When we transition from premortal life to earth life, we are given a new name. When we marry, a woman usually takes on the name of her husband. We assume the title of mother or father when we take on the role of parenting. When our children have children, we take on a new role and the new name of grandparent. Boys take on the titles of deacon, teacher, priest, and elder as they progress through the offices of the priesthood. Particularly interesting is a missionary's title of elder or sister. For missionaries, first names are all but forgotten, symbolizing the setting "aside of their own identity and interests to be joined to the purposes of the Lord."[20] A man takes on the name bishop or president

---

18 John H. Groberg, *In the Eye of the Storm* (Salt Lake City: Deseret Book Company, 1993), 219–220.

19 Thomasson, 4.

20 Janette C. Hales Beckham, "Your Good Name," *BYU Speeches 1995–1996* (Provo, Utah: Brigham Young University, 1996), 2.

when he is called to those positions in the Church, again setting aside his personal interests for those of the Lord.

Receiving a new name frequently entails special privileges and honors. When Joseph becomes Pharaoh's right-hand man, the vizier of Egypt, he takes on the name of Zaphnath-paaneah.[21] When a man became a king, he frequently took a throne name and received powers, honors, and privileges.[22] In the Book of Mormon, King Benjamin says that on the morrow he will give "this people a name, that thereby they may be distinguished above all the people which the Lord God hath brought out of the land of Jerusalem" (Mosiah 1:11). In other words, they are to receive a new name and a special honor or new status. Inasmuch as King Benjamin's people were already commandment keepers, their new name and status may have to do with "the higher blessings associated with the Melchizedek Priesthood and the fulness of the gospel," or, in other words, temple blessings.[23]

Not all name changes are for the better. After experiencing the devastating loss of husband and sons, which equates to losing not only the companionship of loved ones but everything which provided security to a woman in the ancient world, Naomi cries, "Call me not Naomi [delight], call me Mara [bitter]: for the Almighty hath dealt very bitterly with me" (Ruth 1:20). When one of Jeremiah's chief adversaries, Pashur, beats Jeremiah and puts him in the stocks, the Lord changes Pashur's name to *Māgôr-missābîb*. Without knowing Hebrew, one may think the name change isn't too significant. However, *magor* means "terror" or "destruction," and *missabab* means "surrounding, encompassing." His new name amounts to a curse. Terror and destruction will encompass him.

---

21 The meaning of Joseph's new name is debated. The following interpretations have all been suggested: "God speaks and he lives" or "the god has said: he will live" or "the man who knows things" or "the sustainer of life" or "sustenance of the land is the living" (or, is this living one). See Victor P. Hamilton, *The Book of Genesis: Chapters 18–50* (Grand Rapids, Michigan: William B. Eerdmans Publishing Company, 1995), 507–508.

22 In Israel, for example, Shallum was the personal name of King Jehoahaz. Jedidiah was the personal name of King Solomon. Coniah was the personal name of King Jehoiakin.

23 See Rodney Turner, "Christ's Church in Ancient America," *Ensign*, March 2000, 51. See also M. Catherine Thomas, "Benjamin and the Mysteries of God," *King Benjamin's Speech*, 284, 290.

Name changes occurred at significant moments in a person's life and at times of transition. Additionally, it was almost universal in the ancient world that when one entered into a covenant, he took on a new name. When Abram, Sarai, and Jacob received their new names, it was in connection with receiving or renewing the Abrahamic covenant. When Hosea's children (typifying Israel and Judah) received their new names—names indicative of covenant faithfulness and loyalty—they did so in the presence of the heavens and the earth, which frequently served as witnesses of covenant making (see Hosea 2:21; see also Isaiah 1:2; Deuteronomy 4:26, 32:1; Alma 1:15). The changing of a name in a covenant setting is actually a token or a seal of the covenant.[24] Since covenants are an integral part of the temple, it is not surprising that names are of paramount importance. Truman Madsen explains:

> In the temple ritual setting, names are not seen as mere labels. They mark degrees or attributes or roles in one's transformation process. They are symbolic of new births or beginnings. Thus, an individual, while retaining his identity, may take on several names as he moves through stages toward the divine.[25]

The names we take on in our religious covenants are usually some form of the name of Christ. The difference between *Abram* and *Abraham* and *Sarai* and *Sarah* is in both cases the letter *h*. *H* is the dominant letter in the divine name of Yhwh. This may indicate that Abraham and Sarah, whose names are already pretty impressive (Exalted Father and Queen[26]), are taking on another dimension of the name and nature of God. Jacob takes on the name Israel. *Israel* comes from two roots: *śār* meaning "one who rules, a chieftain, ruler prince" and *ʾēl*, God. While there is no scholarly consensus as to the meaning of the name *Israel*, one of the possible interpretations is "he rules as God." "Now it is plain that he who rules or will rule as God is Jehovah, himself, or Jesus

---

24 See Andersen and Freedman, 286. See also Janet Hovorka, "Sarah and Hagar: Ancient Women of the Abrahamic Covenant," *Astronomy, Papyrus, and Covenant*, eds. John Gee and Brian M. Hauglid (Provo, Utah: FARMS, 2005), 151.

25 Truman G. Madsen, "'Putting on the Names': A Jewish-Christian Legacy," *By Study and Also By Faith*, 1:459.

26 Sarai "means 'princess' in Hebrew but 'queen' if based on Akkadian *sharratu*." Sarna, Genesis, 87.

Christ. The new name for Jacob is also a name of God himself."[27] This name is significant for us since we bear the name "children of Israel" and "house of Israel." Based on the meaning of the word *Israel*, we are the children of Christ and the house or family of Jehovah.[28]

When men receive the Melchizedek Priesthood, they take upon themselves the priesthood of the King of Righteousness, *melek* meaning "king" and *zedek* meaning "righteousness." In other words, they take on a name or title of Christ. When we are baptized into the Church, we take upon us the name of Christ and are called "the children of Christ" (Mosiah 5:7). All who believe in Christ bear His name. They are Christians. As seen by these examples, we don't take on the name of Christ just once but in almost every covenant. Baptism is just the beginning.

Only occasionally, even in our world, do we determine the names we take on. We had no say about what our parents named us, and the surnames men are born with are usually the ones they keep. Even women who take on their husband's name at marriage do not strictly choose the name. Several years ago, we were watching a nighttime talk show and saw an interview with Deion Sanders. He had just moved from playing football for the Dallas Cowboys to the Washington Redskins. The host asked Deion about getting a new nickname. Deion responded, "A nickname can't be made up. It's got to be given, by another, by your homies. It's got to be earned."[29] So it is with new names. Names "are acquired by legitimate means, through ritual."[30] While the scriptures don't give a lot of details about this ritual process, we do read that Jacob wrestled with an angel through the long night at the ford of Jabbok. According to Hugh Nibley, *wrestled* can just as well be translated as *embraced*. "It was in this ritual embrace that Jacob obtained a new name and the bestowal of priestly and kingly power at sunrise."[31]

---

27 Chauncey C. Riddle, "Code Language in the Book of Mormon," transcript (Provo, Utah: FARMS, 1992), 17.

28 See ibid.

29 *The Tonight Show*, NBC, Burbank, California, June 8, 2000.

30 Thomasson, 4. See also Madsen, "Putting on the Names," 458.

31 Nibley, "On the Sacred and the Symbolic," 580.

God and Names

"In secularized Western societies we often take names far too lightly."[32] For the most part, they are merely labels of identification, words we use to distinguish one person from another. In ancient thought, a name conveyed the very essence of a person. It revealed a person's character and nature. To know a person's name was to know the person. The same is true for God. "God's self, his real person, is concentrated in his name."[33] Therefore, to know God's name is to know God. Consequently, it is not surprising that God has many names. For instance, the names of God our Heavenly Father include Father, Father in Heaven, Heavenly Father, God the Father, Elohim, Ahman, and Man of Holiness. The names of Jesus Christ (who is almost exclusively the God we are referring to in this chapter) are even more numerous. Many names are needed to teach the rich and diverse aspects of His nature and mortal ministry. For instance, Christ is called the Lamb of God to represent His submission, His atoning sacrifice, and His perfection. Like the sacrificial lambs of Israel, He is without blemish. On the other hand, Christ is also the Lion of Judah. A lion is a royal image. Even today, a lion is known as the king of the jungle. "The lion was an emblem of strength, majesty, courage, and menace. . . . It also was symbolic of intellectual excellence."[34] The lion, with its ferocity, was an image of security for Israel. For them, the lion represented the protecting and defending power of God. Lion of Judah and Lamb of God are only two of the many names needed to teach us the character of Jesus Christ. In an appendix to his book *Christ and the New Covenant*, Elder Jeffrey R. Holland lists some of the names or titles for Christ that are found in the Book of Mormon. He lists 101.[35]

Sometimes, multiple names are given at the same time. For instance, in Revelation 1:8, Christ says, "I am Alpha and Omega, the beginning and the ending, . . . the Almighty." In the surrounding verses, John refers to Christ as "Jesus Christ," "the faithful witness," "the first begotten of the dead," "the prince [or ruler] of the kings of the earth," "Amen,"

32 Thomasson, 8.

33 *Interpreter's Dictionary* 2:408; quoted in Dallin H. Oaks, *His Holy Name* (Salt Lake City: Bookcraft, 1998), 49.

34 Ford, 85.

35 See Holland, *Christ and the New Covenant* (Salt Lake City: Deseret Book Company, 1997), 353–355.

and "him which is, and which was, and which is to come," which is perhaps another way to say "Yahweh," or "I am that I am," the name God revealed to Moses on Sinai (Exodus 3:14; Revelation 1:4–8). It appears that a multiplicity of names is a rich outpouring of grace, an invitation to know God. To know His name "entails a certain kind of relationship. . . . A relationship without a name inevitably means some distance. Naming the name is necessary for closeness. It makes for a great intensity of presence, a certain concreteness that would not otherwise be there for God."[36] Therefore, when God reveals His name, it is an invitation to become more intimate with Him and to establish an even closer relationship with Him.

In Exodus 33, Moses beseeches God, "Shew me thy glory." God responds, "I will proclaim the name of the Lord before thee" (Exodus 33:18–19). The next day, Moses ascends Mount Sinai and the Lord descends in a cloud and "stood with him there, and proclaimed the name of the Lord." The name God proclaims is, "The Lord, The Lord God, merciful and gracious, longsuffering, and abundant in goodness and truth, Keeping mercy for thousands, forgiving iniquity and transgression and sin" (Exodus 34:6–7). Some of these names/titles appear more like a description than a name. However, such is not out of place in a culture where names *were* descriptions of a person. It is also worth noting that "thirty-two words may seem an impossibly long appellation, even for a god."[37] However, the "multiplication of names was one way to express the power and station of the deity"[38] in the ANE.

Another scripture worth examining is Mosiah 3:8. In his great farewell address, King Benjamin "solemnly disclosed for the first time an extended name of Jesus Christ and gave it to the entire multitude by way of covenant."[39] This name had been revealed by an angel who awakened King Benjamin in the middle of the night and prophesied of the coming of Jesus Christ, of His healings and ministry and His

36 Freitheim, 100.

37 William H. C. Propp, *Exodus 19–40*, Anchor Bible (New York: Doubleday, 2006), 609.

38 John H. Walton, *Ancient Near Eastern Thought and the Old Testament* (Grand Rapids Michigan: Baker Academic, 2006), 92.

39 John W. Welch, "Ten Testimonies of Jesus Christ from the Book of Mormon," *Doctrines of the Book of Mormon: The 1991 Sperry Symposium*, eds. Bruce A. Van Orden and Brent L. Top (Salt Lake City: Deseret Book Company, 1992), 231–232.

Atonement. The angel then said, "And he shall be called Jesus Christ, the Son of God, the Father of heaven and earth, the Creator of all things from the beginning." When King Benjamin finished his speech, the people all fell to the earth and "cried aloud with one voice" (Mosiah 4:2) for God to have mercy on them through the atoning blood of Christ. They finish their appeal by citing the name that King Benjamin had earlier revealed: "For we believe in Jesus Christ, the Son of God, who created heaven and earth, and all things" (Mosiah 4:2). The fact that all the people simultaneously fell down and spoke certain words in unison strongly suggests that this name took on a ceremonial significance among the Nephites.[40] Many years later, Samuel the Lamanite used this same name/title when calling the people to repentance, indicating this name may have become "standard confessional language among the believing generations."[41]

Isaiah also prophesied of the coming of Christ by citing several names. Isaiah 9:6 states: "For unto us a child is born, unto us a son is given: and the government shall be upon his shoulder: and his name shall be called Wonderful, Counsellor, The Mighty God, the everlasting Father, The Prince of Peace." Joseph Blenkinsopp translates the phrase "the government shall be upon his shoulder" as "the emblems of sovereignty rest on his shoulders."[42] Blenkinsopp suggests this phrase points "to investiture with a robe or other symbol of authority."[43] This other symbol of authority may have been a key of considerable size that was slung from the shoulder. Whether key or robe, placing governing powers upon a person suggests the enthronement of a king. Therefore, the names listed in this verse may be the new throne names that the child will assume when he eventually takes the throne. Since divinely given throne names may be "indicative of what the new king and his

---

40 See Terrence L. Szink and John W. Welch, "Benjamin's Speech in the Context of Ancient Israelite Festivals," *King Benjamin's Speech*, 188. See also Welch, "Ten Testimonies," 232.

41 John W. Welch, "Benjamin, the Man: His Place in Nephite History," *King Benjamin's Speech*, 46.

42 Joseph Blenkinsopp, *Isaiah 1–39*, Anchor Bible, 246. This is the only place in the Bible where the word translated as *government* in the King James Version is used, making its meaning less than certain.

43 Ibid., 250.

rule are to be,"[44] these names reveal the nature of the Messiah and deserve a closer look.

Many translations omit the comma between *Wonderful* and *Counsellor*, making the first title *Wonderful Counselor*. The word for "wonderful," *pele'*, has the connotation of something that is extraordinary, surpassingly marvelous, even supernatural. Here, it may refer to either the counselor or the counsel. In either case, it is beyond the realm of natural man.[45]

The next title, *mighty God*, is literally "God Warrior." The image of God as the Divine Warrior was an important one in the ANE. Kings were to protect and defend their people. "Ancient nations could not establish internal peace or stability without first securing their borders and maintaining national security. Effective military leadership by the king, therefore, was vital to society's well-being."[46] It was no small thing that when God appeared to Joshua on the eve of their assault on Jericho, He did so as the Divine Warrior, with a drawn sword, introducing Himself with the title "captain of the host of the Lord" (Joshua 5:14), or in modern terms, "general of the armies of the Lord."

The third title, *Everlasting Father*, suggests that Christ's role as king entails more than power and authority. It includes loving, nurturing, and even disciplining His people.

The fourth and last title is *Prince of Peace*. Peace, *shalom,* from the Jewish perspective, is more than the absence of hostilities. It is a state of wholeness, the main component of which is being in a right relationship with God. Christ is the Prince of Peace. It is Christ and Christ alone who makes being in a right relationship with God possible.

In the Hebrew text of the Old Testament, two names are predominantly used for deity: Elohim and Yahweh. These names are

---

44 J. Alec Motyer, *The Prophecy of Isaiah: An Introduction and Commentary* (Downers Grove, Illinois: InterVarsity Press, 1993), 102.

45 It may well be that if the phrase so often used of the gospel of Jesus Christ, "a marvelous work and a wonder," were translated into Hebrew, both "marvelous work" and "wonder" would be the same root word, *p-l-'*. It might be "marvel of marvels" or "wonder of wonders," which, like "Holy of Holies," expresses the superlative. Thus the phrase would indicate the most marvelous and wondrous of all works, the work that is not of human hands but truly from God.

46 Todd R. Kerr, "Ancient Aspects of Nephite Kingship in the Book of Mormon," *Journal of Book of Mormon Studies* 1, no. 1 (Fall 1992): 87.

translated into English as *God* and *Lord*, respectively. To Latter-day Saints who recognize Elohim as a sacred name for the Father, it may be surprising to learn that in the Hebrew text *ĕlōhîm*, or the parallel term *'ēl*, is a common word for "gods" or "god." It may even refer to pagan gods as well as to the God of Israel. (We see a similar thing in English where *God*, with a capital *G*, refers to the true God. While *god* with a lower case *g* represents a pagan god.) Sometimes we see the compound name Yahweh Elohim, or Lord God. In this construction, Elohim is again a general name, almost a surname, while Yahweh is the personal, intimate name. Pamela Reis comments, "In English, God has no intimate name. YHWH [Yahweh], however, is considered by Jews to be the sacred, unpronounceable, personal name of God, and it always and only signifies the one God of the covenant and the universe."[47] While other nations used El and Elohim, only Israel used Yahweh. It is the name the God of the Old Testament gave when Moses asked what name he should give to the Hebrews as a sign that he had been in the presence of God (see Exodus 3:13). In ancient times, the name Yahweh was believed to hold magical power. "The name YHWH is properly synonymous with power (to punish and to rescue), sovereignty, holiness, and authorship and control of events."[48] Not only was there power in the name of God, but one who knew His name was believed to exercise a degree of power over the deity. Knowing God's name, one could summon Him to come to one's aid.

Because of the sacredness and power associated with the name Yahweh, the only time it was ever spoken was by the high priest on the Day of Atonement. On this holy feast day, the high priest would "utter this name ten times during the Yom Kippur liturgy."[49] Each time the people would fall prostrate to the ground. The ineffability of this name was impressed upon me in my first semester of studying Hebrew. We were laboring along trying to read the Hebrew text, when a student read aloud the name printed on the page: Yahweh. Immediately, our professor stopped the student and said emphatically we were not to speak the holy name. We were to say "Adonai" whenever we came across

47 Pamela Tamarkin Reis, *Reading the Lines: A Fresh Look at the Hebrew Bible* (Peabody, Massachusetts: Hendrickson Publishers, 2002), 26.

48 Greenberg, *Ezekiel 1–20,* 133.

49 Szink and Welch, 179.

the letters *Y-h-w-h*. To do otherwise would be an egregious affront to any Jews in our class. The translators of the King James Version honored the reverence the Jews had for the sacred name and translated the word *Yhwh* as LORD. However, since *lord* is also used as a title of respect for men, they distinguished between the two "lords" by writing the name for deity with all capital letters, though the font used for the *-ORD* of Lord is smaller.

Ancient Hebrew manuscripts were consonantal. The vowels were not written down. The pronunciation of words was transmitted in the oral tradition. Since the name "Yhwh" was never spoken, the pronunciation became lost. Its pronunciation is only a scholarly guess. The meaning of the name is also unknown. It is usually thought to have come from the word meaning *to be* and as such expresses something about existence. It may mean that God is the one who causes existence. It may express the unchanging nature of God, or it could denote "the eternity of God—that He was, He is, He shall be, or that His presence shall never depart from Israel."[50] Whatever the exact meaning and pronunciation, Yhwh (i.e., Jehovah) is the name of Jesus Christ, the God of the Old Testament.[51] In time, "the Kabbalists gave the name [Yhwh] the title 'tetragrammaton,' 'the word of four letters,' or the square name, or more simply, the square."[52]

God's Name and Swearing

In the ancient world, covenants were sealed or made legally binding with an oath, a name, a sacrifice at an altar, a symbolic act such as a token or sign that represented the punishment to be inflicted upon one who broke the covenant, or any combination of the above. Oaths are solemn statements that formally or legally bind a person. Today, we swear oaths in a court of law when we promise we will speak the truth. In general, however, people today do not consider their word inviolable, so contracts—signed, sealed and notarized—have largely taken the place

50 Madsen, "Putting on the Names," 463.

51 The word *Jehovah* is derived from *Yhwh* being transliterated with the Latin letters *j-h-v-h,* to which the vowels of *Adonai* were added. The vowels used in "Jehovah" (ᵉ-ō-ā) and "Adonai" (ă-ō-ā) are not identical, but this is due to the phonology of Biblical Hebrew. More specifically, the *hataf patakh* (ă) is grammatically identical to the schwa (ᵉ) and replaces it under a guttural letter.

52 Madsen, "Putting on the Names," 470.

of oaths. It was not so in the ancient world. Hugh Nibley explains, "The oath is the one thing that is most sacred and inviolable among the desert people and their descendants: 'Hardly will an Arab break this oath, even if his life be in jeopardy,' for 'there is nothing stronger, and nothing more sacred than the oath among the nomads.'"[53] The most binding oaths were sworn by the life of something. When a person swore an oath by his own life, he in essence placed his life on the line if he failed to live up to his oath. The most serious and binding of all oaths was "by the life of God" or "as the Lord liveth." When one swore an oath in the name of God, he invoked God as "the guarantor of any obligation which a man may take upon himself. In the event of a breach of any undertaking or agreement Yhwh would be expected to visit the covenant-breaker with judgment."[54] When Nephi promised safety and freedom to Zoram, Laban's servant, he did so with a double oath, "As the Lord liveth, and as I live" (1 Nephi 4:32). There is nothing Nephi could have said or done that would have avouched his pledge more forcefully.

Often, an oath included a self-execrative statement such as, "May God do so to me and more also if I fail to keep my oath." The consequence is not usually explicitly stated, but it is accompanied by a gesture such as drawing one's finger across one's throat.[55] Consider for instance the story of Ruth when she declares her undying commitment to her mother-in-law. Ruth's famous words—"Whither thou goest, I will go; . . . and where thou diest, will I die, and there will I be buried"—are immediately followed by the less famous words, "The Lord do so to me, and more also, if ought but death part thee and me" (Ruth 1:16–17). This oath transforms Ruth's beautiful expression of loyalty into a sacred and solemn oath. "It was presumably accompanied by a symbolic gesture, something like our index finger across the throat."[56] The Nephites who were stirred by Moroni's title of liberty and call for patriotism seal their oaths by rending their garments and casting them at Moroni's feet, inviting God to rend them and cast them at the feet of

---

53 Hugh Nibley, "Portrait of Laban," *CWHN*, 129.

54 Thompson, 237.

55 See Delbert R. Hillers, *Covenant: The History of a Biblical Idea* (Baltimore: The Johns Hopkins University Press, 1969), 41.

56 Edward F. Campbell, Jr., *Ruth*, Anchor Bible, 74.

their enemies if they violate their covenants. When Elijah has the priests of Baal slain, Queen Jezebel responds in fury, "So let the gods do to me, and more also, if I make not thy life [Elijah's life] as the life of one of them [the slain priests] by tomorrow about this time" (1 Kings 19:2). As in most cases, the symbolic action is not explicitly stated, but its footprint is there. The footprint is even fainter in the rather disturbing account in Judges of the man whose concubine is repeatedly raped until she dies. The man cuts her body up and sends the pieces throughout Israel. It is very likely that each of these pieces meant, "If ye will not come and avenge my wrong, may ye be hewn in pieces like this abused and murdered woman." In oath making, a symbolic gesture and using the name of God are "intended to strengthen the validity and credibility of the oath and to reinforce the oathtaker's determination to fulfill it."[57]

A somewhat enigmatic symbolic gesture occurs in Genesis 24 when Abraham sends his trusted servant to the land of his birth to find a wife for Isaac. Abraham instructs his majordomo to put his hand under Abraham's thigh. Since the thigh is a standard euphemism for genitalia, this gesture may have invoked the curse of sterility upon the servant if he broke his oath. Alternatively, "taking the membrum—now circumcised as a covenant sign—into the hand is a way of invoking the presence of God" at this moment of oath taking.[58] Either way, it was a serious and weighty symbolic act used to reinforce the gravity of this oath. Abraham then instructs his servant to "swear by the Lord, the God of heaven, and the God of the earth, that thou shalt not take a wife unto my son of the daughters of the Canaanites, among whom I dwell" (Genesis 24:3). To enter into covenants and oaths in the name of God and then to break those covenants was to have taken the Lord's name in vain. This was the primary way in which an Israelite in Old Testament times would have understood "thou shalt not take the name of the Lord thy God in vain" (Exodus 20:7).

God may swear an oath in His own name. As God sends Adam and Eve out of the Garden, He says, "For as I, the Lord God, liveth, even

57 Sarna, *On the Book of Psalms*, 114.

58 Hamilton, *Genesis 18–50*, 139. "Note that words such as *testimony*, *testify*, *attest* have their origin in Latin 'testes,' suggesting the possibility that Roman society had some kind of symbolic gesture of touching (some)one's genitals when an oath was taken." Hamilton, *Genesis 18–50*, 139.

so my words cannot return void, for as they go forth out of my mouth they must be fulfilled" (Moses 4:30). Paul tells us that when God established the Abrahamic covenant, "he could sware by no greater, [because] he sware by himself" (Hebrews 6:13). Bruce R. McConkie explains, "Because the blessings of Abraham exceed anything else on earth or in heaven, Deity uses the most solemn language known to man to confirm their verity. . . . When God Himself swears with an oath, He puts His own Godhood on the line: either what He promises shall come to pass or He ceases to be God."[59] In establishing the Abrahamic covenant, we do not have record of God using the phrase, "As I live" or "by my own life"; however, He does say, "For I am the Lord thy God" (Abraham 2:7) and "I am the Almighty God" (Genesis 17:1). According to William Propp, "I am so-and-so" is a statement of power and often functions as an oath. Thus, "I am Yahweh" and "As I [Yahweh] live" appear to have much the same force.[60] Another phrase God uses in swearing to Abraham is "my name is Jehovah" (Abraham 2:8). This appears to be another way in which God swears by His own name. After Abraham expresses ultimate obedience and trust in God by nearly sacrificing his son Isaac, God reiterates the promises of the Abrahamic covenant. This time He prefaces the promises by saying, "By myself have I sworn" (Genesis 22:16). God has responded to Abraham's ultimate sacrifice by giving him the ultimate promise, the promise of Abraham's calling and election made sure,[61] which "is as immutable as an oath by Himself."[62]

God's Name and Reputation

The scriptures reveal that God's name "is to be blessed, praised, exalted, magnified, glorified, rejoiced and exulted in, thanked, hallowed, feared, loved, remembered, proclaimed, declared, waited on, walked in, desired, and sought."[63] From this list, it is clear that God's name

59 Bruce R. McConkie, *New Witness,* 317.

60 See William H. C. Propp, *Exodus 1–18*, Anchor Bible, 270. This does not mean, however, that the two statements are necessarily interchangeable. "I am Yahweh" may serve other purposes. See Propp, *Exodus 1–18,* 271.

61 See Bruce R. McConkie, *DNTC,* 3:164.

62 Hyrum Andrus, *Principles of Perfection* (Salt Lake City: Bookcraft, 1970), 352.

63 Ryken, Wilhoit, Longman, 584.

can be simply another way of referring to God. Even today, many Jews use the term *haShem* or "The Name" when referring to God, to avoid saying the sacred word *Yhwh* or even the less sacred *Adonai* (Lord). Based on this understanding, to have faith in the name of God is to have faith in God. To bless the name of God is to bless, or praise, God. The scripture, "There is no other name given whereby salvation cometh" (Mosiah 5:8) means there was no alternative savior and no alternative plan.

A name may also refer to one's fame and reputation. In today's world, a good name and reputation is a valuable asset. It was even more important in the honor-shame society of the biblical world. A good name was of paramount importance in every public action. It was what gave purpose and meaning to their lives. It was the basis for people's interactions with each other. It was much like money is in our culture. "In the United States, an auto dealer won't sell you a new car unless your credit rating is good. In the Mediterranean world, no one would freely associate with you in covenant relationship unless your honor ratings were good, and so a good name and family reputation are the most valuable of assets."[64] To have one's name ridiculed was deeply offensive and insulting. It is not surprising, therefore, that we sometimes read in scripture about God acting for His name's sake. In Isaiah 48:9–11 we read of God deferring his anger "for my name's sake." He will not punish Israel because He does not want His name profaned by the surrounding nations who would view God as incapable of defending His people and would claim ascendancy for their gods. Thus, God states, "I will not give my glory unto another" (Isaiah 48:11). What might at first seem a rather self-serving reason for a perfect being to act may rather reflect God's commitment to mankind. If God's honor and reputation were impugned, His value as a covenant partner is diminished. A bad reputation would hinder His work of bringing to pass salvation.

There is yet another reason God acts for His name's sake. In Jeremiah 14:7, Jeremiah pleads, "O Lord, though our iniquities testify against us, do thou it for thy name's sake." Jeremiah is fully aware that nothing Israel has done merits God's saving intervention. Therefore, he petitions the Lord solely on the basis of Yahweh's name. Since one's name reflects

64 Bruce J. Malina, *The New Testament World: Insights from Cultural Anthropology* (Louisville, Kentucky: Westminster/John Knox Press, 1993), 38.

one's character, Jeremiah may be asking God to act because His name and character are "merciful and gracious, [and] longsuffering" (Exodus 34:6). We close our prayers in the name of Jesus Christ because He is the intercessor between God and man, but we could also do so because His name (i.e., His character) is loving, merciful, generous, and wise—characteristics that elicit a divine response to our mortal concerns.

The Hidden Name of God

In Revelation 19, John sees in heaven a majestic rider on a white horse. He has many crowns upon his head, symbolizing great power and authority. This rider has many names: Faithful and True, The Word of God, and King of Kings and Lord of Lords. He also has "a name written, that no man knew, but he himself" (Revelation 19:12). The idea of having or receiving a name that must be kept hidden from others is widely attested in antiquity.

Rabbinic literature frequently mentions the hidden names of God, referencing a four-letter name, a twelve-letter name, a forty-two-letter name, and a seventy-two-letter name.[65] According to Jewish folklore, God has a secret name, a name other than Yahweh, which was supposedly engraved on Moses's staff.[66] This staff is called in Exodus 4:20 "the rod of God" or the "rod of Elohim." This can be understood in one of two ways. It may mean that the rod belongs to God, just as we might write our names upon something to mark it as our possession. Alternatively, sometimes the word *elohim* is used as an abstract noun connoting the supernatural. Therefore, the rod of elohim "might mean that the rod gives its wielder miraculous powers."[67] This is not too far from Doctrine and Covenants 130:11, which tells us that everyone who enters into the celestial kingdom will be given an object, a white stone, upon which "a new name [is] written, which no man knoweth save he that receiveth it." This object will grant its owner great knowledge and therefore power.

In Egypt, one of the designations for a god was "He whose name is hidden."[68] The importance of "the hidden name of god" is illustrated in the following myth of Re and Isis:

65 See Porter and Ricks, 509.

66 See Propp, *Exodus 1–18,* 224.

67 Ibid., 216.

68 Porter and Ricks, 508.

> According to this myth, Isis desired to learn the hidden name of Re so that she might gain some of the power which he possessed. Since Re had become old, he frequently drooled. Isis took some of Re's saliva which had fallen to the ground, kneaded it with earth, and formed a serpent in the shape of a pear. Subsequently, the serpent bit him [Re], causing him to cry out in pain as the "flame of life" began to depart from him. Isis offered to alleviate Re's suffering through magic (an art at which she was particularly adept) if he would agree to reveal to her his secret name. At first he attempted to satisfy her by a repetition of names which were already well known to her. Isis refused to provide him any relief until Re, tormented and in the depths of despair, revealed his secret name to her.[69]

Knowing the secret name of God was a supreme privilege for a human being. First of all, this knowledge was believed to confer some of God's power upon humans.[70] In addition, it was believed to prevent evil powers from gaining control of an individual. Finally, the name of God was a password or a key word that permitted a person to enter into the presence of God (see D&C 130:11).[71] According to the Egyptians, once in the presence of the gods, a person became like them.[72]

Frequently in scripture we read about or are enjoined to call on God's name. For instance, in Alma 9:17, we read, "For the Lord will be merciful unto all who call on his name." This is an obvious reference to prayer. However, it literally means to call on God by name. "The name is, from the human point of view, the means by which God is approached and known."[73] Indeed, the very pronunciation of the divine name was thought to bring a person into direct contact with God.[74] This means that names were more than designations; they were invocations, ways to

69 Ibid.

70 See Propp, *Exodus 1–18*, 224.

71 See Gaye Strathearn, "Revelation: John's Message of Comfort and Hope," *The Testimony of John the Beloved: The 27th Annual Sidney B. Sperry Symposium* (Salt Lake City: Deseret Book Company, 1998), 292–293.

72 See Porter and Ricks, 510.

73 Ryken, Wilhoit, and Longman, 584.

74 See Madsen, "Putting on the Names," 464.

summon and commune with God.[75] Therefore, when God reveals His names to His people, as He did to Moses on Sinai, He is granting them unprecedented access to Him.[76]

Taking on the Name of God

With the Fall of Adam, man experienced spiritual death, or alienation from God, which is "in a sense a disinheritance from the royal family."[77] Consequently, we are "nameless and familyless, spiritual orphans, and thereby alone in the world."[78] When we enter into the covenant of baptism, we are adopted into the family of Christ. He becomes our Father, and we take His name upon us. The giving of a name is a significant event for both father and child.

> As the crown of womanhood is in granting life, so the crown of manhood is the conferring upon one's posterity the family name. Often ceremony and ritual are associated with a father placing his name, his most prized possession, upon the newborn. In the giving of a name, the father declares the child to be his; he makes of him or her a rightful heir of all that he possesses, and effectually promises to love and protect his progeny, for the child is but the manifestation of his own flesh and blood. The children in return are taught to love and respect their parents, and to so live as to bring honor to the name that has been given them as a sacred trust.[79]

To take on the name of Christ as our spiritual father is to enter into a relationship of intimacy and belonging. We are entitled to

75 See ibid., 463.

76 See Gerald H. Wilson, *The NIV Application Commentary: Psalms, Volume 1* (Grand Rapids, Michigan: Zondervan, 2002), 433.

77 Robert L. Millet, "The Only Sure Foundation: Building on the Rock of Our Redeemer," *The Book of Mormon: Helaman through 3 Nephi 8, According to Thy Word*, eds. Monte S. Nyman and Charles D. Tate Jr. (Provo, Utah: Religious Studies Center Brigham Young University, 1992), 17–18.

78 Ibid., 18.

79 Joseph Fielding McConkie, "The Testimony of Christ Through the Ages," *The Book of Mormon: Jacob through Words of Mormon, to Learn with Joy*, eds. Monte S. Nyman and Charles D. Tate Jr. (Provo, Utah: Religious Studies Center Brigham Young University, 1990), 164.

unparalleled blessings and to His watch-care and protection, but we also bear certain responsibilities. We are subject to His authority.

Taking on the name of Christ means taking on His identity. One of the delights (and sometimes banes) of parenting is seeing your children take on your identity. It begins with physical resemblances. In our family, my husband and I have pictures of our children as babies that are nearly identical to our own baby pictures, the only distinguishing factor being whether the pictures are in black-and-white or color. As our children have grown, it has been amazing to see them not only look like us but act and talk like us, even sharing the same facial expressions and gestures. Now that our children are adults, we have even seen that they often think and feel like we do. When we take on Christ's name, we are to take on His identity. We are to grow up in Christ, to take on His attributes, to act as He acts, and even to feel and think as He does. Ultimately, "we will exhibit divine characteristics not just because we think we should, but because that is the way we are."[80] This transformation is effected through the power of the Holy Ghost.

In addition to taking on His identity, taking on the name of Christ also includes having the delegated authority of Christ. To Abraham, God said, "I will take thee, to put upon thee my name, even the Priesthood of thy father, and my power shall be over thee" (Abraham 1:18). This verse clearly states that God's name is synonymous with priesthood authority. This is supported by our definition of priesthood, "the power and authority to act in God's *name.*" Priesthood ordinances are performed in the name of Jesus Christ, indicating they are performed with Christ's authority.

Priesthood holders are not the only ones who labor in Christ's name. Speaking in general conference but specifically to the sisters of the Church and even more specifically to visiting teachers, General Relief Society President Barbara Winder explained that because we go in Christ's name, we can see, say, and do things beyond our natural capacities.[81] This is true anytime we serve in the Church. When we receive a calling, it comes through one who has been given priesthood keys to preside in our ward or stake. We are set apart by the laying on

80 Hafen, *The Broken Heart*, 18.

81 See Barbara W. Winder, "Striving Together: Transforming Our Beliefs into Action," *Ensign*, November 1984, 98.

of hands by those whom God has authorized. This means, as President Eyring stated in the October 2002 general conference, that in our callings we represent the Savior. We are His hands and His voice.[82]

We take upon ourselves the identity of Christ when we enter into covenants with Him, beginning with baptism and culminating in the covenants of the holy temple. We do this not only by making covenants in His name, but also by ritual identification. When we are baptized, we "*imitate* or *participate* in Christ's death, burial, and resurrection."[83] In scripture, water symbolizes universal death, specifically death consequent to disobedience to God.[84] Consider, for instance, the waters of the great flood and the waters of the Red Sea that destroyed the Egyptian armies. Our submersion into the waters of death represents the death and burial of the natural man. However, our death is brief, and we are raised up unto new life, just as Christ was resurrected (see Doctrine & Covenants 128:12–13). We are now a new person, alive in Christ. Paul uses this analogy in Romans 6:5: "For if we have been planted together in the likeness of his death, we shall be also in the likeness of his resurrection." In the next verse, he introduces a different image of Christ's death, crucifixion. "Knowing this, that our old man is crucified with him, that the body of sin might be destroyed, that henceforth we should not serve sin" (Romans 6:6). Our man of sin might be drowned or crucified or both. It doesn't much matter. What is important is that we become like the Savior in as many ways as possible.

Becoming like Christ is one of the purposes of the temple. In the temple we are anointed. The titles *Christ* and *Messiah* both mean "the anointed one." We dress in sacred clothing evocative of the splendid clothing worn by the ancient high priest, clothing that made him godlike in his appearance.[85] We make covenants that will make us

82 See Henry B. Eyring, "Rise to Your Call," *Ensign*, November 2002, 76.

83 Jennifer C. Lane, "'Come, Follow Me': The Imitation of Christ in the Later Middle Ages," *Prelude to the Restoration: From Apostasy to the Restored Church: The 33rd Annual Sidney B. Sperry Symposium*, (Salt Lake City: Deseret Book and Brigham Young University Religious Studies Center, 2004), 125.

84 See Allen J. Christenson, "The Waters of Destruction and the Vine of Redemption," *A Witness of Jesus Christ: The 1989 Sperry Symposium on the Old Testament*, ed. Richard D. Draper (Salt Lake City: Deseret Book Company, 1990), 37.

85 See Meyers, *Exodus*, 244.

more Christlike. When we marry, we do so remembering the atoning sacrifice of the Savior. This teaches us much about the nature of a celestial marriage. It is a lesson well understood by one non–Latter-day Saint scholar. Joseph Campbell wrote that when he married his wife, "I felt it was a crucifixion. The bridegroom does go to the bride as to the cross. The bride gives herself equally. It's a reciprocal crucifixion. In marriage you are not sacrificing yourself to the other person. You are sacrificing yourself to the relationship."[86] We sacrifice our life as a sole proprietor. *I* becomes *we*. *We* become *God's*. We are also becoming like Christ. As Paul wrote, "Husbands, love your wives, even as Christ also loved the church, and gave himself for it" (Ephesians 5:25). So much of the temple is to help us take on the name, nature, and identity of Christ. Only then can we truly know God. Only then can we be one with Christ.

Writing the Name

Today, when we want to assert our ownership of an item, we write our name on it. When we want to attest the verity of a document, such as a tax return, we sign our name. When we promise to perform in accordance with certain agreements, we sign our name on a contract. In the ancient world, names were often written, inscribed, or stamped on things—and even people—for the same reasons. One way in which this was done was with a seal, a small object with a pictorial image or a person's name. The seal would be pressed into a soft substance such as clay.

The two basic kinds of seals used in the ANE were cylinder seals and stamp seals. "Cylinder seals were small, engraved cylinders that were rolled in clay or wax to create a continually repeating impression."[87] In Israel, Egypt, and the other smaller kingdoms of the eastern Mediterranean area, stamp seals were more common. Stamp seals were frequently attached to a cord and worn around the neck as we would wear a necklace. A seal could also be set in a ring and worn upon the finger. These were called

86 Joseph Campbell, *A Joseph Campbell Companion: Reflections on the Art of Living*, ed. Diane K. Osbon (New York: HarperPerennial, 1991), 51–52.

87 Dana M. Pike, "Seals and Sealing among Ancient and Latter-day Israelites," in *Thy People Shall Be My People*, 101–102. I recently viewed one of these in the Museum of Natural History in New York City. It was no more than an inch long and looked like an elaborately decorated bead. Cylinder seals were commonly used in Mesopotamia.

signets.[88] A seal, whether a cylinder seal, a stamp seal, or a signet, "was a highly personal object that performed the function of the signature in modern society, a kind of extension of the personality."[89] "It served as the religious and legal surrogate for the person who wore it."[90] We see this in the story of Tamar in the book of Genesis (see Genesis 38:16–26).

Seals and signets were used to seal documents.[91] In some instances, a document was written on papyrus, folded, and secured with a string. A piece of damp clay was placed on the knot of the string and then stamped with the sender's seal.[92] Sometimes a document was folded and signed on the back by a witness and then folded again and signed on the back by a different witness. This could be repeated a number of times. The greater number of witnesses the greater the importance of the document.[93] The document, or scroll, that contains the destiny of the world in Revelation is sealed with seven seals, the number of perfection and wholeness.

The seal marked a document as authentic and ensured that the document would not be tampered with, at least not without detection. The seal also represented the owner and conveyed his authority. A document with the seal of a king was a regal decree and must be carried out. Even in cases of lesser authority, the one whose seal was on a document was responsible for carrying out any agreements contained in the document. The seal made him responsible for all the consequences in the case of noncompliance.[94]

In the ancient world, names were not only written on documents. Herodotus noted that "devotees of the various gods in Egypt often wrote the name of their particular god on their bodies. Slaves were

88 See ibid., 102.

89 Sarna, *JPS Genesis*, 268.

90 E. A. Speiser, *Genesis*, Anchor Bible, 298.

91 Sometimes to further seal a document, it was pierced with a nail. "In recent decades, over a hundred Greek and Roman curses that have been inscribed on small lead sheets that were folded up and pierced with a nail have been recovered from tombs, temples, and especially wells near the law courts." "Cursing a Litigant with Speechlessness," *Insights: An Ancient Window, The Newsletter of the Foundation for Ancient Research and Mormon Studies*, no. 120 (October 1998): 2.

92 See Pike, 103.

93 See Ford, 93.

94 See Speiser, 298.

often tattooed with their owners' names."[95] Soldiers were also branded, often on their hands. In Israel, tattooing was explicitly prohibited (see Leviticus 19:28). The Israelites did, however, wear upon their foreheads and upper arms *tephillim*, or phylacteries—little boxes that contained verses from Deuteronomy and Exodus expressing their devotion to the one God of Israel. This form of writing the name of God upon them was as close to tattooing as they could come. However, there are references in scriptures, probably figurative, that refer to tattooing. For instance, Isaiah 44:5 states, "One will say, 'I belong to the Lord'; another will call himself by the name of Jacob; still another will write on his hand, 'the Lord's,' and will take the name Israel" (Isaiah 44:5 NIV). In Isaiah 49:15–16, we read, "Can a woman forget her sucking child, that she should not have compassion on the son of her womb? yea, they may forget, yet will I not forget thee. Behold, I have graven thee upon the palms of my hands." Here, God is affirming His love for Israel in the strongest possible way. First, He uses the ultimate image of personal attachment, a mother's womb. "As the locus of birth, the womb is one of the most profound symbols of human love. Surely no woman can fail to show womb-love for the child of her own womb."[96] Second, he swears an oath using a comparison with the impossible: Can a mother forget her nursing baby? The proper, exaggerated way to make an oath is to compare it to something that is impossible and say that it is more possible that this impossible thing happens (or doesn't happen, depending on the analogy) than for my word to not be fulfilled.[97] Third, God writes Israel's name upon the palms of His hands. This is a reversal of the common practice of the master's name being written on the servant. Here, the servant's name is written upon the master's hands. In actuality, the name is not a name at all but the marks of nails. These marks are tokens of excruciating pain but also of boundless love.

In the book of Revelation, we read, "Him that overcometh will I make a pillar in the temple of my God, and he shall go no more out: and I will write upon him the name of my God, and the name of the

---

95 John N. Oswalt, *The Book of Isaiah Chapters 40–66* (Grand Rapids, Michigan: William B. Eerdsmans Publishing Company, 1998), 168.

96 Trible, 51.

97 See Bruce J. Malina and Richard L. Rohrbaugh, *Social Science Commentary on the Synoptic Gospels* (Minneapolis: Fortress Press, 1992), 147.

city of my God, which is new Jerusalem . . . and I will write upon him my new name" (Revelation 3:12). Pillars are permanent fixtures in a building. They connote strength and stability. They are imposing and beautiful. For Saints to be declared a pillar is for them to be promised a permanent place in the eternal kingdom of God. But the promise in Revelation goes beyond this. These pillars have the name of God written upon them. Elder Bruce R. McConkie explains, "God's name is God. To have his name written on a person is to identify that person as a God. How can it be said more plainly?"[98] But the pillars (the exalted Saints) not only have the name of God written on them. Almost as a second witness, they also have the name of God's city inscribed on them. To bear the name of a city is a sign of citizenship of that city. A person who lives in Phoenix is a Phoenician. A person who lives in Boston is a Bostonian. A person who resides in the city of God—this too is plain. That person is a god.

No Name

Given the importance of a name in the ancient world and the fact that it represented the essence of a person, it is not surprising that "possessing no name was equivalent to nonexistence. An Egyptian text describes pre-creation as the time 'when no name of anything had yet been named.'"[99] A man was not considered complete until he received his name. Then he was whole, having body, soul, and name.[100] The connection between existence and a name holds true even for deity. To remember the name of deity is "the acknowledgement of that deity's existence and power. Thus, not mentioning the god's name is like cutting the name off: it denies the very reality of the idol or deity so designated."[101] By extension, when we do not call upon God in prayer, we effectually cut Him off in our lives and deny His existence in our world.

There have been times in history and in scripture when names have been intentionally removed. In the fourteenth century BC, Pharaoh Akhenaten made "a series of sweeping and evidently unpopular

98 Bruce R. McConkie, *DNTC*, 3:458.

99 Sarna, *JPS Exodus*, 7.

100 See Porter and Ricks, 502.

101 Carol L. Meyers and Eric M. Meyers, *Zechariah 9–14,* Anchor Bible, 370.

changes. . . . With the end of the dynasty, . . . the next dynasty did everything in its power to erase the memory of the heretic king, even to the dismantling of his temples and shipping the stones to opposite ends of the kingdom."[102] Earlier, a pharaoh by the name of Thutmosis III acted similarly following the death of his mother and coregent, Hatshepsut. He "defaced her monuments, removed her name from royal inscriptions, effaced her portraits, and otherwise did all in his power to destroy her name and to remove her memory from the historical recollection of the Egyptians."[103] In a culture where great value was placed on having one's name live on—through one's posterity or works—this was devastating beyond comprehension. However, it not only negated Hatshepsut's whole mortal existence, it jeopardized her life in the next world. It was believed that "a nameless being could not be introduced to the gods, and as no created thing exists without a name, the man who had no name was in a worse position before the divine powers than the feeblest inanimate object."[104]

In Israel, names could be removed or cut off by removing them from the official lists and registrars of the citizens of Israel. This was a serious act with dire consequences. "Those inscribed in the lists had the privilege of sharing in the goods of the community. If one's name were blotted out, . . . one would be denied this privilege and practically, it meant that one was condemned to death."[105] The names may have been literally blotted out by immersing the parchment in water, causing the names to be erased. Interestingly, at the time of Noah when the world was immersed in wickedness and violence, God said, "I will destroy man whom I have created" (Genesis 6:7). The Hebrew word used for *destroy* means "to erase by washing." Not just a list of their names, but the wicked themselves were to be erased by immersing them in the waters of the flood.

The register of citizenry in Israel parallels the book of life kept in heaven. In this heavenly registry "the names of the faithful and

---

102 Oswalt, *Isaiah 1–39*, 325.

103 Porter and Ricks, 504.

104 E. A. Wallis Budge, *Egyptian Magic* (London: Routledge and Kegan Paul, 1971), 166; quoted in Porter and Ricks, 504.

105 Ford, 409.

an account of their righteous covenants and deeds"[106] are recorded. These are they who are citizens of the kingdom of God and who will inherit eternal life. Their names will never be cut off, and therefore they have everlasting names.[107] Perhaps it is no coincidence that in the dedicatory prayer of the Kirtland Temple, Joseph Smith prayed, "We ask thee, Holy Father, to establish the people that shall worship [in the temple], and honorably hold a name and standing in this thy house, to all generations and for eternity" (D&C 109:24).

The scribes who kept the sacred records understood the importance of a name and at times used naming and anonymity to serve their purposes. For instance, when we first meet Potiphar, he is called, "Potiphar, an officer of Pharaoh, captain of the guard, an Egyptian" (Genesis 39:1). His full name and titles are given "to draw attention to the aristocratic nature of the household into which Joseph is sold."[108] In Exodus 1:15, we learn that the midwives who defied Pharaoh's orders to kill the male infants of the Hebrews were named Shiphrah and Puah. In general, midwives are not important people in society. They are not among the rich or the powerful. Yet, the courage and character of these two midwives earned them a right to have their names recorded for posterity. On the other hand, the mighty pharaoh who commanded a nation, who held the fate of the Hebrews in his hands, remains nameless. Not only is this a snub to the pharaoh, it is the way "the biblical narrator expresses his scale of values. All the power of the mighty pharaoh, the outward magnificence of his realm, the dazzling splendor of his court, his colossal monuments—all are illusory, ephemeral, and in the ultimate reckoning, insignificant."[109]

Names are of monumental importance in the eternities, both the names we bear and the names we know. Like the Tongans, we do well to bear several names to mark our advancement through mortality and our spiritual progression. It is imperative that we take on the names of Christ, with all that taking on His name entails—taking on His identity, His nature, and His work. If we live worthy, we may receive

106 Bruce R. McConkie, *Mormon Doctrine*, 97.

107 See Meyers and Meyers, 369.

108 Sarna, *JPS Exodus*, 271.

109 Sarna, *Exploring Exodus: The Origins of Biblical Israel* (New York: Schocken Books, 1996), 25.

the extraordinary privilege of learning the hidden names of God, names that will grant us spiritual power and intimate access to our Father, even to His presence. The greatest blessings that names have to offer are to be had in the temples of our God. Little wonder the temple is called a house for the name of God (see 1 Kings 8:17).

The Temple and the Scriptures

"In general, we know that we only see the tip of the iceberg in the scriptural record."[1] So much is left unsaid. Nephi's vision fills eleven pages of scripture, yet Nephi says, "I have written but a small part of the things which I saw" (1 Nephi 14:28). Regarding the brother of Jared's transcendent experience with the Lord, Moroni writes, "I could not make a full account of these things" (Ether 3:17). John concludes his gospel by saying, "And there are also many other things which Jesus did, the which, if they should be written every one, I suppose that even the world itself could not contain the books that should be written" (John 21:25). The enquiring mind is curious about that which is left unwritten. Some things are omitted because space is limited. Some things are left unwritten because they are too holy for the unendowed and the uninitiated. In these cases, the tip of the iceberg is often visible—enough to pique the interest of one who knows the rest of the story.

This chapter is devoted to examining some temple-related scriptural passages. Some of the passages will exemplify or expound on temple-related ideas we have previously discussed. Others will reflect or illuminate an aspect of the temple not yet addressed. Still others focus on application. Some are short. Some are more detailed. They are not inclusive. Rather, they are a sampling and a springboard to help you recognize the tips of the icebergs and to glance beneath the surface to see eternal truths.

---

1 John W. Welch, *The Sermon at the Temple and the Sermon on the Mount: A Latter-day Saint Approach* (Salt Lake City and Provo, Utah: Deseret Book Company and FARMS, 1990), 16.

GENESIS 11

After the flood, the descendants of Noah spread out across the earth. One migrating group settled in a plain in the land of Shinar (i.e., Mesopotamia). The location provided water, food, and tranquility[2] but limited stone. Consequently, bricks for building were made from molded, sun-dried clay. With the discovery of the technique of firing bricks in a kiln, the bricks became stronger and more durable. The use of bitumen for mortar gave the bricks further strength, cohesion, and impermeability. With these advancements, it became possible to erect multistoried buildings. A new era of monumental temple building began.[3] This is the background of Genesis 11, wherein the people of Babel declare, "Go to, let us make brick, and burn them thoroughly. And they had brick for stone, and slime [bitumen] had they for mortar. And they said, Go to, let us build us a city and a tower, whose top may reach unto heaven" (Genesis 11:3–4). This tower in Babel is not simply a tall building. It was "to reach into heaven," which is a phrase used in Mesopotamian building inscriptions, particularly with reference to ziggurats.[4] Ziggurats were stair-stepped structures "designed to provide stairways from the heavens (the gate of the gods) to earth so that the gods could come down into their temple and into the town and bring blessing."[5] The ziggurats had no rooms, chambers, or passageways inside of them. They were a frame made of sun-dried bricks and filled with dirt and rubble. The whole purpose of the structure was to hold up the stairway.[6]

The ziggurat of Babel was a false temple. It was built by the descendants of Nimrod, a descendant of Ham. They lacked priesthood keys and the authority to build temples and administer the ordinances thereof. However, they did not lack a total understanding of or appreciation for the power of the temple. They built their copycat temple in order to "make us a name" (Genesis 11:4) and "lest we be scattered abroad upon the face of the whole earth" (Genesis 11:4). The

---

2 Westermann, *Genesis 1–11*, 544.

3 See Sarna, *JPS Exodus*, 82.

4 See Sarna, *JPS Exodus*, 82–83.

5 John H. Walton and Victor H. Matthews, *The IVP Bible Background Commentary: Genesis–Deuteronomy* (Downers Grove, Illinois: InterVarsity Press, 1997), 33.

6 See ibid., 34.

idea that temples are associated with gathering and to prevent scattering is seen in our dispensation. Joseph Smith stated, "God gathers together His people in the last days, to build unto the Lord a house to prepare them for the ordinances and endowments, washings and anointings, etc."[7] Without the sealing work that is performed inside the temple, "the whole earth would be utterly wasted at his [Christ's] coming" (D&C 2:3). "One meaning of the word 'wasted' at Joseph Smith's time was 'destroyed by scattering.'"[8]

God was not pleased with the citizens of Babel. They wanted the right things, but they went about it in the wrong way. Five times in Genesis 11:4, the pronouns *us* or *we* are used: "And they said, Go to, let *us* build *us* a city and a tower, whose top may reach unto heaven; and let *us* make *us* a name, lest *we* be scattered abroad upon the face of the whole earth" (italics added). They were attempting to ascend into heaven on their own terms and by their own power. To prevent the defilement of His ordinances, the Lord scattered the people and confounded their language. The word in Hebrew for "to confound" is *nabal* נבל, "to make senseless." The word for "to make brick" is *laban*, לבן. The three root consonants are a mirror image: *n-b-l* and *l-b-n*. "To confound" is the reverse of "to make bricks." Does the reversal of sounds suggest a reversal by God of the human machinations? Will he "unbrick" what they brick? It appears so but only temporarily. Immediately following this incident, God introduces the Abrahamic covenant—the covenant of gathering, the covenant of taking the gospel into all nations, and the covenant of temple and priesthood blessings. The gospel reverses the effects of Babel. Today, the reversal is expanding at a rapid pace. People all over the world are hearing the gospel and reading the sacred texts of scripture in their own languages. They are joining the Church and coming to the temple, where they can gather their ancestors and receive the blessings of heaven.

Genesis 15:7–21

Genesis 15 is one of the five occasions in Genesis in which God affirms the Abrahamic covenant to Abraham. It is set apart from the other

---

7 Joseph Fielding Smith, *Teachings of the Prophet Joseph Smith*, 308.

8 Lee Donaldson, V. Dan Rogers, and David Rolph Seely, "I Have a Question," *Ensign*, February 1994, 60.

Abrahamic covenant pronouncements by some fascinating and unique features. It begins with God's assurance, "Fear not, Abram: I am thy shield" (Genesis 15:1). Since a shield was the primary defensive weapon for a warrior in the ANE, it was an apt metaphor for protection. In this instance, God is promising not only to protect Abraham but also to be "the guarantor and protector of the covenant."[9] God next promises Abraham that he will have a child. As incredible as this promise is to the aging patriarch, Abraham believes the Lord and it is accounted unto him for righteousness (see Genesis 15:6). God is not finished making staggering promises. He next promises that the land in which Abraham wanders will be his. Apparently, this promise was even harder to believe than that of having a child, for Abraham asks for a sign. In response, God instructs Abraham to perform an ordinance, a ritual that seals and ratifies a covenant. This ritual may have been "God's way of making a solemn oath to Abram, much as elsewhere God swears by himself."[10] God commands Abraham to take a heifer, a she-goat, a ram, a turtledove, and a pigeon. God does not spell out what Abraham is to do with these animals, but Abraham's actions indicate that he is familiar with this rite and proceeds to do all that is implied in God's terse command.

The scriptural text gives just the barest account of what follows, but a passage in Jeremiah and the covenant ceremonies of the ANE reveal a custom where the sacrificial animals were slain and the parts of the animals were placed in two rows of equal length, opposite each other, forming an aisle.[11] The covenanting parties then "walked in a dignified procession down the aisle. . . . It is quite likely that they took an oath which may have sounded like this: 'If I transgress the terms of the covenant may my blood be spilled as the blood of this animal was spilled!'"[12] All this is implied in the cryptic statement in Genesis 15,

---

9 S. Kent Brown, "Man and Son of Man: Issues of Theology and Christology," in *The Pearl of Great Price: Revelations from God*, eds. H. Donl Peterson and Charles D. Tate Jr. (Provo, Utah: Religious Studies Center Brigham Young University, 1989), 66.

10 Hamilton, *The Book of Genesis: Chapter 1–17,* 433.

11 See Jeremiah 34:18–20.

12 Ronald Youngblood, *The Heart of the Old Testament* (Grand Rapids, Michigan: Baker Book House, 1971), 39.

"And he took unto him all these, and divided them in the midst, and laid each piece one against another" (Genesis 15:10).[13]

Some time after this covenant ceremony, but before night, vultures[14] swoop down on the animal pieces, and Abraham drives them away. This is more than the food chain at work. With its association with death, uncleanness, and preying on that which is vulnerable, a vulture is a symbol of Satan. Thus, the powers of evil are attacking the sacrifice of God and opposing the covenant. As the sun goes down, a deep sleep falls upon Abraham. The word for "deep sleep," is *tardēmâ*. It is the same word used for the sleep that comes upon Adam when his rib is taken from him and for the sleep that Jonah experiences in the ship on the way to Tarshish. It is an abnormally deep sleep, even a divinely induced sleep. J. Hartley suggests it is "a stupor that God causes to fall on a person, blocking out all other perceptions, in order that the person may be completely receptive to the divine word."[15] Indeed, what follows for Abraham is a revelation and a theophany but not before another encounter with evil. This time, it is not vultures but "an horror of great darkness" (Genesis 15:12). This parallels Joseph Smith's experience in the grove when he was "seized upon" by a power of darkness so violent that it seemed to him for a time that he was doomed to sudden destruction (Joseph Smith—History 1:15). As with so much in this pithy account, Abraham's deliverance is not detailed. The account skips to God's somber warning that Abraham's descendants will experience enslavement and oppression in a land that is not theirs.

When night falls, God performs the rite at the heart of this pericope: God walks down the covenantal aisle created by the sacrificial animals. However, the anthropomorphic terms have been removed. M. Catherine Thomas explains:

---

13 Robert Alter purports, based on the Hebrew text, it is not the animals that face each other but the covenanting parties. Thus, "existing translations fudge the vivid anthropomorphism of the Hebrew here." Robert Alter, *The Five Books of Moses* (New York: W. W. Norton & Company, 2004), 75.

14 "Unaccountably, most English translators render this collective noun as 'birds of prey,' though their action clearly indicates they belong to the category of vultures, not hawks and eagles." Alter, 75.

15 J. Hartley, *Book of Job*, NICOT (Grand Rapids: Eerdmans, 1998), 112; quoted in Hamilton, *Genesis 1–17*, 434.

> At least by the intertestamental period (the period following Malachi, between the Old Testament and the New), the scribes and rabbis found the anthropomorphisms in the Hebrew Bible offensive and made small textual changes, which they described as "biblical modifications of expression." . . . For example, in place of "I [God] will dwell in your midst," they substituted, "I shall cause you to dwell," avoiding the idea that God would dwell with men. The text of Exodus 34:24 was subtly altered from "to see the face of the Lord" (*lir'ot 'et-pene yhwh*) to the phrase "to appear before the Lord" (*lera'ot 'et-pene yhwh*). Again, the effect is to distance and dematerialize God.[16]

In a similar vein, instead of stating that God walked down the covenantal aisle, Genesis 15:17 says a smoking furnace (i.e., a firepot made of earthenware that functioned as an oven) and a burning lamp passed between the pieces. Smoke and fire are both signs of the presence of God (see Exodus 19:18; Numbers 9:16; D&C 110:3; Revelation 1:14). Fire particularly represents God's glory. To say a smoking furnace and a burning lamp passed between the pieces of the sacrificed animals is simply a nonanthropomorphic way of saying God passed between these pieces. It must be remembered that this "oath ritual rests on 'the parallel fate of the animal and the one who takes the oath.'"[17] By this act, God binds himself, under punishment of death, to fulfill His covenant. Since an eternal being cannot die, God is stating in the strongest terms possible that He *will* fulfill His covenant with Abraham. To do otherwise is simply an impossibility.

The Abrahamic covenant is our covenant. The blessings promised to Abraham are sealed upon us when we enter into the covenants of a temple marriage. Like Abraham, we have absolute surety that God will fulfill His promises if we keep our covenants. We have God's solemn and immutable word.

---

16 M. Catherine Thomas, "The Provocation in the Wilderness and the Rejection of Grace," *Thy People Shall Be My People*, 171.

17 Claus Westermann, *Genesis 12–36: A Continental Commentary*, trans. John J. Scullion (Minneapolis: Fortress Press, 1995), *12–36*, 228.

GENESIS 28:10–22; 32:24–32

In Genesis 28, we find Jacob, the son of Isaac and the brother of Esau, journeying to Haran. The purpose of his trip is twofold: to find a bride from among his mother's family and to escape the murderous intentions of Esau. Jacob provoked Esau's fury by assuming Esau's identity (at the behest of his mother, Rebekah) in order to secure the oral deathbed benediction from Isaac. Such pronouncements had the same legal validity as a last will and testament.[18] As Jacob travels from Canaan, he comes upon a place where he will spend the night. Genesis 28:11 tells us that Jacob "lighted upon a certain place," meaning he happened upon it. The randomness of his choice is emphasized. Three times this verse uses the word *māqôm* (place, spot) for the site at which Jacob lodges. Each of the three times, *māqôm* is qualified with the definite article *ha*-(the). This is not any ordinary place. Jacob happens upon *the* place. Furthermore, *māqôm* frequently has the connotation of a sacred site. Some cultures of the ancient world "believed that a [sacred] location accumulated power with time. Once the portal to the Otherworld was opened, once the points of power were set in place, the membrane between the worlds was made thinner with subsequent use."[19] Whether Jacob believed this or not is immaterial for he is apparently unaware of the sacred associations of this place and his mind is focused on sleep, not a theophany.

Jacob sleeps, and while he sleeps, he dreams. His dream is not an ordinary dream but a divine manifestation and glorious vision. He sees a ladder set upon the earth, the top of which reaches into heaven. Angels are ascending and descending the ladder, and at the top of it stands the Lord Himself.[20] In this sacred encounter, the Lord renews the promises given to Abraham and reaffirmed with Isaac. Three times

18 See Nahum M. Sarna, *Understanding Genesis* (New York: Schocken Books, 1966), 187.

19 Linda Schele and David Freidel, *Forest of Kings: The Untold Story of the Ancient Maya* (New York: Quill William Morrow, 1990), 122.

20 Some scholars suggest that the Lord stood beside Jacob, for the Lord *speaks* to Jacob, rather than *calls* to him. Also, a few verses later, Jacob says, "The Lord is in *this place*," presupposing "Yahweh's immediate presence in the place, rather than in heaven at the top of the stairway" (Hamilton, Hamilton, *Genesis 18–50*, 241). However, it may also be that when Jacob says, "The Lord is in this place," Jacob had ascended the ladder and entered the presence of the Lord (Joseph Fielding McConkie, *Gospel Symbolism*, 123).

in two verses, the Lord references Jacob's seed and once promises that his seed would inherit the land where Jacob lies. Such would be particularly meaningful to Jacob, whose life is in danger, who is leaving his homeland, and who is on a mission to find a worthy wife. The Lord next extends to Jacob an amazing promise of protection and divine assistance: "And, behold, I am with thee, and will keep thee in all places whither thou goest, and will bring thee again into this land; for I will not leave thee, until I have done that which I have spoken to thee of" (Genesis 28:15).

Following this extraordinary vision, Jacob declares, "Surely the Lord is in this place; and I knew it not. . . . This is none other but the house of God, and this is the gate of heaven" (Genesis 28:16–17). He names the place Beth-el, which means "house of God," and sets up a stone as a pillar. This stone/pillar serves several functions. First, stones were often set up to mark the site of a theophany and to serve as a visible symbol of the divine presence. In addition, stones functioned as boundary markers, in this case marking the boundary between the holy and the profane. Stones were also set up to serve as witnesses to covenants and to sacred events (see Joshua 4:19–24; 24:27). Finally, the erect stone or pillar might have been a symbol of the stairway to God. Jacob anoints the pillar with oil, further sanctifying the site and the marker, and covenants to live in complete harmony with God's will.

Jacob's experience at Beth-el is, according to Michael Wilcox, "one of the finest descriptions of a temple in scripture."[21] Indeed, the very name of this place, Beth-el, the house of God, begs us to make this connection. Beth-el was a holy place, a place where a ladder or a stairway was revealed that provided access to heaven and to the Lord. Our temples are holy places that provide access to heaven and to God. The covenants we make are like the rungs of Jacob's ladder.[22] Each one lifts us farther above the profane world and moves us closer to God. Having completed all the necessary covenants, we are brought into the presence of God at the gate of heaven. Just as God renewed the Abrahamic covenant

---

21 S. Michael Wilcox, *House of Glory: Finding Personal Meaning in the Temple* (Salt Lake City: Deseret Book Company, 1995), 103.

22 See Marion G. Romney, "Temples—The Gates to Heaven," *Ensign*, March 1971. https://www.lds.org/ensign/1971/03/temples-the-gates-to-heaven?lang=eng.

with Jacob, those portions of the Abrahamic covenant "which pertain to personal exaltation and eternal increase are renewed with each member of the House of Israel who enters the order of celestial marriage."[23] Finally, just as angels ascended and descended Jacob's ladder, the temple is a "place where those who have preceded us in the spirit world descend to us while we ascend to them."[24] Indeed, given all these associations, it is clear that "Jacob received his endowment at Bethel."[25]

Jacob's return to Canaan more than twenty years later is no less eventful than his trip from Canaan. First, he is met by angels. He declares, "This is God's host" (Genesis 32:2), or in Hebrew, "This is God's camp." He calls the place Mahanaim, meaning "two camps." The word *camp* can mean a place of encampment, a large company, or an army. In this instance, the word reveals that Jacob must have seen a vast number of angels; otherwise, *camp* would be meaningless.[26] The military nuance of *camp* also captures the tension and possible peril of Jacob's return. Jacob and Esau had not parted on good terms. Has Esau's bitter hatred mellowed or intensified over the intervening years? Is Jacob risking his life and his family by returning to his homeland? Jacob sends a message to Esau, announcing his return and his acquisition of oxen, asses, flocks, and servants. By this, Jacob tells his brother that he is not sneaking in behind Esau's back, nor has he returned to claim inheritance rights.[27] He has sufficient for his needs, even an abundance. Esau comes to meet Jacob with four hundred men, the standard size of a militia.[28] This is not the welcome wagon. This is a "crisis of staggering proportion. In Jacob's mind, his family, as well as the covenant itself, faced annihilation."[29] In an attempt to preserve at least part of his covenantal family, Jacob divides his party in half and sends them across the ford of Jabbok. He sets apart a generous portion of his flocks as a gift for Esau. Then Jacob prays—all through the night.

---

23 Bruce R. McConkie, *Mormon Doctrine*, 13.

24 Wilcox, *House of Glory*, 103.

25 Andrew C. Skinner, "Jacob in the Presence of God," *Thy People Shall Be My People*, 139.

26 See Westermann, *Genesis 12–36*, 505.

27 See Walton and Matthews, 65.

28 See Sarna, *JPS Genesis*, 224.

29 Skinner, "Jacob in the Presence of God," 141.

Jacob's first theophany occurred at Beth-el, which Jacob declared to be "the gate of heaven" (Genesis 28:17). Jacob's second theophany will occur at the ford of Jabbok. "River crossings or fords function in much the same way as gates. Both are entrance ways giving access in and out of territory."[30] Once again, Jacob is at the border of the profane and the sacred. He is again at the gate of God. The scriptures record, "And Jacob was left alone; and there wrestled a man with him until the breaking of the day" (Genesis 32:24). The record is clear that Jacob is alone. So who is this man and from where did he come? Though the text is translated as "a man," *'ish* "is a generic term, covering both human and divine beings who have the same appearance."[31] In addition, "the word conventionally translated by 'wrestled' can just as well mean 'embraced.'. . . It was in this ritual embrace that Jacob received a new name and the bestowal of priestly and kingly power at sunrise."[32] It is interesting to note that the Holy of Holies was also called the *bet ha kapporet*, the house or room of the atonement, or the house or room of the embrace,[33] giving Jacob's interaction with this divine being a temple setting.

While the wrestling between Jacob and this angel is represented as a physical struggle, this may be metaphorical for the exhaustive spiritual wrestlings that precede the greatest blessings from God. "President Brigham Young said that all of us are situated 'upon the same ground [as Jacob],' in that we must 'struggle, wrestle, and strive, until the Lord bursts the veil and suffers us to behold His glory, or a portion of it.'"[34] With steely determination, Jacob strives with this angel until he is rewarded with an endowment of power. "The bestowal upon Jacob of that rich gift, or endowment, of power followed a familiar pattern. Jacob was asked first to disclose his given name, and then he was given a new name, Israel."[35] As mentioned previously, there is no scholarly consensus as to the meaning of the name *Israel*, but one possible interpretation is "He rules as God." "Now it is plain that he who rules

30 Walton and Matthews, 65.

31 Andersen and Freedman, 608.

32 Nibley, "On the Sacred and the Symbolic," 580.

33 See Thomas, "Zion and the Spirit of At-one-ment," 7.

34 Skinner, "Jacob in the Presence of God," 145.

35 Ibid.

or will rule as God is Jehovah himself. The new name for Jacob is also a name of God himself."[36] In other words, Jacob takes upon him the name of God. To take on the name of God is, according to Elder Bruce R. McConkie, "to identify that person as a god."[37] Having received a new name, Jacob says to the angel, "Tell me, I pray thee, thy name" (Genesis 32:29). "Perhaps he was really asking what name or personage the messenger represented and by whose authority the messenger bestowed the new name and new power. . . . A name of power was a symbol of authority."[38]

Following this conversation, the record states that the angel blessed Jacob (see Genesis 32:29). It does not elaborate on the nature of this blessing. However, the next thing Jacob says is, "I have seen God face to face, and my life is preserved" (Genesis 32:30). Indeed, this is an iceberg event. The most important part of this exchange is under the surface. Since Jacob received his endowment twenty years earlier, it would seem that this experience is something more. It may well be that "the event occurring between verses 29 and 30, though only implied, was no less than the ultimate theophany of Jacob's life—his being ushered into the presence of God to have every promise of past years sealed and confirmed upon him."[39]

Exodus 19; 20:18–26; 24

Following their miraculous deliverance from Egypt, the Israelites traveled in the wilderness until they came to Sinai. They arrived "in the third month" (Exodus 19:1), or at the third new moon, which marked the culmination of six weeks of travel.[40] Thus, the experience that awaits them at Sinai will take place in the seventh week. The number seven is a sacred number, symbolizing that which is whole, perfect, and complete. The Israelites will experience one of the most significant events in the spiritual and political life of Israel at a sacred place and in sacred time. In addition, the Hebrew root, *šbʿ*, from which the number seven is derived, also gives us the word "to swear" or "to take an oath."

---

36 Riddle, 17.

37 McConkie, *DNTC*, 3:458.

38 Skinner, "Jacob in the Presence of God," 146.

39 Ibid., 146–147.

40 See Meyers, *Exodus*, 143.

At a sacred place, at a sacred time, the Hebrews will make sacred covenants that alter the course of their history. They will no longer be a group of descendants of Jacob. They will be the children of Israel, a new nation. God will be their king; He will establish their laws. He will protect and defend them. This is not, however, just a political event. God declares, "Ye shall be unto me a kingdom of priests, and an holy nation" (Exodus 19:6). Israel is to be God's covenant people. As such, the whole nation will be required to live by rules of separation and holiness not usually required of laypeople. But with this requirement also come the opportunities that, in the ancient world, were reserved solely for priests. The whole nation will be privileged to approach God, to hear and see Him (see Exodus 19:9, 11). As a kingdom of priests and kings, Israel is to be to the world what priests and pious kings are to a nation. Israel is to be the channel through which God's blessings will flow to the world.

In the process of making this political-religious covenant, Moses makes several trips up and down Mount Sinai. The scriptural text at this point is not strictly chronological,[41] nor are the ascents and descents clearly delineated, making it difficult to keep track of all Moses's trips. However, it is clear that Moses did not learn all he needed to know and do the first time he climbed this temple-mountain. Following his first conversation with God, Moses descends the mountain and lays before the elders of Israel the invitation of the Lord to be His people, a kingdom of priests. While the people are not free to set the terms of the covenant, they may freely choose whether to enter into the covenant or to reject it. Their response is positive. "All the people answered together, and said, All that the Lord hath spoken we will do" (Exodus 19:8).[42]

Moses then instructs the people to wash their clothes. This cleansing was a necessary prerequisite to performing sacred functions in ancient Israel.[43] The men are also required to refrain from sexual relations with their wives. A limited period of celibacy was not an

41 See ibid.

42 "This is the semantic equivalent of the word 'amen,' the actual word used in Sumerian covenant ceremonies." John M. Lundquist, "Temple Symbolism," in *Isaiah and the Prophets: Inspired Voices from the Old Testament*, ed. Monte S. Nyman (Provo, Utah: Religious Studies Center, 1984), 39.

43 See Tvedtnes, "Priestly Clothing," 688.

unusual requirement for those who were about to enter into a temple or who were serving therein. This was customary among the Egyptians, Babylonians, Syro-Palestinians, and desert nomads. "This temporary continence does not imply that sex was sinful for Israelites and other ancient Near Easterners—any more than eating is sinful because people sometimes fast for religious reasons. Rather, one subjects oneself to a trial by forgoing a licit pleasurable activity."[44] It may also be that since in many ancient religions, "sexual rites were commonly used as a means of communion with the gods, sex was empathically separated from [Israelite] worship."[45] Finally, "the emission of bodily fluids (i.e., semen) renders one temporarily less than whole and [therefore] imperfect."[46] In addition to these requirements, Moses sets bounds around the mountain that has become, in essence, a temple.[47] Typically, sacred space is marked off from ordinary space by walls, fences, and borders. Inside sacred space, gates, doors, and passageways divide holy space from holier space.

Moses ascends Mount Sinai, which is smoking and quaking and seems to be on fire. It appears that the mountain is a volcano—but there are no active volcanoes in the Sinai Peninsula.[48] The earth is responding to the sacred presence of God with the prototypical elements used to mark a theophany: smoke, fire, and quaking.[49] Exodus 19:20 tells us that the Lord comes down to the top of Sinai and calls to Moses, who ascends to the top. "Likely God has been moving back and forth between heaven and Sinai, just as Moses shuttles back and forth between the camp and Sinai."[50] God tells Moses to return down the mountain and to make sure the people do not break through the barrier. Moses, who apparently does not relish the idea of a third strenuous trip down and up this precipitous mountain, suggests that the measures he has already taken are sufficient. Indeed, they may well be

---

44 William H. C. Propp, *Exodus 19–40*, Anchor Bible, 163.

45 Rousas John Rushdoony, *The Institutes of Biblical Law* (United States of America: The Presbyterian and Reformed Publishing Company, 1973), 293.

46 Meyers, *Exodus*, 154.

47 See Propp, *Exodus, 19–40*, 161.

48 See Meyers, *Exodus*, 155.

49 These smoke and fire recall Genesis 15:11.

50 Propp, *Exodus 19–40*, 160–161.

sufficient. This may simply be a test of obedience that Moses must pass before he can enter into God's presence. God rejects Moses's appeal and commands, "Away, get thee down, and thou shalt come up, thou, and Aaron with thee" (Exodus 19:24). Apparently, Moses must personally escort Aaron across the barrier.[51]

Moses again ascends the mount, presumably having done all that God commanded him, and receives the Ten Commandments. Moses returns down the mountain and approaches the people. They have been frightened by the thunderous, fiery tokens of God's presence and are cowering afar off. They plead with Moses to excuse them from encountering God in all His majesty and dread.

To understand this response, we must realize that in the ancient world "divine power can be lethal."[52] It was believed that no man could see God and live. Thus, "faced with the overpowering experience of the holy, man escapes into death."[53] Only God's grace enables one to survive the experience. The common response in the Old Testament and the Book of Mormon—people falling to the ground in the presence of God, angels, or even men with great priesthood power—is a death-feigning response. Being lifted up from this prone position is a quasi-resurrection.[54] However, the Israelites are by no means sure that they will merit God's grace and beg Moses to approach God for them. Moses rejoins, "Fear not: for God is come to prove [test] you" (Exodus 20:20). In other words, Israel must pass through some kind of test before entering into the presence of God. Some scholars, however, think "prove," *nissâ,* is not a test but instruction, a training, or an initiation by ordeal.[55] Despite Moses's pleadings, the Israelites refuse "to exercise the faith to go up. The upper reaches of the mount are, to be sure, not for the faint-hearted."[56] Consequently, they tarry in the foothills of spiritual experience.[57] This rejection of the privilege

51 See ibid., 165.

52 Meyers, *Exodus*, 153.

53 Propp, *Exodus 1–18*, 410.

54 See ibid.

55 See Propp, *Exodus 19–40,* 162, 182.

56 M. Catherine Thomas, "Hebrews: To Ascend the Holy Mount," in *Temples of the Ancient World*, 481.

57 See ibid., 479.

of seeing the face of God amounts to the rejection of the Melchizedek Priesthood (see D&C 84:19–22). God grants their request and gives them the Aaronic, not Melchizedek, Priesthood.[58] For the rest of the Mosaic dispensation, the high priest alone will have the spiritual responsibilities and privileges originally intended for all Israel.

In Exodus 24, the Mosaic covenant is sealed and ratified. First, God commands Moses to bring Aaron; his two sons, Nadab and Abihu; and seventy of the elders to the mount. They are, however, not to approach too closely. They are to "worship . . . afar off. And Moses alone shall come near the Lord" (Exodus 24:1–2). The word translated as *worship* means "to bow down" and is usually translated as such. Nahum Sarna compares this to Jacob's elaborate bowing down from afar, done no less than seven times, as he approached Esau after his prolonged residence in Haran and after Jacob's encounter with the divine.[59] "And he passed over before them, and bowed himself to the ground seven times, until he came near to his brother" (Genesis 33:3). As Jacob draws closer to his brother, the gestures of approach become more intimate. Esau "ran to meet him, and embraced him, and fell on his neck, and kissed him: and they wept" (Genesis 33:4).

Next, Moses tells the people all the words (the Decalogue) and judgments of the Lord (the ritual legislation in Exodus 21–23). The public reading of the covenant was an important aspect of covenant making. In Exodus 24:3–11, we see the actions that are typical for sealing and ratifying covenants in the ancient world: an oath, a sacrifice or the shedding of blood at an altar, a token or sign, and a punishment. The first ratifying act is the oath. "And all the people answered with one voice, and said, All the words which the Lord hath said will we do" (Exodus 24:3). Notably, they answer with a unified voice. This was a ritual response often done when making a covenant (see Mosiah 4:2, 5:2; 3 Nephi 4:30, 20:9). Moses builds an altar and instructs the young men of Israel to offer burnt offerings and peace offerings upon it, shedding blood to seal the covenant. Moses also sets up twelve pillars. These pillars represent the twelve tribes of Israel. The token or sign of this covenant consists of Moses sprinkling the blood of the sacrifice

58 The golden-calf incident also contributed to this diminishing of spiritual powers and privileges.

59 Sarna, *The JPS Torah Commentary: Exodus*, 151.

on the altar, which represents God, and on the people, or perhaps on the twelve pillars which represent the people.[60] In this symbolic act is the implied punishment. The fate of the slaughtered sacrificial animals will be Israel's if they fail to live up to their covenants. One element of sealing a covenant that is not mentioned is a change of name. However, it is at this time that the Hebrews officially become the children of Israel.

Following this covenant ceremony, Moses, Aaron, Nabad, Abihu, and the seventy elders ascend Mount Sinai. They see the God of Israel. The elders eat and drink, or celebrate with a covenant meal. Exodus 24:11 states, "Upon the nobles [elders] of the children of Israel, he [God] laid not his hand." The Hebrew word for "to lay a hand" is *šalaḥ.* It carries the connotation of doing violence or harm, but it also may mean simply "to stretch out." If we read this phrase without its menacing connotation, we see that the divine arm is not stretched out to the elders of Israel, perhaps because "Moses alone shall come near the Lord" (Exodus 24:2). To Moses alone will God stretch out His hand and pull him into His presence.

At Mount Sinai, "all Israel heard with their own ears God himself speak each of the words of the Ten Commandments. . . . All that generation of Israel participated in that preparatory endowment."[61] Yet, so much more had been available to them. In the temples of this dispensation, we have the privilege of enjoying all the temple blessings that God has to offer. Yet we too can tarry in the foothills of spiritual experience. For a variety of reasons, we might absence ourselves from the temple and in effect allow someone else to take our place on the mountain of God. May we accept the invitation of the Lord to enjoy His richest blessings. It is up to us to accept the invitation, to climb the temple-mountain, to seize the hand of the Lord, and to enter into the joy of intimate association with God our Father and the Redeemer of mankind.

Isaiah 6

Isaiah 6 contains Isaiah's account of his ascension into heaven and into the throne room of God, the celestial Holy of Holies. For Isaiah, this

60 See Sarna, *JPS Exodus*, 151, and Propp, *Exodus 19–40*, 294.

61 Ehat, 55.

constituted his call as a prophet. In the ANE, the calling of a prophet was often accompanied by a vision of a heavenly council that was believed to govern the affairs of the universe.[62] The prophet returned from his heavenly ascent and proclaimed the will of God to the people. This experience was viewed as being the proper credentials for a prophet, and he would often document it and place it at the beginning of his record.[63] In this dispensation, Joseph Smith said, "Every man who has a calling to minister to the inhabitants of the world was ordained to that very purpose in the Grand Council of heaven before this world was."[64] It appears that some prophets "have had that mission reiterated, and a specific commission given, in a heavenly council to which they were carried in vision while they were in mortality."[65]

As in most cases, Isaiah reports part but not all of his experience with God. What we have is, again, the tip of the iceberg. What he does share is laced with symbolism. It is apparent that words break down when one attempts to describe a theophany. "The experience is too personal, too awesome, too all-encompassing for mere reportage. Each one of us must aspire to our own experience of his presence."[66]

Isaiah first records that he sees the Lord sitting upon a throne, "high and lifted up" (Isaiah 6:1). The fact that the throne is "high and lifted up" presumes that "the throne is at a high elevation presumably approached by steps."[67] Such would mirror the temple in Jerusalem, which had a series of stairs so that as one made his way from profane to holy space, the journey was one of ascent. Like the temple in Jerusalem,

> the heavens were conceived of as a vast palatial temple-complex, composed of a series of concentric courts, halls, chambers, and shrines. . . .To move between the various sections or *hekhalot* of the celestial temple, the visionary initiate must pass through a series of doors or

62 See Bokovoy, 130–131.

63 See Blake Thomas Ostler, "The Throne-Theophany and Prophetic Commission in 1 Nephi: A Form-Critical Analysis," *BYU Studies*, vol. 26, no. 4 (Fall 1986): 67–68.

64 Smith, *TPJS*, 365.

65 Joseph Fielding McConkie and Robert L. Millet, *Doctrinal Commentary on the Book of Mormon* (Salt Lake City: Bookcraft, 1987), 1:24.

66 Oswalt, *Isaiah 1–39*, 178.

67 Blenkinsopp, 224.

> gates, each guarded by angels. . . . [These angels] will allow the visionary to pass only if he knows the proper passwords—often secret names of the angels—and has the proper token or seals.[68]

Each of the levels represents a different degree of glory. God himself dwells within the highest, most sacred, and innermost sanctuary—the Holy of Holies of the celestial temple. It may be that this temple in heaven was "accessed through the earthly temple, which in Isaiah's case was located in Jerusalem."[69]

When Isaiah sees God on his throne in the Holy of Holies, he notes that his "train filled the temple" (Isaiah 6:1). As noted in the chapter on clothing, the hem of a garment was a statement about the power, authority, and rank of an individual. A train is an extension of the back of a gown or robe that trails on the ground. It is an expansion of the hem. Those who have seen footage or pictures of the wedding of Prince Charles and Princess Diana might remember the magnificent train on Princess Diana's wedding dress. The twenty-five-foot-long train helped create a stunning image of majesty and stateliness as Diana ascended the steps of the cathedral and walked down the aisle. Though impressive, her train pales in comparison to God's train that fills the temple. God's ample train is a way of expressing His omnipotence and glory. Since a train is that which follows or comes behind, it might also be symbolic of those who follow God. Notably, the image is one of plenitude. There are multitudes, enough to fill the celestial temple.

Above the throne were seraphim. *Seraphim* comes from the Hebrew word *śrp,* "to burn." These celestial beings are endowed with power and glory and are ministering to and attending on God. Their radiance and glory symbolize their power. Isaiah describes them as having six wings. According to Doctrine and Covenants 77:4, wings represent power, the power to move and to act. In general, wings also "depict divinity, spiritual nature; the moving, protecting, and all-pervading power of the deity, the power to transcend the mundane world; the never-weary; . . . freedom; victory."[70] The fact that these seraphim have six, not two, wings indicates their high rank and authority. The seraphim use two

68 Hamblin, "Temple Motifs in Jewish Mysticism," 452.

69 Parry, Parry, Peterson, *Understanding Isaiah*, 65.

70 Cooper, 193.

of their wings to fly, but the other four are used to cover their faces and their feet. They may cover their faces to represent their deference for being in the presence of God or perhaps to protect them from the glory of God. *Feet* is often a euphemism for genitalia. Thus, the seraphim have the power to cover their nakedness. They stand before God without shame. They are covered by the Atonement of Christ.

The seraphim cry out to one another, "Holy, holy, holy, is the Lord of hosts: the whole earth is full of his glory" (Isaiah 6:3). Hebrew uses repetition to express superlatives or to indicate totality. For instance, in Genesis 14:10 the Hebrew "pits, pits" is translated into English as "full of slimepits." Describing the Lord as "holy, holy" means He is full of holiness. However, only here do we find a threefold repetition: holy, holy, holy.[71] The holiness of God is unbounded and supreme.

Isaiah also notes that "the posts of the door moved at the voice of him that cried, and the house was filled with smoke" (Isaiah 6:4). Doors in the ANE did not have hinges as we know them. Rather, the doors were attached to large posts that pivoted in a socket. The doorposts had to be massive and strong enough to bear the prodigious weight of large doors that were often covered in metal.[72] Thus, it is no small thing that this locus of strength and stability was quaking. "Shaking is the customary reaction of earth to the divine presence."[73] When God descended to Mount Sinai, "the whole mount quaked greatly" (Exodus 19:18). The shaking doorposts and thresholds might be shaking because of their proximity to God or perhaps because they are acting as deterrents or barriers to unauthorized entrance into the presence of God. In addition to the shaking doorposts, Isaiah notes the heavenly temple was filled with smoke. In Revelation, the celestial temple is filled with smoke from the glory of God "and no man was able to enter into the temple" (Revelation 15:8). At this point in Revelation, the judgments of God were to go forth upon the earth. The time for mercy had passed. No one was to enter the temple to make propitiation.[74] Similarly, the

71 See Motyer, 76.

72 See Paul Hoskisson, "A Latter-day Saint Reading of Isaiah in the Twentieth Century: The Example of Isaiah 6," *The Old Testament and the Latter-day Saints: Sperry Symposium 1986* (Salt Lake City: Randall Book Company, 1986), 197.

73 Motyer, 76.

74 See Draper, 169.

smoke and shaking pillars may have prohibited Isaiah from entering the presence of God because at this point he has not yet been purified.

Feeling unworthy and unclean, Isaiah cries out, "Woe is me! for I am undone; because I am a man of unclean lips" (Isaiah 6:5). It was a common belief in the ANE that one could not look upon the countenance of a god and live. But Isaiah's concern is not just death. He is afraid of being undone, which is to be cut off, ruined, and destroyed. It is even stronger than "I will die." *Undone, nidmêti,* comes from the root *dāmâ*, "to be silent," "which is used of the silence following disaster or death. 'Silenced' would be telling in this context, i.e. excluded from the heavenly choir, forbidden even to join from afar in adoration."[75] In response, one of the seraphim takes a coal and places it in Isaiah's mouth. This is a rite of cleansing and purification. It bears similarities to the Egyptian Opening of the Mouth rite. "Isaiah could now fully participate with the heavenly host in offering praises to the Lord. He had become a member of the heavenly court."[76] According to Mesopotamian thought, Isaiah could now stand before the gods. He is granted the status of quasi-divine.[77]

Isaiah approaches God. His proximity is revealed in the fact that they now enter into a conversation whereas before Isaiah saw God from afar (see Isaiah 6:1, 8). God asks whom He shall send. Isaiah responds, "Here am I; send me" (Isaiah 6:8). This is the traditional Hebrew idiom of readiness. Isaiah is declaring, "I am here, prepared to do Thy will." He is pledging all he is and all he has to the service of God, and he is doing so before God, angels, and a mortal being (himself), who all stand as witnesses. God gives Isaiah his mission call and forewarns him that he will serve amongst a hard-hearted and stubborn people. Their hearts are fat, their ears heavy, and their eyes shut. In other words, their heart, ears, and eyes are all nonfunctioning, emphasizing a total inability to comprehend the spiritual message Isaiah will deliver. However, Isaiah's work does not depend on his success. He has stood in the presence of God and received a divine commission from the mouth of the Almighty. He will return to a world where his fellow Israelites will flounder because they lack faith and because their

75 Motyer, 77.

76 Bokovoy, 134.

77 See ibid.

enemies will press hard upon them, threatening their physical existence and contaminating their spiritual lives. But Isaiah has seen the bigger picture. He knows who he is, what he is to do, and what his future will be—and that makes all the difference.

Isaiah 22:15–25

In Isaiah 22 we meet Shebna, a member of the king's cabinet. He is called the treasurer, but this title doesn't covey how important and powerful he is. He is essentially the prime minister, second perhaps only to the king. At this time, Jerusalem is in a precarious situation. An enemy is poised to attack.[78] The king has been out assessing the strengths of their walls and their water supply. Shebna, on the other hand, has ridden in his elaborate carriage to see a sepulchre, a memorial to himself that he has been building. At a time when he should be acting in the interests of the people, Shebna is focused completely on himself. God sends Isaiah to deliver a divine censure. The first hint of God's displeasure is in the way He refers to Shebna. God tells Isaiah to go to "this treasurer, even unto Shebna." *This*, when used in a phrase such as "this man" or "this fellow," is often contemptuous. God's displeasure is also conveyed by the omission of any reference to Shebna's father. Shebna is not "Shebna the son of ____." He is simply Shebna. "Patronyms were a normal indicator of status and honor."[79] The omission of this indicator in a person of such political importance is a glaring omission.

It appears that Isaiah physically goes to the site of Shebna's tomb to deliver the judgment of God, for in the next verse the word *here* is used three times, including in the phrase, "Thou hast hewed thee out a sepulcher *here*" (Isaiah 22:16; italics added). Isaiah next declares that instead of being buried with great honor, Shebna will be cast aside like a filthy rag.[80] In cultures of the ANE, burial in one's ancestral homeland was considered extremely important. Shebna, however, will be hurled into a foreign land like a ball thrown a great distance. He will be demoted from his office, and it will be given to another. As a

78 The majority of writers take this event to be the deliverance from Sennacherib, the king of Assyria in 701 BC. However, the historical setting could be anywhere from 711 to just before 701.

79 Blenkinsopp, 338.

80 See Oswalt, *Isaiah 1–39*, 420.

replacement to the position of the right-hand man to the king, God will "call my servant Eliakim the son of Hilkiah" (Isaiah 22:20).

My servant is a title of great significance in the book of Isaiah. It is at times applied to Isaiah and to Israel, but it is also a title for Jesus Christ. The poignant prophecy of the Atonement in Isaiah 53 is known as "the Suffering Servant" prophecy. Here, in Isaiah 22, God's servant Eliakim is a type of Christ. The name *Eliakim* means "may God raise" or "God will cause to arise," an appropriate title for Christ, who effected the resurrection of all mankind. The LDS edition of the Old Testament explicitly states in the footnote to Isaiah 22:20 that in the next five verses Eliakim is a type of the Savior.

What follows is the description of enthronement rites for Eliakim. First, he is clothed with the robes of royalty. Next God says, "I will commit thy government into his hand" (Isaiah 22:21). This was probably accompanied by a physical act, like extending a cupped hand. In ancient enthronement rites or in the rites of consecration of a priest, the person would extend his hand in a cupping shape. This would probably be the left hand because the left hand symbolized the receiving principle; the right hand was the giving principle. In other words, the right hand was extended when presenting an offering; the left hand was extended to receive something. If a king were being enthroned, a scepter would be placed into his hand. If a priest were being consecrated, he would be given oil for anointing. If the high priest were being consecrated, the Urim and Thummim might have been placed in his hand.[81]

Eliakim is also given the key of the house of David (see Isaiah 22:22). This may have been a literal key of considerable size that was threaded on a cord and slung from the shoulder. This key was a symbol of the governing powers. It also included the power and authority to admit or exclude people from the king's presence. Such power would only be given to one whom the king trusted explicitly.[82]

81 The term "to fill the hand" is used to describe the consecration of Aaron and his sons in Exodus and in Numbers, although the phrase doesn't make it through the translation process. In English, the text reads, "Thou shalt consecrate Aaron" (Exodus 29:9) and "These are the names of the sons of Aaron . . . whom he consecrated to minister in the priest's office" (Numbers 3:3). The Hebrew reads, "Thou shalt fill the hand of Aaron" and "These are the names of the sons of Aaron whose hands are filled for the priesthood."

82 See Oswalt, *Isaiah 1–39*, 422.

Next, God states, "And I will fasten him as a nail in a sure place" (Isaiah 22:23). The literal image of this rather enigmatic phrase is that of a peg set firmly in the wall. It is able to bear the weight of all the vessels, bowls, and cups that will be hung upon it without apparent strain (see Isaiah 22:24). Thus, this is a metaphor for Eliakim's exalted status and weighty responsibilities as second only to the king. Jesus Christ, of whom Eliakim is a type, is a nail in a sure place. The prodigious weight of all mankind hangs on Him and His Atonement. Hugh Nibley enlightens us with an additional meaning of a nail in a sure place. "When a servant in Israel, out of pure love, wished to be sealed to a master for the rest of his life, even though free to go his own way, his bond was made sure by fixing his ear to the door of his master's house with a nail driven through it (see Deuteronomy 15:16–17)."[83] This ear piercing was a symbolic act that signified the servant "would never walk out on his lord; he was now bound by a sure sign. The nail as a sure fixing of covenants is one of the most ancient symbols."[84] Today, at the Western Wall in Jerusalem, there are thousands of nails pounded into the wall. Daniel Rona explained that this is an ancient custom and many Jews don't know why it is done. One day Daniel met a very old rabbi who told him that a hundred years ago, Jews would bring their sins and the tragedies of life to the wall and nail them in a sure place.[85] Thus, "nails in a sure place" are an image of the Atonement of Jesus Christ, not only of His suffering and death, but also of that aspect of the Atonement expressed in Alma 7:11–12—that of bearing our sorrows and heartaches. In addition, the nail in a sure place is an image of a covenant that will never fail. It is the promise of a loving Savior, of the saving power of the Atonement. It is the promise of loving servants that they will never walk out on their Lord.

Psalm 15

Psalms 15 and 24 are considered entrance liturgies. They probably reflect ceremonies that took place at the entrance of the temple. Both psalms were probably chanted antiphonally, that is, with alternating

---

83 Nibley, "On the Sacred and the Symbolic," 555–556.

84 Ibid., 559.

85 See Daniel Rona, *Israel Revealed Tour*, September 25, 2005.

voices. One group or person would make an inquiry; another group or person would answer. This ritual was likely enacted during one of the three annual pilgrimage festivals of ancient Israel: Passover, the Feast of the Harvest, and the Feast of Tabernacles/Day of Atonement. These were holy days of great rejoicing and spiritual renewal. We might think of them like general conference and Christmas rolled into one. While these two psalms might be considered a type of temple recommend, their purpose was not to keep anyone out of the temple but to impress upon the minds of worshippers that entering into God's presence is a sacred and solemn privilege and is not to be done unworthily or thoughtlessly. It requires preparation of body, mind, and spirit.[86] "Presence in the sacred place and the worship of God are not to be mechanical observances or routine formalities, not even simple conformity with religious requirement."[87]

The psalm begins with the worshippers asking the priest what the qualifications are for entrance into the holy place. "Lord, who shall abide in thy tabernacle? who shall dwell in thy holy hill?" (Psalm 15:1). The word *abide* is *gûr*. The noun form of this word is *gēr* and is the regular term for *stranger*. In ancient Israel, a *gēr* was basically a legal alien. We might think of a *gēr* as a foreigner who has a green card or a temporary visa. He resides legally in a country but is not a citizen. Anciently, a *gēr* had a right to live in Israel, but being without clan or kinfolk he had no claim to protection against violence and exploitation. Because of this, God frequently included the *gēr* on the list of the most vulnerable in society. Along with widows and orphans, strangers were not to be exploited but treated with social justice. Among the seminomads of the Near East and among the bedouin of the desert to this day, a *gēr* is a natural enemy unless he enters a tent, in which case it becomes a matter of honor for the host to protect him. However, this obligation is temporary and lasts for only three days. In the book of Hebrews, the human race is likened unto *gērîm* (the plural of *gēr*). We are, as Paul says, "strangers and pilgrims on the earth" (Hebrews 11:13). However, we have the privilege of entering into God's tent, the temple. To do so is to be His houseguest and to enter into His protection. In God's holy house, we can enjoy a needed respite from our wanderings.

86 See Wilson, 301.

87 Sarna, *Psalms*, 103.

To the question posed by the pilgrim(s) regarding who shall dwell in the temple, the priest responds on behalf of the Lord, listing eleven qualities and standards of behavior. "A passage in the Talmud states that at Sinai the Israelites received six hundred and thirteen commandments; David came and reduced them to eleven—as set forth in this psalm."[88] In other words, while the psalm lists only eleven guidelines, it represents obedience to all the laws and demands of the gospel. Psalm 15:2 states, "He that walketh uprightly, and worketh righteousness, and speaketh the truth in his heart." The verbs used here are participles; they express continuing action. These actions are a way of *being*, not something to *do*. The next verse lists things a worthy temple patron is not to do: backbite with his tongue, do evil to his neighbor, or cast slurs against or discredit his neighbor.[89] The message is sobering. Our words are not inconsequential. What we say can not only hurt and destroy someone else but can also defile our spirit. We simply cannot be in a right relationship with God unless we are in a right relationship with our fellow man.

Psalm 15:4 warns against being a person "in whose eyes a vile person is contemned." The word *abhorrent* could be used instead of *contemned*, yielding a clearer understanding. The injunction is to not reject human beings but to reject evil. Verse 4 adds as a standard, "He that sweareth to his own hurt, and changeth not." We might say one who keeps his promises and covenants, even when the cost is great. Verse 5 speaks of not putting out money to usury and not taking bribes. The idea is honesty and integrity in all our financial dealings. Lending money with interest was not wrong in principal, but it normally involved exploitation and abuse. Thus, financial integrity extended beyond what was legal to what was ethical. Verse 5 concludes with a blessing: "He that doeth these things shall never be moved." The verb *moved* (shaken) "is often used in the Bible in contexts that describe seismic activity: when 'the earth's foundations tremble' and the earth itself is said to 'totter.'. . . [Standing in such upheaval is] an image of stability, solidity, firmness and strength."[90] It evokes the promise given in Revelation:

---

88 Sarna, *Psalms,* 111.

89 See Derek Kidner, *Psalms 1-72* (Downers Grove, Illinois: InterVarsity Press, 1973), 81.

90 Sarna, *Psalms*, 120.

"Him that overcometh will I make a pillar in the temple of my God, and he shall go no more out" (Revelation 3:12). Pillars don't walk out of the temple. They are an integral part of it. They are permanent fixtures in the temple of God. They will stand by God throughout the eternities.

Psalm 24

Psalm 24 has three parts. The first part, verses 1 and 2, reads: "The earth is the Lord's and the fulness thereof; the world, and they that dwell therein. For he hath founded it upon the seas, and established it upon the floods" (Psalm 24:1–2). These verses praise the Lord for the creation of the world and for His dominion over it. Verse 2 tells us that the Creation involved subduing the rebellious and chaotic waters. God did this by banishing them to the regions below the earth and above the heavens. With these limits and boundaries in place, God controlled how much and how often the waters flowed into the earth, bubbling up as springs or coming down as rain.[91] Thus, the first stanza of Psalm 24 focuses on the creation of the earth and God's absolute sovereignty over it. "Sovereignty confers the power and thus authority to impose standards of behavior upon those who reside in His realm."[92] God also has the power to impose the standards for those who would enter His holy house, the topic of the next part of Psalm 24.

The second part, verses 3–6, has been identified as another entrance liturgy. The pilgrims ask, "Who shall ascend into the hill [or mountain] of the Lord? or who shall stand in his holy place?" (Psalm 24:3). The priest responds, "He that hath clean hands, and a pure heart; who hath not lifted up his soul unto vanity, nor sworn deceitfully" (Psalm 24:4). The southern approach to Herod's temple had numerous small ritual baths in which the worshippers would cleanse themselves before approaching the temple. However, this should not mislead us into thinking that germ-free hands constituted temple readiness. "Hands are the essence of the individual. Hands communicate our attitudes and perform our deeds. They speak more eloquently than our words, since the actions of the hands come from the heart."[93] Thus, having

91 See Wilson, 449.

92 Sarna, *Psalms*, 123.

93 Ryken, Wilhoit, Longman, 362.

clean hands and a pure heart is parallelism. It reflects the same thought, not two different kinds of purity.

The next two requirements are stated in the negative—what the temple pilgrim is to not have done. The pilgrim must not have lifted his soul to vanity or sworn deceitfully. To lift up one's soul is to offer one's deepest commitment, one's whole soul, to something. Isaiah uses the term *vanity* to describe idols, which appears to be the meaning here (see Isaiah 44:9). Many Diaspora Jews made the pilgrimage to the temple from foreign lands. In their homelands, they would have faced great pressure to accept foreign religious practices. The ability to declare that they had not lifted up their souls to idols was no small thing.

Finally, the pilgrim was not to have sworn deceitfully. He was not to have reneged on his vows or oaths. However, this requirement is not merely about past behavior. The pilgrim should not enter into any solemn oaths in the temple without the intention of fulfilling them.

A temple pilgrim who lived according to these requirements would receive a "blessing from the Lord, and righteousness from the God of his salvation" (Psalm 24:5). *Righteousness* is a legal term. It was used by a judge to declare that a person had properly fulfilled the expectations of justice. To say of a temple pilgrim that he has been given righteousness from the Lord is tantamount to declaring him worthy to enter the temple. However, the literal reading—the temple pilgrim is given righteousness from the Lord—is also true. In Revelation 19, the Saints are likened unto the bride of Christ. At the time of the eschatological wedding, the bride is "granted that she should be arrayed in fine linen, clean and white: for the fine linen is the righteousness of saints" (v. 8). The operative point for our discussion is that the beautiful garments (righteousness) are *granted* or *given* to the bride. Because of the many promises in scripture that God will bless us when we keep the commandments, it is easy to think that we must white-knuckle our way to righteousness with gritted teeth. Then, when we are righteous the Lord will bless us. Psalm 24 and Revelation 19 suggest otherwise. Though we must do our best, ultimately our righteousness is a function of grace. This grace is extended to every person who comes to this earth through the light of Christ. "By virtue of this endowment all men automatically and intuitively know right from wrong *and are encouraged and enticed to do what is right.*"[94] The Holy Ghost labors more intensely with us, reshaping our hearts and our desires, purifying our natures, and giving us the mind of Christ (see 1 Corinthians 2:16). In this spiritually renovated condition, we want to be righteous. These godly influences are essential in our quest for righteousness.

The next verse in this entrance liturgy reads, "He shall receive the blessing from the Lord" (Psalm 24:5).[95] What is this blessing the worthy pilgrims will receive? The key is in verse 6, though not as it stands in the King James Version. The KJV of Psalm 24:6 states, "This is the generation of them that seek him, that seek thy face, O Jacob." Donald Parry translates this verse, "This is the *circle* of them that *inquire* of him, that seek the face *of the God of Jacob.*"[96] The Hebrew word for *generation*, *dôr*, is only one vowel different from the word *circle*, *dur*. Since vowels were added many hundreds of years after the original Hebrew texts were written, they are subject to some uncertainty. Parry translates the KJV "seek thy face" as "inquire," a legitimate choice that better fits "the prayer setting of this hymn."[97] In addition, somewhere along the way, the word *elohim* has fallen out of this verse between the words *face* and *Jacob*. Most translations now render this phrase something like "seek thy face, God of Jacob."[98] Putting this all together, we have the temple pilgrim who, after being found worthy to enter the temple and praising the God of creation, participates with a circle of worshippers "in the rites and ceremonies, including prayer, where the temple visitor 'inquires' after the Lord and 'seeks his face.'"[99]

The third part of Psalm 24 is also a conversation, this time between the gatekeepers of the temple and those who are carrying the ark of the covenant. The basic underlying image of this section is the return of the ark from war. The ark would be taken out on the battlefield because it

94 Bruce R. McConkie, *Mormon Doctrine*, 156; italics added.

95 Donald Parry translates this as, "He will lift up a blessing from Yahweh." This is a literal translation of the Hebrew, and it accords with the fact that prayers in the temple were spoken with upraised arms. Donald W. Parry, "Temple Worship and a Possible Reference to a Prayer Circle in Psalm 24," *BYU Studies*, vol. 32, no. 4 (1992): 58, 61.

96 Ibid., 58; italics added.

97 Ibid., 59.

98 Ibid., 60.

99 Ibid.

symbolized God's presence. When the Israelite armies were victorious, they returned the ark to the temple in joyous triumphal procession. Its return was viewed as the return of the victorious Divine Warrior to His holy place.[100] In verse 7, those carrying the ark cry out, "Lift up your heads, O ye gates; and be ye lift up, ye everlasting doors; and the King of glory shall come in." "Everlasting doors" can also be translated as "entrances of eternity"[101] or "gates of eternity."[102] The gatekeepers ask, "Who is this King of glory?" (Psalm 24:8). The ark bearers respond with their testimony of God. "The Lord strong and mighty, the Lord mighty in battle" (Psalm 24:8). This has application in the lives of modern temple patrons, spiritual warriors who are returning home victoriously. To walk through the gates of eternity, we need to know our Savior, to bear His name and His character. Truly, He is the Lord, strong and mighty.

Psalm 42, 43[103]

Aron Ralston was hiking in the remote canyons of Utah when an eight-hundred-pound boulder tumbled loose and pinned his right hand and wrist against the canyon wall. Unable to free himself, he spent six agonizing days bound to a rock. He details his harrowing battle for survival in his book *Between a Rock and a Hard Place*. On day four, he exhausted his meager supply of food and water. For the previous two and a half days, he had been severely rationing his water, sipping the smallest amounts, forcing himself to pull the bottle away from his lips before the inside of his lower lip was even fully wet. He tried to capture his humidified breath in a bag as he breathed out during the chilly nights, hoping to get a few drops of moisture. He would soon be drinking his urine. "Nothing, nothing," he related, "compares to the

---

100 See Peter C. Craigie, *Word Biblical Commentary: Psalms 1–50* (Thomas Nelson Publishers, 2004), 214.

101 Parry, "Temple Worship," 58.

102 Brian M. Hauglid, "Temple Imagery in the Psalms," *Covenants, Prophecies, and Hymns of the Old Testament: The 30th Annual Sidney B. Sperry Symposium* (Salt Lake City: Deseret Book Company, 2001), 264.

103 "There is extensive agreement among the majority of interpreters that Pss 42 and 43 should be interpreted as a single psalm for the following reasons: (a) many Heb. mss present the psalms as a single unit; (b) Ps 43 has no title, which is surprising in Book II of the Psalter; and (c) they are joined by a common refrain (42:5, 11; 43:5)." Craigie, 325.

anguish of my thirst: unslakable . . . unquenchable . . . unsatisfiable . . . insuppressible . . . in-extinguishable. I find myself wishing [for death] to get this all over with simply to bring relief to the thirst."[104] Such is the human need for water. The spirit's need for living water is just as intense.

The psalmist begins Psalm 42 by crying out, "My soul thirsteth for God, for the living God" (42:2). What will slake his thirst? Entering the temple of God. He pleads, "O send out thy light and thy truth: let them lead me; let them bring me unto thy holy hill, and to thy tabernacles. Then will I go unto the altar of God, unto God my exceeding joy" (Psalm 43:3–4). When our spirits are thirsty, we can go to the temple. There we can drink of living water[105] until our souls are satisfied and refreshed.

Psalm 133

Psalms 120–134 are a series of psalms that bear the subtitle "A Song of Degrees." This subtitle may also be translated as "Psalms of Ascent." Scholars generally agree that these psalms were sung by pilgrims on their way to the temple. For the Diaspora Jews, the pilgrimage was one of great distance. For the Galileans, the journey was about ninety miles, typically a five-day journey by foot. It was a demanding journey. Nevertheless, the journey was one of great joy and anticipation. The pilgrims eagerly looked forward to entering the holy city and the sacred temple precincts. Psalms 120–134 may also have been sung or recited within the temple complex by worshippers as they ascended the great stairway in the Court of the Women. They may have sung one psalm as they stood on each of the fifteen steps. In this setting, the psalms were literally psalms of going up by degrees, one step at a time, paralleling the spiritual ascent of pilgrims as they journey to God. The psalms address the characteristics one needs to have, the things one needs to cast away, and the challenges one faces on this journey. A thorough examination of these psalms would require a small book in and of itself. Therefore, we will limit our discussion to Psalm 133. Psalm 134 is the last Psalm of Ascent, but it reads

104 Aron Ralston, *Between a Rock and a Hard Place* (New York: Aria Books, 2004), 194.

105 What exactly is living water? In the book of John, living water is both the teachings and revelations of Christ and the Holy Ghost. It is not Jesus Himself but something spiritual that flows from Him, something He offers (see John 4:10–14). In Lehi's dream, living waters are the love of God (see 1 Nephi 11:25).

almost like a blessing once the pilgrim has arrived. Thus, Psalm 133 is the last requirement, the ultimate demand in the approach to God.

Psalm 133 begins, "Behold, how good and how pleasant it is for brethren to dwell together in unity" (133:1). *Pleasant* may also be translated as "delightful, beautiful." It can be used in a musical context when everything is in harmony. Unity is a vital issue to God. In the Doctrine and Covenants, God says, "Thou shalt live together in love" (D&C 42:45). "Thou shalt" is a strong imperative. It is the language of the Ten Commandments. An even stronger command comes in Doctrine and Covenants 38:27: "Be one; and if you are not one ye are not mine." We are not to be merely a group of righteous individuals. We are to be a covenant community, a Zion community of one heart and one mind. The fact that unity is a part of the temple endowment and is the subject of the penultimate psalm of ascent informs us that unity is not a nicety. It is a prerequisite for entering into the presence of God and being like God. In Psalm 133, unity is illustrated by two metaphors: the oil of anointing and the dew of Mount Hermon.

Psalm 133:2 says unity "is like the precious ointment upon the head, that ran down upon the beard, even Aaron's beard; that went down to the skirts of his garments." Exodus 29 tells us that Aaron, the high priest, was to be washed with water and clothed with the holy garments of the priesthood. "Then shalt thou take the anointing oil, and pour it upon his head, and anoint him" (Exodus 29:7). In the anointing of a king or priest, a ram's horn was filled with oil and then poured upon the head of the king or a priest. In Psalm 133, so much oil is used that it runs down upon the beard, down upon the garments, all the way to the hem of the priestly robe. Oil is a symbol of the Holy Ghost. George Q. Cannon explained, "One of the peculiarities of the Holy Ghost, as we read of its effects in the scriptures, was to unite the hearts of those who received it and to make them one."[106] The Holy Ghost is the key to unity. When we have the Spirit, we are more inclined to love, peace, long-suffering, gentleness, and goodness (see Galatians 5:22). The temple is where we "receive a fulness of the Holy Ghost" (D&C 109:15). Therefore, the temple makes possible a rich outpouring of the Holy Ghost into our lives, like oil that runs down from the head of the high priest onto his beard, his robes, and the

106 Cannon, 1:179.

hem of his garment. However, the reference here is not merely to an individual. The body of the high priest symbolized the body of Israel. Similarly, in the New Testament, the Church was considered the body of Christ. We are members of that body. Through the power of the Holy Ghost, members of the Church, from the head to the hem, can be unified in purpose and in love.

Verse 3 introduces the second metaphor of this psalm. Unity is "as the dew of Hermon." Mount Hermon is a majestic mountain on the border between Israel and Lebanon. It is the highest mountain peak in all of Israel. Most of the year it is capped in snow. The dew that falls on the slopes of Mount Hermon is particularly abundant. One scholar stated, "The dews of Syrian nights are excessive; on many mornings it looks as if there had been heavy rain."[107] In general, Israel has a rainy season (winter) and a dry season (summer). In the summer, dew is of vital importance. It is the main source of water during this five- to six-month season when little or no rain falls. Because of this, dew became a symbol for life. Dew is also "a metaphor of abundance and reinvigoration, a symbol of God's beneficence."[108] In poetry, dew represents any beneficial effect produced by quiet means. It connotes well-being. It also symbolizes resurrection.

Psalm 133:3 begins, "As the dew of Hermon, *and as the dew* that descended upon the mountains of Zion." The italics indicate that these words were added by translators to yield a smoother translation or clearer meaning. In this case, it reads better without the addition. "As the dew of Hermon descended upon the mountains of Zion" suggests that the dews of Hermon are so abundant that they flow all the way down to the arid land of Judea and to Mount Zion, the place of the temple. Thus, the imagery of the dew and the oil are the same. The blessings flow from head to toe, from the beard to the robe, from Galilee to Judea. Unity blesses the whole of Israel with life, abundance, and well-being, and it does so without fanfare or excitement.

It is worth noting that dew is considered a gift of God. It comes down from above. As such, it parallels the anointing oil, symbolic of the Holy Ghost, which also comes from heaven. The ability to live

107 G. A. Smith, *The Historical Geography of the Holy Land,* 25th ed. (London, 1931), 65; quoted in Mitchell Dahood, *Psalms III: 101–150,* Anchor Bible, 252.

108 Sarna, *JPS Genesis,* 192.

together in unity and love comes from above. "A Zion society is the product of the personal choice of every person in it; and yet, it is also a function of the grace of the Lord Jesus Christ."[109] It takes both the Saints' best efforts and the grace of heaven to exult with the Psalmist, "How good and how pleasant it is for brethren to dwell together in unity!" (Psalm 134:1).

The psalm finishes with the statement, "For there the Lord commanded the blessing, even life for evermore" (Psalm 133:3). The referent of *there* is ambiguous. It may mean Mount Zion or more particularly the temple that stood on Mount Zion. But *there* may also be referring to unity. Unity and love are an essential aspect of eternal life and are the conditions of the celestial kingdom (see D&C 105:3–5). M. Catherine Thomas reflects:

> I suggest that one reason we have come to earth is to learn the principles of peace and at-one-ment in the face of considerable opposition, and to take them with us into the kingdom. We knew these principles in the premortal world, but here we may have forgotten how they work. . . . It is sobering to realize how readily we trade inner peace for something less, for some sort of upset; how readily we take offense and then escalate the disturbance around us—in home or office or even church. How easily we have unsatisfied expectations of how others should treat us or what they should be doing for us—and we grow cold or irritable to retaliate for this real or imagined slight! How eagerly we insist on being right at the expense of precious relationships. . . . I have asked myself, How long could I last in Zion? How long would it be before I single-handedly dismantled Zion?
>
> Maybe I have thought that at the last judgment someone would wave a magic priesthood wand over me and I would suddenly acquire a heavenly personality. But it's clear to me now that the Lord expects me to practice here and to involve Him in these kinds of personal challenges until the heavenly personality becomes mine.[110]

---

109 Thomas, *Spiritual Lightening*, 80.

110 Ibid., 78–80.

John 2:1–11

The first public miracle Jesus performed was the turning of water into wine at the wedding in Cana. This was more than a miracle to relieve the distress of an anxious mother. It was a profoundly symbolic act. Since water is a symbol for universal death and wine is a symbol for atonement, this miracle foreshadowed Christ's mission of turning spiritual and physical death into reconciliation with God. This miracle also illuminates Christ's transforming power. Christ takes existing elements and transforms them into something better.[111] He turns ordinary water into superb wine. He takes five barley loaves and two small fishes and turns them into sustenance for thousands. He takes ordinary fishermen and turns them into Apostles. He transforms the natural man into a spiritual man with the power and potential for godliness. The miracle at Cana also revealed the Savior's interest and concern for the ordinary pressures and problems of life.[112] In addition to all this, this miracle gives us insight into a temple wedding.

The running out of wine at a wedding feast, which might last as long as a week, was not a mere inconvenience or an embarrassment. It was a serious threat to one's honor, the preeminent virtue in the ancient Mediterranean world. Though inconceivable to us, it could even entail a heavy pecuniary liability and the possibility of legal action.[113] In addition, close friends often sent wine before the wedding as a gift. Thus, a lack of wine implied a lack of friends. Since Mary responds to the lack of wine with some urgency, it may well be that the dishonor of running out of wine would fall upon her and perhaps, by extension, Jesus.[114] Mary approaches her son and informs Him of the predicament. Jesus tells her to have six waterpots of stone, each containing about twenty

---

111 See Cecelia M. Peek, "Early Galilean Ministry and Miracles," *The Life and Teachings of Jesus Christ: From Bethlehem through the Sermon on the Mount*, eds. Richard Neitzel Holzapfel and Thomas A. Wayment (Salt Lake City: Deseret Book, 2005), 1:303.

112 See Robert E. Lund, "Women in the Writings of John," *The Testimony of John the Beloved: The 27th Annual Sidney B. Sperry Symposium* (Salt Lake City: Deseret Book Company, 1998), 127.

113 See Leon Morris, *The Gospel According to John* (Grand Rapids, Michigan: William B. Eerdmans Publishing Company, 1995), 156.

114 See Bruce J. Malina and Richard L. Rohrbaugh, *The Social-Science Commentary on the Gospel of John* (Minneapolis: Fortress Press, 1998), 66–67.

gallons, filled with water. Most village families would have no more than one such waterpot, indicating that five waterpots may have been borrowed from neighbors for this occasion. When these waterpots are filled, Jesus transforms the water into wine of superb quality. Presumably, not all six waterpots of wine were needed to entertain the guests for the remainder of the feast. In which case, "Jesus was making a bountiful wedding gift to the couple, who were evidently poor. Not only did he rescue them from what might well have been a crippling liability, but he provided that they began their married life with an unexpected asset."[115]

When we marry in the temple, we marry in the house of the Lord. Thus, we may consider Christ "the ruler of the feast" (John 2:9) and an honored and important guest. As in John 2, the Lord gives the new couple a wedding gift—actually gifts, for they are numerous and abundant. He gives the gift of eternal riches unfathomable to the mortal mind. He gives the gift of the promise of an abundance of the Holy Ghost to help us make our marriages as sweet as they are intended to be. He gives the gift of wine or at least that which wine symbolizes. Throughout the Old Testament, an abundance of wine is symbolic for the joy of the final days (see Amos 9:13–14; Hosea 14:7; Jeremiah 31:12).[116] Thus the Lord's gift is a promise of an eventual abundance of joy in marriage. For many couples, there will be difficult times in the interim, but the promise of joy in the final days is real. In October 2000, Elder David B. Haight declared at conference, "Now, after we have been married seventy years, I can say to all of you that it gets better, that it gets better year after year, with the preciousness and tenderness and the realization of some of the eternal blessings that lie ahead of us."[117] The Savior's wedding gift is the transforming power that changes water to wine and the union of two people into a loving companionship of eternal joy and celestial glory.

ACTS 1:3

Following His Resurrection, Christ showed Himself to His Apostles "by many infallible proofs" (Acts 1:3). In the Greco-Roman world,

115 Morris, 162.

116 See Raymond E. Brown, *The Gospel According to John I–XII*, Anchor Bible, 105.

117 David B. Haight, "Be a Strong Link," *Ensign*, November 2000, 19.

much like today, acceptable evidence arose from sensory experience—seeing, touching, and hearing. During the forty-day ministry, Jesus was seen, felt, and heard by His disciples. The Greek words translated as *infallible proofs* could also be rendered as "sure signs or tokens."[118] As a sure sign that He was indeed the resurrected Lord, Christ proffered the sure signs of crucifixion and death—the nail prints in His hands, feet, and wrists and the mark of the sword in His side—to believers in both the old and the new worlds.

Revelation 14:4–5

In Revelation 14, John sees the Savior on Mount Zion with 144,000 who have the Father's name written on their foreheads (see Revelation 14:1). John reveals that these are they "which were not defiled with women; for they are virgins. These are they which follow the Lamb whithersoever he goeth. These were redeemed from among men. . . . And in their mouth was found no guile: for they are without fault before the throne of God" (Revelation 14:4–5). The description of these 144,000 as virgins has generated much discussion among scholars. Does it endorse celibacy? Is it figurative? Have these "virgins" kept themselves free from spiritual adultery, i.e., idolatry? Is it a metaphor for the Church as the bride of Christ? As perplexing as this is to scholars, these verses are clear to Latter-day Saints. Michael Wilcox explains:

> Though not a complete list, these qualities define the essential aspects of character the Lord expects of those who will stand with him. They have lived the law of chastity, keeping all their desires within the boundaries established by God. They have lived the law of obedience, as indicated by their willingness to follow the Lamb in all things, in all places, and in all circumstances.[119]

They have applied the power of the Atonement in their lives. They are honest. "There was no deceit in their communication or dealings with their fellowman."[120] In other words, the 144,000 represent temple-worthy Saints.

---

118 Andrew C. Skinner, "The Garden Tomb," *The Savior's Final Week* (Salt Lake City: Deseret Book Company, 2014), 185.

119 Wilcox, *Revelation*, 202–203.

120 Ibid., 203.

2 Nephi 9:41

Jacob's speech recorded in 2 Nephi 6–10 is a covenant speech (see 2 Nephi 9:1).[121] In Nephi's record, this speech follows the establishment of the Nephite state and the building of the temple. This is not a mere coincidence. "The construction of a temple was an important sign in the ancient world that a new society was soundly based and that the leader had been divinely authorized."[122] Jacob's speech may even have been "delivered at the newly completed temple of Nephi."[123] Therefore, it is not surprising to find some tip-of-the-iceberg references in 2 Nephi 6–10. One of these is 2 Nephi 9:41. In this verse, Jacob states, "The way for man is narrow, but it lieth in a straight course before him." Solomon's temple in Jerusalem, upon which the Nephite temple was patterned (see 2 Nephi 5:16), was built in a "straight course." The three sacred areas—the courtyard, the Holy Place, and the Holy of Holies—stood one behind the other in a straight line. The high priest walked in a straight course from the altar to the Holy of Holies.

According to Jacob, at the end of this straight path is a strait gate, a narrow entrance. Christ also refers to this strait gate in the Sermon on the Mount: "Enter ye in at the strait gate: for wide is the gate, and broad is the way, that leadeth to destruction, and many there be which go in thereat: Because strait is the gate, and narrow is the way, which leadeth unto life, and few there be that find it" (Matthew 7:13–14). Standing there is the keeper of the gate, the Holy One of Israel. Jacob tells us that "he employeth no servant there; and there is none other way save it be by the gate; for he cannot be deceived, for the Lord God is his name" (2 Nephi 9:41). Elder Neal A. Maxwell reflects on the keeper of the gate and His purpose there:

> Once, I assumed, with partial correctness . . . that Jesus would be there to certify, because He knows perfectly well who could enter and who could not. . . . But I will tell you . . . out of the conviction of my soul . . .what I think the major reason is as contained in another Book of Mormon scripture which says He waits for you "with open arms" (Mormon 6:17). That's why He's there! He

---

121 See Welch, "The Temple in the Book of Mormon," 334.

122 Ibid., 327.

123 Ibid., 334.

> waits for you "with open arms." That's imagery that is too powerful to brush aside. . . . It is imagery that should work itself into the very center core of one's mind—a rendezvous impending, a moment in time and space, the likes of which there is none other. And that rendezvous is a reality. I certify that to you.[124]

When we experience that rendezvous in reality, perhaps we will have the privilege of being clasped in the arms of the Savior. To be so embraced "symbolizes the fulfillment of His Atonement in our personal lives, here as well as in heaven, becoming literally 'at one' with Him, belonging to Him, as He will belong to us."[125]

Ether 2–3

The brother of Jared has a formidable task at hand. At the Lord's command, he is to build barges that will take his party across an ocean. The Lord has given him design plans, but in the course of building the barges, the brother of Jared becomes aware of some significant problems. They will have no light and no air in the barges. The Lord reveals the answer to the problem of air but not to the problem of light. Rather, He asks the brother of Jared, "What will ye that I should do that ye may have light in your vessels?" (Ether 2:23). The pattern here is worth noting. God freely gives us air and life (see Mosiah 2:21).[126] However, light and knowledge we have to work for. Elder Richard G. Scott taught, "Profound spiritual truth cannot simply be poured from one mind and heart to another. It takes faith and diligent effort. Precious truth comes a small piece at a time through faith, with great exertion, and at times wrenching struggles. The Lord intends it to be

---

124 Neal A. Maxwell, "But a Few Days," prepared by the Church Educational System, 1983, 7; quoted in Bruce A. Van Orden, "The Seed of Abraham in the Latter Days," in *The Old Testament and the Latter-day Saints: Sperry Symposium 1986* (United States of America: Randall Book Company, 1986), 65.

125 Bruce C. Hafen and Marie K. Hafen, *The Belonging Heart*, 102.

126 See Thomas R. Valletta, "Jared and His Brother," *The Book of Mormon: Fourth Nephi through Moroni, from Zion to Destruction*, eds. Monte S. Nyman and Charles D. Tate Jr. (Provo, Utah: Religious Studies Center Brigham Young University, 1995), 313–314.

that way so we can mature and progress."[127] Though the Lord expects the brother of Jared to come up with a viable solution, He doesn't leave the brother of Jared completely to his own wisdom. He reveals things that won't work, such as windows and fire, but then reiterates His original question, "What will ye that I should prepare for you?" (Ether 2:25). So ends Ether 2. Chapter 3 begins, "And it came to pass," indicating that the brother of Jared has wrestled with this problem for a period of time. Eventually, he comes up with a solution.

The brother of Jared ascends a mountain "they called the mount Shelem, because of its exceeding height" (Ether 3:1). However, *shelem* does not mean "great height." It comes from the root *šlm*, which is the same root from which we get *shalom*, peace. *Shelem* means "peace offering," that offering made to establish friendship between God and man. The mount is called *Shelem* because its exceeding height makes it "a place that is suitably high for temple activity."[128]

The brother of Jared carries sixteen small stones up the mountain. These aren't ordinary stones. They are white, clear, and transparent like glass. These adjectives are more than descriptions. Along with his statement that he "did molten [them] out of a rock" (Ether 3:1), the text suggests the brother of Jared has labored over his stones, refining, polishing, and removing the rough edges. According to Jung, the stone is a symbol for the self.[129] In the ancient world, no one approached God without an offering. The brother of Jared carries in his outstretched hands his offering: his whole self. He is doing what Amaleki will charge his brethren to do in a few hundred years: "I would that ye should come unto Christ. . . . Yea, come unto him, and offer your whole souls as an offering unto him" (Omni 1:26).

It is worth noting that stones are also closely related with covenant making. The Ten Commandments were written on tables of stone. Altars, the place where covenants were made, were made by piling stones

---

127 Richard G. Scott, "Acquiring Spiritual Knowledge," *Ensign*, November 1993, 88.

128 M. Catherine Thomas, "The Brother of Jared at the Veil," *Temples of the Ancient World*, 391.

129 Wikipedia contributors, "Self in Jungian Psychology," Wikipedia, *The Free Encyclopedia,* https://en.wikipedia.org/wiki/Self_in_Jungian_psychology, (accessed February 17, 2016).

into shapes that resembled miniature mountains. Stones were erected as witnesses of covenants and reminders of times when God intervened to save His people because of their covenants. In Daniel's vision, the gospel of Jesus Christ in the latter days, the new and everlasting covenant, is likened to a stone cut without hands. The brother of Jared ascends a mountain with the tokens of covenants.

At the top of Shelem, the brother of Jared prays with deep humility, acknowledging his mortal weaknesses and limitations and God's transcendent power and holiness. He asks God to touch the stones with His finger that they might shine in the darkness of their boats. In spite of the fact that the Lord does exactly what the brother of Jared has requested, the brother of Jared is astounded to see a finger reaching through the cloud-veil. He falls to the ground in shock and fear. A question-and-answer exchange follows wherein the Lord tests the brother of Jared. The Lord asks, "Believest thou the words which I shall speak?" (Ether 3:11) The brother of Jared professes, "Yea, Lord, I know that thou speakest the truth, for thou art a God of truth, and canst not lie" (Ether 3:12). With this profession, the brother of Jared affirms the nature and character of God. The Lord declares the brother of Jared is redeemed from the Fall, innocent through the Atonement of Christ. He is found worthy. The Lord then parts the veil, and the brother of Jared is brought back into presence of the Lord (see Ether 3:13). The brother of Jared sees the Lord face-to-face. The Lord reveals His name and His mission: "I am Jesus Christ. I am the Father and the Son. In me shall all mankind have life, and that eternally" (Ether 3:14). Their dialogue continues but then is abruptly cut short, with Moroni explaining that he cannot give a full account of all that went on. Again, we see but the tip of the iceberg.

Elder Jeffrey R. Holland points out that Ether 1–3 takes pains to portray the brother of Jared as an ordinary human being. He is reprimanded by the Lord when his prayers become bland and lackluster.[130] He frets about his offering not being good enough or sophisticated

130 Given the spiritual stature of the brother of Jared, it is likely that his error was not ceasing to pray altogether but allowing "his prayers to become less fervent, more casual and routine." McConkie and Millet, *Doctrinal Commentary*, 4:270.

enough. But for all his humanity, his faith in God is unparalleled.[131] Because of this, he was granted remarkable spiritual experiences. And so it is for us who are mere mortals in terms of the gospel (Scout leaders, Primary teachers, counselors, and other everyday members). In the temple the Lord can part the veil, and we can have intimate communion with Him. We might see the Lord face-to-face, but more likely we will receive divine counsel, feel exquisite peace, and experience ineffable love. If our experience is less spectacular than the brother of Jared's, it is sufficient—sufficient to change our lives and our hearts, sufficient to know that God knows us individually, sufficient to have us climb the mountain over and over just to have a foretaste of what we will one day experience when we are wrapped in the loving embrace of our God.

131 See Jeffrey R. Holland, "Rending the Veil of Unbelief," in *Nurturing Faith through the Book of Mormon: The 24th Annual Sidney B. Sperry Symposium* (Salt Lake City: Deseret Book Company, 1995), 24.

Epilogue

Abraham Heschel wrote, "It is hard for us to imagine what entering a sanctuary or offering a sacrifice meant to ancient man. The sanctuary was holiness in perpetuity, a miracle in continuity. . . . In offering a sacrifice, man mingled with mystery [and] reached the summit of significance."[1] The intention of this book is to help you, in some degree, enter the ancient world and to experience how ancient man thought, dressed, and worshipped. Having done so, Heschel's statement hopefully becomes not only comprehensible but representative of our experience as we enter into the temples of this dispensation.

Some years ago, at the dedication of the temple in Buenos Aires, Argentina, Elder Boyd K. Packer said, "If the outside [world] knew about what was happening here, the cars would stop, planes would not take off, and people would gather to see what the Lord hath wrought. This work we have a part in; it is cause for great rejoicing."[2] Hopefully, this book helps you understand a little better what is happening inside the walls of the holy temple. May we stop our cars, our planes, and our lives long enough to enjoy the privilege of entering the holy temple, the house of God. May our time therein be a cause for great rejoicing.

---

1 Abraham J. Heschel, *The Prophets* (New York: Harper and Row Publishers, 1962), 1:197.

2 *Church News,* January 26, 1986; quoted in E. Dale LeBaron, "Elijah's Mission: His Keys, Powers, and Blessings from the Old Testament to the Latter Days," *Thy People Shall Be My People*, 72.

Glossary of Symbols

Ablutions (washings): Ablutions denote the cleansing of the soul from sins and iniquities. They return man to his primordial purity.[1] They were also believed to bestow the recipient with life and strength and to avert evil. Washings were a part of a sequence of ordinances. Usually, they were followed by an anointing and clothing in special raiment.

Altar: An altar is a place of offering sacrifices and making covenants. Altars were erected at places where God appeared to man and thus places where God is likely to return. Consequently, altars are associated with the presence of God. In ancient Israel, altars were also places of refuge. A man accused of a crime could claim asylum by grabbing hold of the horns of the altar. His safety was assured until facts could be gathered and the case tried.

"In rabbinic and Talmudic times the phrase 'building an altar' was used as a metaphor to mean not only the observance of the commandments, but also the total consecration of all one possessed—even the laying down of one's own life—for the sanctification of God's name. Some of the ancient rabbinic sages, therefore, coined expressions like 'as if an altar was erected in his heart' to portray those individuals who were willing to do all that God required."[2]

---

1 Cooper, 10.

2 Andrew C. Skinner, "Genesis 22: The Paradigm for True Sacrifice in Latter-day Israel," in *The Old Testament and the Latter-day Saints: Sperry Symposium 1986* (United States of America: Randall Book Company, 1986), 77.

Anonymity: "Anonymity can symbolize the loss of identity, hence absorption into the divine."[3] "In Egyptian initiation rites one puts off his former nature by discarding his name, after which he receives a new name. Prior to coronation, the candidate is presented to the gods without his own personal name. In order to pass the obstacles, he recites the name of his god and thus is allowed to pass. If the candidate cannot produce the name, the gatekeepers are aggressive and unyielding."[4]

Arms: The arm is the part of the body that best symbolizes personal strength. When a person wants to demonstrate his strength, he or she flexes his arm. Similarly, "the arm of the Lord" symbolizes His power. The "stretched out arm" (Exodus 6:6), or upraised arm, is frequently used to describe the Lord's power to deliver His people from bondage. When God declares, "Mine arm is not shortened" (D&C 35:8; see also 133:67), He is saying that His arm is not too short (i.e., too weak) for the task. The Lord makes His arm bare to reveal His strength (see Isaiah 52:10; D&C 109:51, 133:3) much like people today roll up their sleeves to show their flexed muscles.

Upraised arms denote supplication, prayer, and surrender. "To raise the hands" is even a synonym for "to pray" in several Semitic languages.[5] In ancient Israel, when the high priest gave the priestly blessing, he did so with both arms stretched above his head with palms forward. Although not mentioned in the Talmud, the *Midrash Rabbah* refers to the practice of the priest separating the little finger and the ring finger from the middle and pointer fingers, forming a v. The thumbs are outstretched and touching. Thus, the hands form the Hebrew letter *shin* ש. *Shin* stands for *Shaddai*, one of the divine names for God. In later periods, this hand position became symbolic of the priesthood and was known as the Aaronic sign.[6] This hand gesture can be seen in Jewish cemeteries on the headstones of *kōhănîm* (the priests), the descendants of Aaron (see figure G-1). The spread fingers of the priests form "windows" through which God's blessings flow to the congregation. Some Jews

3 Cooper, 13.

4 Madsen, "Putting on the Names," 459.

5 Sarna, *Exploring Exodus*, 122.

6 Alfred J. Kolatch, *The Jewish Book of Why* (Middle Village, New York: Jonathan David Publishers, Inc., 1981), 158.

Image couretsy of www.jcam.org
Figure G-1. The Aaronic sign.

believe that the spread fingers symbolize the cloven hooves of a sacrificial lamb. Thus, to pray with raised arms and spread fingers would be to take on the identity of the crucified Lamb of God.[7]

Praying with raised arms also signified the Crucifixion. Early Christians considered this position an imitation of the upright cross.[8] To pray in this position is to identify with the crucified Christ.[9] At the same time, it symbolically transformed the person into a tree of life. "Each person who is raised up in the form of the tree will have eternal life."[10] In early Christianity, these two symbols merged into one. "The cross is, in early traditions, the tree of life, bringing us back into the presence of God through the Savior's Atonement."[11]

Praying with outstretched arms also symbolizes purity. "The gesture exposes to God both the breast and the palms of the petitioner to show that they are pure (clean)."[12] Additionally, when you enter the presence of a great one, you raise both hands to show that you are not armed and that you bear no ill will. It is tantamount to saying that you trust the Great One completely.

Axis Mundi: The axis mundi is the vertical axis that passes through each of the three major planes of existence: the underworld, the world, and the heavens. This axis is "the point of intersection of those regions. It is here that the break-through to another plane is possible, and at the same time, communication between the three regions."[13] The axis mundi marks the center of each plane. In the realm of symbolism and

---

7 See John A. Tvedtnes, "Temple Prayer in Ancient Times," in *The Temple in Time and Eternity*, 86, 90.

8 See Welch, *The Sermon at the Temple*, 76–77.

9 See Nibley, "The Early Christian Prayer Circle," 4:58, 59.

10 Welch, *The Sermon at the Temple*, 76.

11 Tvedtnes, "Temple Prayer in Ancient Times," in *The Temple in Time and Eternity*, 85.

12 Ibid., 84.

13 Mircea Eliade, *Images and Symbols*, trans. Philip Mairet (Princeton, New Jersey: Princeton University Press, 1991), 40.

imagery, the center is sacred space. The axis mundi may be represented as a ladder (see Genesis 28), a cosmic tree (or tree of life), a mountain, a pillar, a pole, a staff, or a nail.[14] The temple is an axis mundi, a sacred space that unites all three cosmic regions. Saving ordinances for the living and the dead allow individuals to break through to another plane or ascend to a higher realm.

Bell: Bells represent consecration. "Small bells sounding in the breeze symbolize the sweet sounds of paradise."[15]

Birds: Birds symbolize, among other things, the divine power that descends into the world. We see this in the dove, which is the sign of the Holy Ghost,[16] a sign instituted before the creation of the world. We also see this in Facsimile 1 of the book of Abraham. There, the angel of the Lord that comes to rescue Abraham is portrayed as a hawk, a bird that was believed to fly between heaven and earth. Similarly, the eagle was "thought to be able to fly up to the sun and gaze unwaveringly upon it and to identify with it. Thus, the eagle represents the spiritual principle in man which is able to soar heavenwards."[17] It is therefore significant that Israel is promised that she shall "mount up with wings as eagles" (Isaiah 40:31). In the temple, Israel participates in ordinances that enable her to soar heavenward and to gaze unwaveringly upon the Son.

Not all birds are beneficent. There are birds that feed on corpses, making them not only unclean but linked with the realm of the dead. Birds that are active at night were viewed as being on errands of evil and creatures of a dark realm. Because ruins were believed to be cursed, birds that frequented them were associated with dark, supernatural forces.[18]

---

14 See Cooper, 16.

15 Ibid., 20.

16 As is often the case, truth finds its way into legend. In legends and literature, birds take on some of the functions of the Holy Ghost. For instance, birds frequently accompanied a hero on his quest or in slaying a dragon. The birds could also give him secret advice. Consider the saying, "A little bird told me." The communication from birds symbolized heavenly communication or the help of celestial powers such as angels. Ibid., 21.

17 Ibid., 58.

18 See Ryken, 93. See also Isaiah 13:21.

Birds are also symbols of escape and safety. In Revelation, the Church is symbolized by a woman clothed with the sun. She is given the wings of a great eagle that she might fly into the wilderness to safety, away from the devouring dragon. In Matthew 23, Christ laments that Israel has not availed herself of the safety beneath His wings.

Bones: Bones were the gauge of the body's vitality. They become dry and brittle with age and illness. Symbolically, dry bones represent despair and grief. In Ezekiel 37:11, the bones that represent the house of Israel say, "Our bones are dried, and our hope is lost." On the other hand, "high spirits and good cheer are figured as moist, oily, or sappy bones."[19] Bones full of marrow are a picture of robust health. "Figuratively, a soul who has 'marrow and fatness' (Psalm 63:5; Isaiah 25:6) or 'marrow to [his] bones' (D&C 89:18; Proverbs 3:8) is one who has received an abundance of temporal blessings from God."[20]

Cap: A cap represented nobility and freedom; slaves went bareheaded.[21]

Cave: The cave was a place of safety and rescue, a place where people went to hide from enemies (see Joshua 10:16; 1 Samuel 13:6). A cave was considered a sacred center, a holy place. It was the meeting place of the divine and the human, as in the case of Elijah's theophany in 1 Kings 19:9–18. It symbolized that which was hidden and thus esoteric knowledge. It was a place of initiation, mystery, increase, and renewal.

As a place of initiation, it was also a secret place, not visible to the profane world. Entering a cave required a difficult and exacting journey through a labyrinth or dangerous passage. The entrance was often guarded by some monster or supernatural person, and entry could only be gained by overcoming the opposing force. However, when one succeeded at passing through the cave, he experienced a change of state. The cave is also the place of the sacred marriage between kings and queens.[22]

19 Moshe Greenberg, *Ezekiel 21–37*, Anchor Bible, 745.

20 Joseph Fielding McConkie and Donald W. Parry, *A Guide to Scriptural Symbols* (Salt Lake City: Bookcraft, 1990), 82.

21 See Cooper, 29.

22 See ibid., 31.

The Center: Center symbolizes sacred space, absolute reality, pure being, and the origin of all existence. In the center, time and space are transcended. The journey away from the center is a journey into earthly manifestation. The journey back to the center is a journey to sacred space, to the totality of all possibility, the place of reconciliation, where all opposites disappear. It is the journey to God.[23]

The temple in Jerusalem was a series of concentric circles of holiness. The Holy of Holies was the center and holiest place. The celestial temple, on which the temple in Jerusalem was patterned, was also a "series of concentric courts, palaces, halls, chambers, shrines, or levels. . . . Generally speaking, God himself dwells within the highest, most sacred, and innermost sanctuary—the Holy of Holies of the celestial temple."[24]

Clouds: Clouds represent both the presence of God ("And the Lord went before [the children of Israel] by day in a pillar of a cloud" [Exodus 13:21]) and the hiddenness of God ("The Lord came down and talked with the brother of Jared; and he was in a cloud, and the brother of Jared saw him not" [Ether 2:4; see also Exodus 19:16]). Thus, clouds often accompany theophanies. "A hand, or hands, emerging from a cloud is divine omnipotence."[25] "Clouds represent the veil through which we must pass to stand in the divine presence."[26]

A number of scriptural passages use the imagery of the divine warrior to describe Jesus Christ at the Second Coming. He comes heavily armed with the powers of the thunderstorm: violent winds, lightning bolts (i.e., flaming arrows), and the hosts of heaven (the heavenly armies). Just as earthly kings rode into battle in a chariot, so Christ will travel through the heavens in His majestic chariot, the clouds. The thunder is understood to be the rumbling of the chariot's wheels. The image of the warrior god riding a chariot into battle is an ancient one and one that is common in Mesopotamia. Baal's stock epithet is "rider of the clouds." At that great day of the Lord's Second

---

23 See ibid., 32.

24 Hamblin, "Temple Motifs in Jewish Mysticism," 445.

25 Cooper, *An Illustrated Encyclopaedia of Traditional Symbols*, 38.

26 McConkie and Parry, *A Guide to Scriptural Symbols*, 32.

Coming, we "shall see the Son of man coming in the clouds with great power and glory" (Mark 13:26).

Compass: The compass represents "unerring and impartial justice; the perfect figure of the circle with the central point, the source of life."[27] With the square, the compass defines the limits and the bounds of rectitude. In sacred architecture, the compass represents transcendent knowledge.[28]

Crown: Crowns are a symbol of the highest attainment and victory. Crowns were worn by both kings and high priests. The "crown" of the high priest was the golden diadem worn around his turban.[29] To possess a king's crown connotes sharing or usurping some of that king's power.[30] Crowns were given to the victors at games. Paul employs this image when he writes, "I have fought a good fight, I have finished my course, I have kept the faith: Henceforth there is laid up for me a crown of righteousness" (2 Timothy 4:7–8).

The "shaman's crown, a crown of mountain goat horns, symbolizes the wearer's power to move surely and safely among the high places of the gods."[31] Additionally, crowns are symbols of God's blessings on His people (see Proverbs 10:6). Because crowns are circular, they represent completeness, the circle of time, and endless duration.

Cube: The cube is a symbol of perfection, completion, and eternal stability.[32] Since a cube is always the same regardless of how it is viewed, it represents truth.[33] The Holy of Holies was a cube.

Dancing: In the ancient world, dancing often consisted of forming a ring or a circle. Hugh Nibley cites several ancient documents to support the idea that ancient prayer circles may well have been round dances. "The Greek and Russian Orthodox churches still preserve the ring

27 Cooper, 42.

28 See ibid.

29 See Barker, 105.

30 Ryken, Wilhoit, and Longman, *Dictionary of Biblical Imagery*, 185.

31 Cooper, 47.

32 See Draper, 236.

33 See Cooper, 48.

dance around the altar in that most conservative of rites, the wedding ceremony, when bride, groom, and priest all join hands and circle the altar three times; H. Leisegang connects this definitely with the old prayer circle."[34] J. C. Cooper notes, "In the monotheistic religions, the round or ring dance imitates the dance of angels round the throne of God. In Christianity the Apocryphal Acts of St. John has a round dance in which the Twelve Apostles circle round Jesus as the centre, who would have it called a mystery."[35] Nibley suggests that the when Lehi sees God on his throne "surrounded with numberless concourses of angels in the attitude of singing and praising their God" (1 Nephi 1:8), Lehi is seeing a heavenly prayer circle. "Surrounding concourses are concentric circles."[36]

"Dancing, in its essence, is always symbolic. . . . [It] is primarily a physical and visual means of praising, honoring, and thanking God."[37] In ancient thought, round dances follow the sun's course in the heavens. American Plains Indians in the nineteenth century participated in sun dances, "recreating and confirming the course of the sun through the heavens and giving the dancers a participating share in that course."[38] A round dance was also viewed as enclosing a sacred space. "Dancing round an object encloses it in a magic circle, both protecting and strengthening the object."[39]

Descent: Descent, including man's descent into the mortal world (the Fall), "is equated with the quest for . . . wisdom, rebirth, and immortality. It also represents the understanding of, and redeeming of, the dark side of man's own nature."[40] As Nibley has said, "This is the place to find out all the dirty, nasty, little sides of our nature; it is the only place we can, because we are not in the presence of God and angels here, and it is possible for us to sin."[41] Descent is sometimes

34 Nibley, "The Early Christian Prayer Circle," 53.

35 Cooper, 50.

36 Nibley, "The Early Christian Prayer Circle," 53.

37 Ryken, Wilhoit, and Longman, 188.

38 Cooper, 49.

39 Ibid.

40 Ibid., 50.

41 Hugh W. Nibley, "Funeral Address," *CWHN*, 9:302.

associated with danger and deprivation, as when Joseph and Jeremiah are lowered into pits as places of imprisonment. The ultimate human descent is the descent into Sheol, the abode of the dead.

Another category of descent in the Bible is more positive. God, who dwells above the earth in heaven, comes down to this earth, or sends His angels, to speak to man, to reveal Himself and His truths (see Exodus 19:11, 20; Joseph Smith—History 1:17–20), to investigate rebellion (see Genesis 11:5; 18:21), to display His power, to rescue His own, and to execute righteous judgment. "God's coming down to earth is thus an image of the intervention of a transcendent God into the flow of human activity on earth."[42]

Door: Doors and doorways are places of transition. The doorway, gate, portal, or entryway is often associated with entrance into areas of great spiritual significance. Jesus refers to Himself as "the door" (John 10:9).[43] "An important feature of Egyptian architecture of temple, tomb, and even palace is a door, sometimes shown as a curtain or lattice, through which a spirit can pass, a means of communication between two worlds; and the literature is full of ceremonial and mystical doors and gates and instructions on how to pass them."[44]

The Embrace: In Greek "recognition drama, the embrace is the immediate seal of recognition and love when the identity of the tested party has been proved. . . . The hand clasp and the embrace perfectly express the concept of two separate halves coming together to create a unity."[45]

Fountain: Fountains represent the waters of life or immortality, the source of the legendary fountain of youth and immortality.[46]

Gate: Gates and doors share the symbolism of the door as a threshold, a place of entrance. They mark entry into a new life. "Gates and portals are usually guarded by symbolic animals such as lions, dragons, bulls, dogs, or fabulous beasts. At the gates of the house of Osiris, a goddess

42 Ryken, Wilhoit, and Longman, 204.

43 See Ryken, Wilhoit, and Longman, 215–216.

44 Nibley, *Of All Things*, 51.

45 Compton, 614, 628.

46 See Cooper, 71.

keeps each gate, whose name has to be known."[47] Gates are a point of communication between one world and another, and between the living and the dead. The gate is also associated with wisdom. "Kings sat in judgment at gates, probably as sacred places of divine power."[48]

Gestures of Approach: Before an individual could approach the temple's most sacred spot and receive blessings from God, he would need to participate in certain rituals called "gestures of approach" or "threshold rituals."[49] In ancient Israel, such gestures included removing profane items (such as one's shoes), ritual ablutions or washings, dressing in vestments of the priesthood, and anointing with oil.[50]

The Manual of Discipline of the Dead Sea Scrolls details the three steps of identification that someone who is approaching a sacred site must go through.

> First, at a distance, he seeks admission, giving a visible sign by raising his arms (a greeting that can be seen from afar and is a sign, among other things, that he is unarmed); approaching closer for inspection, he gives his name; then approaching for the final test, he actually makes physical contacts with certain grips, which are the most secret and decisive. His final acceptance is by the most intimate tokens of all, including an embrace, or a *unio mystica* (mystic union), in which the candidate becomes not only identified, but identical, with the perfect model.[51]

Girdle: A girdle—or a belt, cord, or sash worn around the waist—symbolizes binding. "It can depict the circle of life, or sovereignty, wisdom and strength; it can also signify virginity, marital fidelity, or fertility. . . . To put on the girdle, or to gird oneself, is to prepare for, or be bound to, some action or to go forth on a mission or journey."[52]

---

47 Ibid., 73.

48 Ibid.

49 See Donald W. Parry, "Introduction," *Temples of the Ancient World*, xvi.

50 See Parry, "Ritual Anointing," 276.

51 Nibley, "Return to the Temple," 12:58–59.

52 Cooper, 73.

Hands: Hands represent power and strength, agency, and authority. Raised hands represent adoration, worship, prayer, and salutation. Both hands raised suggests supplication, weakness, dependence, surrender, and also invocation and prayer. A hand emerging from a cloud denotes divine power and benefits and majesty.[53] "In early Christian representations, the hand of God reaching through the veil is grasped by the initiate or human spirit who is being caught up into the presence of the Lord."[54]

"The right hand is the 'hand of power.' It is held up in blessing and pledges the life principle. The right arm is raised to the square when bearing witness or taking an oath. Josephus writes: 'None of them will deceive you when they have given the right hands nor will anyone doubt their fidelity.'"[55]

> H. P. L'Orange notes that "the outstretched right hand of the king" is endowed with supernatural powers. The gesture could be used to bless or to curse. "From the outstretched divine hand supernatural powers emanate, repelling all hostile and evil forces. . . . The supernatural redeeming power in the emperor's outstretched right hand presupposes higher powers and abilities dwelling in him. Through the emperor, manifesting his power in this gesture, divine interference in human affairs takes place."[56]

The left hand is the passive aspect of power, receptivity.[57] While the right hand is the giving principle, the left hand is the receiving principle. The priest slaughtered with his right hand and used the right thumb to cover the horns of the altar with the atoning blood. He held the sacrificial blood in the left hand (the receiving principle). The priest also held the oil used in the anointing in his left hand and used his right thumb to anoint. John A. Tvedtnes notes, "In the temple, the priest evidently stood with hand in cupping shape, [probably the left hand,] ready to receive something which was given to him. It was probably

---

53 See ibid., 78.

54 Nibley, "The Meaning of the Atonement," 9:561–562.

55 Cooper, 78.

56 Ricks and Sroka, 253.

57 See Cooper, 78.

incense, though, in the last days . . . it will evidently be the white stone or Urim and Thummim, with the new name written in it."[58]

To fill a hand is to invest with an office or to communicate a dignity. It goes without saying that no man can do this for himself. It must be the act of God. A filled hand also implies a simple offering of gifts, which the offerer brings in his hands. The filled hand is the widespread sign of offering sacrifice.

The Handclasp: The handclasp is a token of recognition, friendship, and agreement. It also suggests love, initiation, arrival, salvation, and union with God. The marriage handclasp "represents uniting, love, equality, sexuality, and treaty between husband and wife as marriage begins."[59]

> In some early Christian depictions of the Ascension of Christ, Christ Himself, approaching heaven, clasps the hand of God, which descends from a stylized upper corner of the composition. This symbolism is arresting: Christ, the Savior, reaches up to be saved, and must be drawn, or at least helped, up into heaven. Perhaps there is a residual emphasis on the unity and equality of the saving handclasp here, but it is nevertheless a saving, diagonal clasp.[60]

Head: The head represents wisdom, mind, control, and rule. As the chief member of the body, the head is the seat of the life force. "Bowing the head lowers the seat of the life force before another in honor or submission. To nod the head is to pledge the life force."[61]

Heaven: "In sacred architecture the heavens are depicted by the dome, stupa . . . or the open central hole of a tepee, tent, or sacred lodge. Universally portrayed as blue in color, but occasionally as black, and as

58 John A. Tvedtnes, quoted in Dr. Lynn M. Hilton, "The Hand as a Cup in Ancient Temple Worship," a paper presented at the Thirtieth Annual Symposium on the Archaeology of the Scriptures, held at BYU, September 26, 1981.

59 Compton, 618.

60 Ibid., 621.

61 Cooper, 80.

round or domed in shape."[62] "Heaven is, as it were, one vast 'temple without walls,' because God's presence fills that space, and the temple is, by definition, a model of the place where God dwells."[63]

Key: The key symbolizes the powers of opening and closing, binding and loosing. The key also represents freedom, knowledge, mysteries, and initiation.[64] Keys denote power and control access. They are symbols of trust and responsibility.[65]

Ladder: The ladder is an axis mundi. It typifies the passage from one plane to another and the breakthrough to a new ontological level. In Genesis 29, Jacob's ladder allowed heavenly beings to descend and Jacob, a mortal being, to ascend. The ladder is a means of access, but it is also removable. "Originally a ladder existed between heaven and earth in paradise and there was uninterrupted communication between God and man, but this was lost at the Fall."[66] The rungs of the ladder represent the degrees of initiation. "In initiation one ascends by knowledge."[67] The two sides of the ladder are the left and right pillars or the two trees of paradise—the tree of life and the tree of knowledge of good and evil, unified by the rungs, or covenants.[68]

Mitre: A mitre is "a flat cap or pad that was meant to support the weight of a crown."[69] It represents authority.[70]

Mountain: The Cosmic Mountain is a holy center through which the axis mundi runs. As the highest point of the earth (often in the clouds), it is the meeting place of heaven and earth.[71] It is also the place where

62 Ibid., 82.

63 John M. Lundquist, "What Is Reality?" *By Study and Also By Faith*, 1:430.

64 See Cooper, 90.

65 See Ryken, Wilhoit, and Longman, 476.

66 Cooper, 94.

67 Ibid.

68 See ibid.

69 Nibley, "The Meaning of the Atonement," 9:578.

70 See Cooper, 106.

71 See ibid., 110.

the gods were thought to live or where the gods descended to in order to meet those who had made the demanding journey up the mountain to be instructed.

Throughout the ANE, the temple was viewed as an artificial mountain on which the Lord dwelt. Temples were constructed in such a way as to preserve their connection with mountains. They were built of natural indigenous materials, many times coming from the mountains. The buildings were of great heights, causing an onlooker to gaze upward, much as one who was standing before a mountain might do. The temple of Solomon was built on a platform so that people literally went up to it. Temples were often built on a mountain or hill upon which sacred events had already transpired.

In addition to the temple connection, mountains are a symbol of refuge and security. They denote permanence and solidity; because of which, they stand as witnesses to covenants. They are places where God's people will dwell in abundance.[72]

Oil: Oil symbolizes "consecration; dedication; spiritual illumination; mercy; fertility. Anointing with oil is infusing new divine life; consecration; bestowing the grace of God or conferring wisdom."[73] Anointing with oil was a great honor. Prophets, priests, and kings were anointed to set them apart. Anointing with oil signifies being invested with the Holy Ghost.

Pillar: A pillar represents the vertical world axis, the axis mundi. It is closely associated with the tree of life. Indeed, a pillar is a tree that has been stripped of its foliage, revealing its changeless center.[74] The pillar raises the sacred above the profane or ordinary. Just as large buildings required pillars to support them, so the earth and the heaven were envisaged as supported by pillars. Thus, pillars both hold apart and join heaven and earth. Two pillars may represent the tree of life and the tree of knowledge. They also "form Heaven's Gate, the necessary way through which to enter the temple or church; this passing between

72 See Ryken, Wilhoit, and Longman, 572.

73 Cooper, 122.

74 See Jeanette W. Miller, "The Tree of Life, a Personification of Christ," *Journal of Book of Mormon Studies* 2, no. 1 (Spring 1993): 96.

two pillars typifies entry into new life, or another world, or eternity."[75] The two pillars of Solomon's temple were named Boaz and Jachin and represented king and priest, throne and altar.[76] (Eternal kingship and priesthood constitute godhood.) "The symbolic function of these huge, magnificent gateposts was probably to indicate that the Lord had passed through them, entered the temple, and dwelt there in the midst of his people. These nonweight-bearing monoliths also symbolized by their sheer size and mass the grandeur and stability of God."[77] God Himself chose to represent His presence among the children of Israel with two pillars, a pillar of fire at night and a pillar of a cloud during the day. These divine pillars represent the King of Kings and the great High Priest Yahweh, the Savior, the ultimate axis mundi, who, through the Atonement, allows mortals to ascend into the heavens.

Plumb: Along with the compass, the square with a plumb bob hanging from it was an instrument of measurement. "In sacred architecture it symbolizes transcendent knowledge; the archetype controlling all works."[78]

Pyramid: A pyramid represents the primeval Sacred Mountain, which is often four sided.[79] It is a sacred center and axis mundi. To the Egyptians of the Old Kingdom, their king was a living god. When he died, he joined the immortal gods. However, if they kept his body safe, his spirit would be able to return to it and his power would preserve Egypt. The pyramid was designed to keep the king's body safe forever. The burial chamber of the pyramid was carved with descriptions of the changes the king would go through until he became a god. On the walls of the burial chamber were false doors, opening to the outer world, through which it was believed the king's spirit could pass.

Threshold: Thresholds are a boundary symbol. They represent the passage from the profane to the sacred. Crossing a threshold is entering

75 Cooper, 130.

76 See ibid., 131.

77 Ryken, Wilhoit, and Longman, 645.

78 Cooper, 134.

79 See ibid.

into sacred space or a new world.[80] Thresholds may be a specific point, such as a doorway, or an extended space, such as an ocean, desert, or wilderness. Standing as they do between two different worlds and as a point of entering the perilous unknown, thresholds are also places of danger. Crossing a threshold in either direction can be hazardous, thus the custom of carrying a bride over the threshold of her new home, avoiding any misfortune should she cross by foot.[81]

Since the temple is a sacred space, there is a threshold that marks the boundary of the sacred and the profane. Thus, the dedicatory prayer of the Kirtland Temple promises that "all people who shall enter upon the threshold of the Lord's house may feel thy power, and feel constrained to acknowledge that thou hast sanctified it" (D&C 109:13).

Experiences at thresholds are often called *liminal*, from the word *limen*, the Latin word for *threshold*.[82] Liminal experiences are times of transformation. The temple itself is a liminal place because it is where people undergo spiritual transformation.[83] In a sense, all mortal life is a liminal event since this world is not our final home.[84]

Wilderness: Wildernesses and deserts represent danger, death, rebellion, punishment, evil, temptation, deprivation, and thirst. They stand in opposition to fertile ground, fruitful fields, and gardens. "The imagery of being in the wilderness was often used in the scriptures to describe separation from family and God. 'Wilderness imagery does not express beauty, success, or security. It crystallizes abject fear, destruction, and desolation.'"[85] When Adam and Eve stepped out of the Garden of Eden, they stepped into a wilderness.

---

80 See Cooper, 171.

81 See Propp, *Exodus 1–18,* 441.

82 See Richard Dilworth Rust, *Feasting on the Word, The Literary Testimony of the Book of Mormon* (Salt Lake City and Provo, Utah: Deseret Book Company and FARMS, 1996), 221.

83 See ibid., 224.

84 See ibid., 223.

85 Daniel L. Belnap, "'We Are Not Cut Off': Separation and Reconciliation through Sacred Covenants," *Living the Book of Mormon: The 36th Annual Sidney B. Sperry Symposium* (Provo, Utah and Salt Lake City: Religious Studies Center, Brigham Young University and Deseret Book Company), 122.

However, wildernesses can also have a positive connotation. They are a place of refuge for a person or group who is fleeing from danger, as in the cases of Elijah running from Jezebel (see 1 Kings 19:4), the children of Israel fleeing from Egypt, and Lehi and his family escaping the impending destruction of Jerusalem. In the wilderness, God delivers His people, provides for them, and gives them divine guidance and revelation. "In both the Old Testament and the Book of Mormon a *wilderness* symbolizes any place in which the people are tested, tried, proven, refined by trials, taught grace, and prepared to meet the Lord."[86]

---

86 Shemaryahu Talmon, "The 'Desert Motif' in the Bible and in Qumran Literature," *Biblical Motifs: Origins and Transformaitons*, ed. Alexander Altmann (Cambridge, MA; Harvard Unviersity Press, 1966), 45. M. Catherine Thomas, "The Provocation in the Wilderness and the Rejection of Grace," 169.

Works Cited

Alter, Robert. *The Five Books of Moses.* New York: W. W. Norton & Company, 2004.

Andersen, Francis I. and David Noel Freedman. *Hosea.* Anchor Bible. New York: Doubleday, 1980.

Andrus, Hyrum. *Principles of Perfection.* Salt Lake City: Bookcraft, 1970.

Asay, Carlos E. "The Temple Garment: 'An Outward Expression of an Inward Commitment.'" *Ensign*, August 1997, 19–24.

Ashton, Marvin J. "The Tongue Can Be a Sharp Sword." *Ensign*, May 1992, 18–20.

Aukschun, Linda. "The Ordinances and Performances That Pertain to Salvation." In *Riches of Eternity: 12 Fundamental Doctrines from the Doctrine and Covenants.* Salt Lake City: Aspen Books, 1993. 131–153.

Barker, Margaret. *The Revelation of Jesus Christ.* London: T & T Clark, 2000.

Barth, Markus. *Ephesians 4–6.* Anchor Bible. New York: Doubleday, 1974.

Beckham, Janette C. Hales. "Your Good Name," *Brigham Young University 1995–96 Speeches.* Provo, Utah: Brigham Young University, 1996. 1–9.

Belnap, Daniel L. "'We Are Not Cut Off': Separation and Reconciliation through Sacred Covenants." In *Living the Book of Mormon: the*

36th Annual Sidney B. Sperry Symposium. Provo, Utah and Salt Lake City: Religious Studies Center, Brigham Young University and Deseret Book Company. 113–124.

Benjamin, Don C. *Old Testament Story—An Introduction.* Tempe, Arizona: Scholargy Custom Publishing, 2003.

Benson, Ezra Taft. *Come, Listen to a Prophet's Voice.* Salt Lake City: Deseret Book Company, 1990.

----------. *The Teachings of Ezra Taft Benson.* Salt Lake City: Bookcraft, 1988.

Blenkinsopp, Joseph. *Isaiah 1–39,* Anchor Bible. New York: Doubleday, 2000.

Bock, Darrell L. and Gregory J. Herrick. *Jesus in Context: Background Readings for Gospel Study.* Grand Rapids, Michigan: Baker Academic, 2005.

Bokovoy, David E. "The Calling of Isaiah." In *Covenants, Prophecies, and Hymns of the Old Testament: The 30th Annual Sidney B. Sperry Symposium.* Salt Lake City: Deseret Book Company, 2001. 128–139.

Brandt, Edward J. "The Law of Moses and the Law of Christ." In *A Witness of Jesus Christ: The 1989 Sperry Symposium on the Old Testament.* Ed. Richard D. Draper. Salt Lake City: Deseret Book Company, 1990. 18–36.

Bright, John. *Jeremiah.* Anchor Bible. New York: Doubleday, 1965.

Brinley, Douglas. "How the Doctrine and Covenants Can Strengthen Marriages." Church Educational System Religious Educators Conference at Brigham Young University, August 2002. 13–15.

Brown, Cheryl. "Complexities, Covenants, and Christ." In *To Rejoice as Women: Talks from the 1994 Women's Conference.* Eds. Susette Fletcher Green and Dawn Hall Anderson. Salt Lake City: Deseret Book, 1995. 145–151.

Brown, Francis, S. R. Driver, and Charles A. Briggs. *The Brown-Driver-Briggs Hebrew and English Lexicon.* Peabody, Massachusetts: Hendrickson Publishers, 2001.

Brown, Matthew B. "Girded about with a Lambskin," *Journal of Book of Mormon Studies* vol. 6, no. 2 (1997): 124–151.

Brown, Raymond E. *The Birth of the Messiah.* Anchor Bible Reference Library. New York: Doubleday, 1993.

-----------. *The Gospel According to John I–XII.* Anchor Bible. New York: Doubleday, 1966.

----------. *The Gospel According to John XIII–XXI.* Anchor Bible. New York: Doubleday, 1970.

Brown, S. Kent. "Man and Son of Man: Issues of Theology and Christology." In *The Pearl of Great Price: Revelations from God.* Eds. H. Donl Peterson and Charles D. Tate Jr. Provo, Utah: Religious Studies Center Brigham Young University, 1989. 57–72.

Campbell, Beverly. *Eve and the Choice Made in Eden.* Salt Lake City: Bookcraft, 2003.

Campbell, Edward F. Jr. *Ruth.* Anchor Bible. New York: Doubleday, 1975.

Campbell, Joseph. *A Joseph Campbell Companion: Reflections on the Art of Living.* Ed. Diane K. Osbon. New York: Harper Perennial, 1991.

Cannon, George Q. *Gospel Truth.* Edited by Jerreld L. Newquist. 2 vols. Salt Lake City: Deseret Book Company, 1974.

Christenson, Allen J. "The Waters of Destruction and the Vine of Redemption." In *A Witness of Jesus Christ: The 1989 Sperry Symposium on the Old Testament.* Ed. Richard D. Draper. Salt Lake City: Deseret Book Company, 1990. 37–52.

Christensen, Kevin. "The Temple, the Monarchy, and Wisdom." In *Glimpses of Lehi's Jerusalem.* Eds. John W. Welch, David Rolph Seely, and Jo Ann H. Seely. Salt Lake City: FARMS, 2004. 449–522.

Compton, Todd M. "The Handclasp and Embrace as Tokens of Recognition." In *By Study and Also By Faith.* Eds. John M. Lundquist and Stephen D. Ricks. 2 vols. Salt Lake City and Provo, Utah: Deseret Book Company and FARMS, 1990. 1:611–642.

Cooper, J. C. *An Illustrated Encyclopaedia of Traditional Symbols.* London: Thames and Hudson, 1978.

Covey, Steven R. "The Abundant Life in Christ." In *The Redeemer: Reflections on the Life and Teachings of Jesus the Christ*. Salt Lake City: Deseret Book Company, 2000. 73–122.

Cowan, Richard O. "Sacred Temples Ancient and Modern." In *The Temple in Time and Eternity.* Eds. Donald W. Parry and Stephen D. Ricks. Provo, Utah: FARMS, 1999. 99–120.

Cox, Paul Alan. "Seeing with New Eyes." In *Brigham Young University 1995–96 Speeches*. Provo, Utah: Brigham Young University, 1996. 39–48.

Craigie, Peter C. *Word Biblical Commentary: Psalms 1–50.* Thomas Nelson Publishers, 2004.

"Cursing a Litigant with Speechlessness." *Insights: An Ancient Window, The Newsletter of the Foundation for Ancient Research and Mormon Studies*, no. 120 (October 1998).

Dahood, Mitchell. *Psalms III: 101–150.* Anchor Bible. New York: Doubleday, 1970.

de Vaux, Roland. *Ancient Israel: Its Life and Institutions*. Trans. John McHugh. Grand Rapids, Michigan: William B. Eerdmans Publishing Company, 1961.

Donaldson, Lee, V. Dan Rogers, and David Rolph Seely. "I Have a Question" *Ensign*. February 1994, 60.

Dosick, Rabbi Wayne. "How Goodly Is Your Temple, O Mormons." *San Diego Jewish Times*, March 25, 1993: 15.

Draper, Richard D. *Opening the Seven Seals: The Visions of John the Revelator.* Salt Lake City: Deseret Book Company, 1991.

Edwards, Douglas. R. "Dress and Ornamentation." In *The Anchor Bible Dictionary*. Ed. David Noel Freedman, vol 2. New York: Doubleday, 1992. 232–238.

Ehat, Andrew F. "'Who Shall Ascend into the Hill of the Lord?' Sesquicentennial Reflections of a Sacred Day: 4 May 1842." In *Temples of the Ancient World*. Ed. Donald W. Parry. Salt Lake City: Deseret Book and FARMS, 1997. 48–62.

Eliade, Mircea. *Images and Symbols.* Trans. Philip Mairet. Princeton, New Jersey: Princeton University Press, 1991.

Endowed from on High: Temple Preparation Seminar, Teacher's Manual. Salt Lake City: The Church of Jesus Christ of Latter-day Saints, 2003.

England, Kathy. "The Washington D.C. Temple." *Ensign*, October 1977, 88.

Eyring, Henry B. "Covenants and Sacrifice." General Authority Address Old Testament Symposium 1995. In *The Nineteenth Annual Church Educational System Religious Educators' Symposium.* Salt Lake City: The Church of Jesus Christ of Latter-day Saints, 1995.

----------. "Rise to Your Call." *Ensign*, November 2002, 75–78.

Fairchild, Cory. Personal Correspondence. December 9, 2003.

"The Family: A Proclamation to the World." *Ensign*, November 1995, 102.

Faulconer, James E. *Scripture Study: Tools and Suggestions.* Provo, Utah: FARMS, 1999.

Faust, James E. "The Forces That Will Save Us." *Ensign*, January 2007, 4–9.

----------. "Search Me, O God, and Know My Heart." *Ensign*, May 1998, 17–20.

Featherstone, Vaughn J. *Incomparable Christ: Our Master and Model.* Salt Lake City: Deseret Book Company, 1995.

Fletcher, Allen J. *A Study Guide to the Facsimiles of the Book of Abraham.* Springville, Utah: CFI, 2006.

Ford, J. Massyngberde. *Revelation.* Anchor Bible. New York: Doubleday, 1975.

Fretheim, Terence E. *The Suffering of God.* Philadelphia: Fortress Press, 1984.

Gaskill, Alonzo L. *The Savior & the Serpent: Unlocking the Doctrine of the Fall.* Salt Lake City: Deseret Book Company, 2005.

Gee, John. "The Keeper of the Gate." In *Temple in Time and Eternity.* Eds. Donald W. Parry and Stephen D. Ricks. Provo, Utah: FARMS, 1999. 233–273.

Gee, John and Daniel C. Peterson. "Graft and Corruption: On Olives and Olive Culture in the Pre-Modern Mediterranean." In *The Allegory of the Olive Tree.* Eds. Stephen D. Ricks and John W.

Welch. Salt Lake City and Provo, Utah: Deseret Book Company and FARMS, 1994. 186–247.

Goelet, Ogden. "Moses' Egyptian Name." *Bible Review*, June 2003: 14–17, 50–51.

Greenberg, Moshe. *Ezekiel 1–20.* Anchor Bible. New York: Doubleday, 1983.

---------. *Ezekiel 21–37.* Anchor Bible. New York: Doubleday, 1997.

Groberg, John H. *In the Eye of the Storm.* Salt Lake City: Deseret Book Company, 1993.

Hafen, Bruce C. *The Broken Heart: Applying the Atonement to Life's Experiences.* Salt Lake City: Deseret Book Company, 1989.

Hafen, Bruce C. and Marie K. Hafen. *The Belonging Heart: The Atonement and Relationships with God and Family.* Salt Lake City: Deseret Book Company, 1994.

Haight, David B. "Be a Strong Link." *Ensign*, November 2000, 19–21.

----------. "Come to the House of the Lord." *Ensign*, May 1992, 15–17.

Hamblin, William J. "Aspects of an Early Christian Initiation Ritual." In *By Study and Also By Faith.* Eds. John M. Lundquist and Stephen D. Ricks. 2 vols. Salt Lake City and Provo, Utah: Deseret Book Company and FARMS. 1:202–221.

----------. "Temple Motifs in Jewish Mysticism." In *Temples of the Ancient World.* Ed. Donald W. Parry. Salt Lake City: Deseret Book and FARMS, 1997. 440–476.

Hamilton, Victor P. *The Book of Genesis: Chapter 1–17.* Grand Rapids, Michigan: William B. Eerdmans Publishing Company, 1990.

----------. *The Book of Genesis: Chapter 18–50.* Grand Rapids, Michigan: William B. Eerdmans Publishing Company, 1995.

Hanks, Marion D. "Christ Manifested to His People." In *Temples of the Ancient World.* Ed. Donald W. Parry. Salt Lake City: Deseret Book and FARMS, 1997. 3–28.

Hardison, Blake. Personal Correspondence. June 23, 2007.

Harris, James R. "The Book of Abraham Facsimiles." In *Studies in Scripture, Volume 2: The Pearl of Great Price.* Eds. Robert L. Millet and Kent P. Jackson. 8 vols. Salt Lake City: Randall Book Company, 1985. 247–286.

Hauglid, Brian M. "Temple Imagery in the Psalms." In *Covenants, Prophecies, and Hymns of the Old Testament: The 30th Annual Sidney B. Sperry Symposium*. Salt Lake City: Deseret Book, 2001. 262–274.

Heinerman, Joseph. *Spirit World Manifestations.* Salt Lake City: Joseph Lyon & Associates, 1978.

----------. *Temple Manifestations.* Salt Lake City: Joseph Lyon and Associates, Inc., 1974.

Heschel, Abraham J. *The Prophets.* 2 vols. New York: Harper and Row Publishers, 1962.

Hiebert, Theodore. "Theophany in the OT." In *The Anchor Bible Dictionary*. Ed. David Noel Freedman, vol 6. New York: Doubleday, 1992. 505–511.

Hill, Andrew E. *Malachi.* Anchor Bible. New York: Doubleday, 1998.

Hillers, Delbert R. *Covenant: The History of a Biblical Idea.* Baltimore: The Johns Hopkins University Press, 1969.

Hilton, Dr. Lynn M. "The Hand as a Cup in Ancient Temple Worship." Presented at the Thirtieth Annual Symposium on the Archaeology of the Scriptures, held at BYU, September 26, 1981. http://www.ldstemplepage.org/spoonl.html, 12/23/00.

Hinckley, Gordon B. "Closing Remarks." *Ensign*, November 2004, 104–105.

----------. "New Temples to Provide 'Crowning Blessings' of the Gospel." *Ensign*, May 1998, 87–88.

----------. *Teachings of Gordon B. Hinckley.* Salt Lake City: Deseret Book Company, 1997.

----------. "The State of the Church," *Ensign*, November 2003, 4–7.

Holland, Jeffrey R. *Christ and the New Covenant.* Salt Lake City: Deseret Book Company, 1997.

----------. "Rending the Veil of Unbelief." In *Nurturing Faith through the Book of Mormon: The 24th Annual Sidney B. Sperry Symposium.* Salt Lake City: Deseret Book Company, 1995. 1–24.

Holland, Jeffrey R. and Patricia T. Holland. *On Earth as It Is in Heaven.* Salt Lake City: Deseret Book Company, 1989.

Holzapfel, Richard Neitzel. *A Lively Hope: The Suffering, Death, Resurrection, and Exaltation of Jesus Christ.* Salt Lake City: Bookcraft, 1999.

Hoskisson, Paul. "A Latter-day Saint Reading of Isaiah in the Twentieth Century: The Example of Isaiah 6." In *The Old Testament and the Latter-day Saints: Sperry Symposium 1986.* Salt Lake City: Randall Book Company, 1986. 197–210.

Hovorka, Janet. "Sarah and Hagar: Ancient Women of the Abrahamic Covenant." In *Astronomy, Papyrus, and Covenant.* Eds. John Gee and Brian M. Hauglid. Provo, Utah: FARMS, 2005. 147–166.

Hunter, Howard W. *The Teachings of Howard W. Hunter.* Ed. Clyde J. Williams. Salt Lake City: Bookcraft, 1997.

Hunter, Milton R. *Archaeology and the Book of Mormon.* Salt Lake City: Deseret Book Company, 1956.

Hyers, Conrad. *The Meaning of Creation: Genesis and Modern Science.* Atlanta: John Knox Press, 1984.

Kerr, Todd R. "Ancient Aspects of Nephite Kingship in the Book of Mormon." *Journal of Book of Mormon Studies*, vol. 1, no. 1 (Fall 1992): 85–118.

Kidner, Derek. *Psalms 1–72.* Downers Grove, Illinois: InterVarsity Press, 1973.

Kimball, Spencer W. "The Blessings and Responsibilities of Womanhood." In *Woman.* Salt Lake City: Deseret Book Company, 1988. 77–85.

----------. *Faith Precedes the Miracle.* Salt Lake City: Deseret Book Company, 1972.

----------. *The Teachings of Spencer W. Kimball.* Ed. Edward L. Kimball. Salt Lake City: Bookcraft, 1982.

Kolatch, Alfred J. *The Jewish Book of Why.* Middle Village, New York: Jonathan David Publishers, Inc., 1981.

Lane, Jennifer C. "'Come, Follow Me': The Imitation of Christ in the Later Middle Ages." In *Prelude to the Restoration: From Apostasy to the Restored Church: The 33rd Annual Sidney B. Sperry Symposium.*

Salt Lake City: Deseret Book and Brigham Young University Religious Studies Center, 2004. 115–129.

Larsen, Dean L. “The Importance of the Temple for Living Members.” *Ensign*, April 1993, 10–12.

LeBaron, Dale E. “Elijah’s Mission: His Keys, Powers, and Blessings from the Old Testament to the Latter Days.” In *Thy People Shall Be My People and Thy God My God: The 22nd Annual Sidney B. Sperry Symposium.* Salt Lake City: Deseret Book Company, 1994. 61–73.

Levine, Amy-Jill. *The Old Testament, Part 1.* CD-ROM. The Great Courses. 2001.

Ludlow, Daniel H. *Selected Writings of Daniel H. Ludlow: Gospel Scholars Series.* Salt Lake City: Deseret Book Company, 2000.

Lund, Robert E. “Women in the Writings of John.” In *The Testimony of John the Beloved: The 27th Annual Sidney B. Sperry Symposium.* Salt Lake City: Deseret Book Company, 1998. 125–140.

Lundquist, John M. “The Common Temple Ideology of the Ancient Near East.” In *The Temple in Antiquity: Ancient Records and Modern Perspectives.* Ed. Truman G. Madsen. Provo, Utah: Religious Studies Center, 1984. 53–76.

----------. “Temple Symbolism.” In *Isaiah and the Prophets: Inspired Voices from the Old Testament.* Ed. Monte S. Nyman. Provo, Utah: Religious Studies Center, 1984. 33–56.

----------. “What Is a Temple? A Preliminary Typology.” In *Temples of the Ancient World.* Ed. Donald W. Parry. Salt Lake City: Deseret Book and FARMS, 1997. 83–117.

----------. “What Is Reality?” In *By Study and Also By Faith.* Eds. John M. Lundquist and Stephen D. Ricks. 2 vols. Salt Lake City and Provo, Utah: Deseret Book Company and FARMS, 1990. 1:428–438.

Luschin, Immo. “Ordinances,” *Encyclopedia of Mormonism.* Ed. Daniel H. Ludlow. 4 vols. New York: Macmillan Publishing Company, 1992.

Madsen, Truman G. “The Olive Press: A Symbol of Christ.” In *The Allegory of the Olive Tree.* Eds. Stephen D. Ricks and John W. Welch. Salt Lake City and Provo, Utah: Deseret Book Company and FARMS, 1994. 1–10.

----------. "'Putting on the Names': A Jewish-Christian Legacy." In *By Study and Also By Faith.* Eds. John M. Lundquist and Stephen D. Ricks. 2 vols. Salt Lake City and Provo, Utah: Deseret Book Company and FARMS, 1990. 1:458–481.

----------. "The Temple and the Atonement." In *Temples of the Ancient World: Ritual and Symbolism.* Ed. Donald W. Parry. Salt Lake City: Deseret Book and FARMS, 1997. 63–79.

Madsen, Truman G. and Steven R. Covey. *Marriage and Family: Gospel Insights.* Salt Lake City: Bookcraft, 1983.

Malina, Bruce J. *The New Testament World: Insights from Cultural Anthropology.* Louisville, Kentucky: Westminster/John Knox Press, 1993.

Malina, Bruce J. and Richard L. Rohrbaugh. *Social Science Commentary on the Synoptic Gospels.* Minneapolis: Fortress Press, 1992.

----------. *The Social-Science Commentary on the Gospel of John.* Minneapolis: Fortress Press, 1998.

Martyn, J. Louis. *Galatians.* Anchor Bible. New York: Doubleday, 1997.

Mathews, Kenneth A. *The New American Commentary: Genesis 1–11:26, vol 1A.* United States of America: Broadman and Holman Publishers, 2002.

Matthews, Robert J. "The Origin of Man." In *Riches of Eternity: 12 Fundamental Doctrines from the Doctrine and Covenants.* Eds. John K Challis, John G. Scott. Salt Lake City: Aspen Books, 1993. 17–29.

Maxwell, Neal A. *All These Things Shall Give Thee Experience.* Salt Lake City: Deseret Book Company, 1979.

----------. *But For a Small Moment.* Salt Lake City: Bookcraft, 1986.

----------. *Not My Will, But Thine.* Salt Lake City: Bookcraft, 1988.

----------. "The Tugs and Pulls of the World." *Ensign,* November 2000, 35–37.

McCarter, P. Kyle, Jr. *I Samuel.* Anchor Bible. New York: Doubleday, 1980.

McConkie, Bruce R. "Christ and the Creation," *Ensign*, June 1982, 9–15.

----------. Conference Report. April 1970.

----------. *Doctrinal New Testament Commentary*. 3 vols. Salt Lake City: Bookcraft, 1974.

----------. *Mormon Doctrine*. Salt Lake City: Bookcraft, 1966.

----------. *A New Witness for the Articles of Faith*. Salt Lake City: Deseret Book, 1985.

McConkie, Joseph Fielding. *Gospel Symbolism*. Salt Lake City: Bookcraft, 1988.

----------. "The Mystery of Eden." In *The Man Adam*. Eds. Joseph Fielding McConkie and Robert L. Millet. Salt Lake City: Bookcraft, 1990. 23–35.

----------. "Obedience and Sacrifice." *Pearl of Great Price Discussions*. BYU Television. August 31, 2006.

----------. "The Testimony of Christ through the Ages." In *The Book of Mormon: Jacob through Words of Mormon, to Learn with Joy*. Eds. Monte S. Nyman and Charles D. Tate Jr. Provo, Utah: Religious Studies Center Brigham Young University, 1990. 157–174.

McConkie, Joseph Fielding and Robert Millet. *Life Beyond*. Salt Lake City: Bookcraft, 1986.

----------. *Doctrinal Commentary on the Book of Mormon*. 4 vols. Salt Lake City: Bookcraft, 1987.

McConkie, Joseph Fielding and Donald W. Parry. *A Guide to Scriptural Symbols*. Salt Lake City: Bookcraft, 1990.

Mercer, Robert L. "Pioneers in Ivory Coast." *Liahona*, March 1999, 16–24.

Merrill, Byron R. *Elijah: Yesterday, Today, and Tomorrow*. Salt Lake City: Bookcraft, 1997.

Meyers, Carol. "Apron." In *The Anchor Bible Dictionary*. Ed. David Noel Freedman, vol 1. New York: Doubleday, 1992. 318–319.

----------. *Discovering Eve: Ancient Israelite Women in Context*. New York: Oxford University Press, 1988.

----------. *Exodus.* Cambridge: Cambridge University Press, 2005.

----------. "Jachin and Boaz in Religious and Political Perspective." In *The Temple in Antiquity: Ancient Records and Modern Perspectives.* Ed. Truman G. Madsen. Provo, Utah: Religious Studies Center, 1984. 135–150.

----------. "Sea, Molten." In *The Anchor Bible Dictionary.* Ed. by David Noel Freedman, vol 5. New York: Doubleday, 1992. 1061–1062.

Meyers, Carol L. and Eric M. Meyers. *Zechariah 9–14.* Anchor Bible. New York: Doubleday, 1993.

Milgrom, Jacob. *Leviticus 1–16.* Anchor Bible. New York: Doubleday, 1991.

----------. *Leviticus 17–22.* Anchor Bible. New York: Doubleday, 2000.

Miller, Jeanette W. "The Tree of Life, a Personification of Christ." *Journal of Book of Mormon Studies*, vol. 2, no. 1 (Spring 1993): 93–106.

Millet, Robert L. *Alive in Christ: The Miracle of Spiritual Rebirth.* Salt Lake City: Deseret Book Company, 1997.

----------. "Another Testament of Jesus Christ." In *The Book of Mormon: First Nephi, the Doctrinal Foundation.* Eds. Monte S. Nyman and Charles D. Tate Jr. Provo, Utah: Religious Studies Center Brigham Young University, 1988. 161–175.

----------. "The Only Sure Foundation: Building on the Rock of Our Redeemer." In *The Book of Mormon: Helaman through 3 Nephi 8, According to Thy Word.* Eds. Monte S. Nyman and Charles D. Tate Jr. Provo, Utah: Religious Studies Center Brigham Young University, 1992. 15–38.

----------. *When a Child Wanders.* Salt Lake City: Deseret Book Company, 1996.

Morris, Leon. *The Gospel According to John.* Grand Rapids, Michigan: William B. Eerdmans Publishing Company, 1995.

Motyer, J. Alec. *The Prophecy of Isaiah: An Introduction and Commentary.* Downers Grove, Illinois: InterVarsity Press, 1993.

Mounce, Robert H. *The Book of Revelation.* Grand Rapids, Michigan: William B. Eerdmans Publishing Company, 1998.

Nelson, Russell M. "Children of the Covenant" *Ensign*, May 1995, 33–35.

Nibley, Hugh. *Ancient Documents and the Pearl of Great Price.* Provo, Utah: FARMS, 1986.

----------. "Before Adam." In *Old Testament and Related Studies.* Vol. 1 of The Collected Works of Hugh Nibley. Eds. John W. Welch, Gary P. Gillum, and Don E. Norton. Salt Lake City and Provo, Utah: Deseret Book Company and FARMS, 1986. 49–86.

----------. "But What Kind of Work." *Approaching Zion.* Vol. 9 of The Collected Works of Hugh Nibley. Ed. Don E. Norton. Salt Lake City and Provo, Utah: Deseret Book Company and FARMS, 1989. 252–289.

----------. "The Circle and the Square." In *Temple and Cosmos.* Vol. 12 of The Collected Works of Hugh Nibley. Ed. Don E. Norton. Salt Lake City and Provo, Utah: Deseret Book Company and FARMS, 1992. 139–173.

----------. "The Early Christian Prayer Circle." *Mormonism and Early Christianity.* Vol. 4 of The Collected Works of Hugh Nibley. Eds. Todd M. Compton and Steven D. Ricks. Salt Lake City and Provo, Utah: Deseret Book Company and FARMS, 1987. 45–99.

----------. "Funeral Address." *Approaching Zion.* Vol. 9 of The Collected Works of Hugh Nibley. Ed. Don E. Norton. Salt Lake City and Provo, Utah: Deseret Book Company and FARMS, 1989. 290–307.

----------. "A House of Glory." In *Temples of the Ancient World.* Ed. Donald W. Parry. Salt Lake City and Provo, Utah: Deseret Book Company and FARMS, 1994. 29–47.

----------. "Law of Consecration." In *Approaching Zion.* Vol. 9 of The Collected Works of Hugh Nibley. Ed. Don E. Norton. Salt Lake City and Provo, Utah: Deseret Book Company and FARMS, 1989. 422–486.

----------. "Leaders to Managers: The Fatal Shift." In *Brother Brigham Challenges the Saints.* Vol. 13 of The Collected Works of Hugh

Nibley. Eds. Don E. Norton and Shirley S. Ricks. Salt Lake City and Provo, Utah: Deseret Book Company and FARMS, 1994. 486–507.

----------. "The Meaning of the Atonement." In *Approaching Zion*. Vol. 9 of The Collected Works of Hugh Nibley. Ed. Don E. Norton. Salt Lake City and Provo, Utah: Deseret Book Company and FARMS, 1989. 554–614.

----------. "The Meaning of the Temple." In *Temple and Cosmos*. Vol. 12 of The Collected Works of Hugh Nibley. Ed. Don E. Norton. Salt Lake City and Provo, Utah: Deseret Book Company and FARMS, 1992. 1–41.

----------. *The Message of the Joseph Smith Papyri: An Egyptian Endowment.* Eds. John Gee and Michael D. Rhodes. Salt Lake City and Provo, Utah: Deseret Book Company and FARMS, 2005.

----------. "A New Look at the Pearl of Great Price." *Improvement Era*, September 1969: 85–95.

----------. Notes to "The World of the Jaredites." Vol. 5 of The Collected Works of Hugh Nibley, Eds. John W. Welch, Darrell L. Matthews, and Stephen R. Callister. Salt Lake City and Provo, Utah: Deseret Book Company and FARMS, 1986. 264–282.

----------. *Of All Things! Classic Quotations from Hugh Nibley*. Ed. Gary P. Gillum. Salt Lake City and Provo, Utah: Deseret Book Company and FARMS, 1993.

----------. "On the Sacred and the Symbolic." In *Temples of the Ancient World.* Ed. Donald W. Parry. Salt Lake City and Provo, Utah: Deseret Book Company and FARMS, 1994. 535–621.

----------. "Patriarchy and Matriarchy." In *Old Testament and Related Studies*. Vol. 1 of The Collected Works of Hugh Nibley. Eds. John W. Welch, Gary P. Gillum, and Don E. Norton. Salt Lake City and Provo, Utah: Deseret Book Company and FARMS, 1986. 87–114.

----------. "Portrait of Laban." In *An Approach to the Book of Mormon.* Vol. 6 of The Collected Works of Hugh Nibley. Ed. John W. Welch, 3rd edition. Salt Lake City and Provo, Utah: Deseret Book Company and FARMS, 1988. 120–131.

----------. "Return to the Temple." In *Temple and Cosmos*. Vol. 12 of The Collected Works of Hugh Nibley. Ed. Don E. Norton. Salt Lake City and Provo, Utah: Deseret Book Company and FARMS, 1992. 42–90.

----------. "Sacred Vestments." In *Temple and Cosmos*. Vol. 12 of The Collected Works of Hugh Nibley. Ed. Don E. Norton. Salt Lake City and Provo, Utah: Deseret Book Company and FARMS, 1992. 91–138.

----------. *Teachings of the Book of Mormon*. 4 vols. Provo Utah: FARMS, 1993.

----------. "Three Degrees of Righteousness from the Old Testament." In *Approaching Zion*. Vol. 9 of The Collected Works of Hugh Nibley. Ed. Don E. Norton. Salt Lake City and Provo, Utah: Deseret Book Company and FARMS, 1989. 308–340.

----------. "Unrolling the Scrolls—Some Forgotten Witnesses." In *Old Testament and Related Studies*. Vol. 1 of The Collected Works of Hugh Nibley. Eds. John W. Welch, Gary P. Gillum, and Don E. Norton. Salt Lake City and Provo, Utah: Deseret Book Company and FARMS, 1986. 115–170.

----------. "What Is Zion? A Distant View." In *Approaching Zion*. Vol. 9 of The Collected Works of Hugh Nibley. Ed. Don E. Norton. Salt Lake City and Provo, Utah: Deseret Book Company and FARMS, 1989. 25–62.

Neuenschwander, Dennis B. "Ordinances & Covenants." *Ensign*, August 2001, 21–26.

Neusner, Jacob. *Genesis Rabbah, The Judaic Commentary to the Book of Genesis.* 3 vols. Atlanta, Georgia: Scholars Press, 1985.

Nielsen, Donna. *Beloved Bridegroom*. United States of America: Onyx Press, 1999.

Norton, Don E. *Temple and Cosmos*. Vol. 12 of The Collected Works of Hugh Nibley. Ed. Don E. Norton. Salt Lake City and Provo, Utah: Deseret Book Company and FARMS, 1992. xv–xix.

Nydle, Rabbi Edward Levi and Levi bar Ido. "White Garments: Significant of wearing white garments on the Shabbat." February

26, 2007. http://www.bnaiavraham.net/teaching_articles/english_teachings/RabbiEd/WHITE_GARMENTS.htm.

Oaks, Dallin H. *His Holy Name.* Salt Lake City: Bookcraft, 1998.

Oman, Richard G. "Exterior Symbolism of the Salt Lake Temple: Reflecting the Faith That Called the Place into Being." *BYU Studies*, vol. 36, no. 4 (1996–1997): 6–68.

Ostler, Blake. "Clothed Upon: A Unique Aspect of Christian Antiquity." *BYU Studies*, vol. 22, no. 1 (Winter 1982): 31–45.

----------. "The Throne-Theophany and Prophetic Commission in 1 Nephi: A Form-Critical Analysis." *BYU Studies*, vol. 26, no. 4 (Fall 1986): 67–95.

Oswalt, John N. *The Book of Isaiah: Chapters 1–39.* Grand Rapids, Michigan: William B. Eerdmans Publishing Company, 1986.

----------. *The Book of Isaiah: Chapters 40–66.* Grand Rapids, Michigan: William B. Eerdmans Publishing Company, 1998.

Otten, Leaun G. and C. Max Caldwell. *Sacred Truths of the Doctrine and Covenants.* 2 vols. Salt Lake City: Deseret Book Company, 1983.

Pace, Glenn L. *Spiritual Plateaus.* Salt Lake City: Deseret Book Company, 1991.

----------. *Spiritual Revival.* Salt Lake City: Deseret Book Company, 1993.

Packer, Boyd K. *The Holy Temple.* Salt Lake City: Bookcraft, 1980.

----------. "Our Moral Environment." *Ensign*, May 1992, 66–68.

Parrish, Alan K. "Modern Temple Worship through the Eyes of John A. Widtsoe, a Twentieth-Century Apostle." In *The Temple in Time and Eternity.* Eds. Donald W. Parry and Stephen D. Ricks. Provo, Utah: FARMS, 1999. 143–182.

Parry, Donald W. "Introduction." In *Temples of the Ancient World.* Ed. Donald W. Parry. Salt Lake City: Deseret Book and FARMS, 1997. Xi–xxiv.

----------. "Ritual Anointing with Olive Oil in Ancient Israelite Religion." In *The Allegory of the Olive Tree.* Eds. Stephen D. Ricks and John W. Welch. Salt Lake City and Provo, Utah: Deseret Book Company and FARMS, 1994. 262–289.

----------. "Sacred Space and Profane Space." In *Temples of the Ancient World: Ritual and Symbolism*. Ed. Donald W. Parry. Salt Lake City: Deseret Book and FARMS, 1997. 413–439.

----------. "Temple Worship and a Possible Reference to a Prayer Circle in Psalm 24," *BYU Studies*, vol. 32, no. 4 (1992): 57–62.

Parry, Donald W., Jay A. Parry, and Tina M. Peterson, *Understanding Isaiah.* Salt Lake City: Deseret Book Company, 1998.

Peek, Cecilia M. "Early Galilean Ministry and Miracles." In *The Life and Teachings of Jesus Christ: From Bethlehem through the Sermon on the Mount.* Eds. Richard Neitzel Holzapfel and Thomas A. Wayment, 2 vols. Salt Lake City: Deseret Book Company. 1:269–305.

Peterson, H. Donl. *The Pearl of Great Price: A History and Commentary.* Salt Lake City: Deseret Book Company, 1987.

Pike, Dana M. "Seals and Sealing among Ancient and Latter-day Israelites." In *Thy People Shall Be My People and Thy God My God: The 22nd Annual Sidney B. Sperry Symposium.* Salt Lake City: Deseret Book Company, 1994. 101–117.

Porter, Bruce H. "Altar." *Encyclopedia of Mormonism*. Ed. Daniel H. Ludlow. 4 vols. New York: Macmillan Publishing Company, 1992.

Porter, Bruce H. and Stephen D. Ricks. "Names in Antiquity: Old, New, and Hidden." In *By Study and Also By Faith.* Eds. John M. Lundquist and Stephen D. Ricks. 2 vols. Salt Lake City and Provo, Utah: Deseret Book Company and FARMS, 1990. 1:501–522.

Propp, William H. C. *Exodus 1–18*, Anchor Bible. New York: Doubleday, 1999.

----------. *Exodus 19–40.* Anchor Bible. New York: Doubleday, 1999.

Quinn, D. Michael. "Latter-day Saint Prayer Circles." *BYU Studies*, vol. 19, no. 1 (Fall 1979): 79–105.

Ralston, Alston. *Between a Rock and a Hard Place*. New York: Aria Books, 2004.

Redd, J. Lyman. "Aaron's Consecration: Its Nature, Purpose and Meaning." In *Thy People Shall Be My People and Thy God My God: The 22nd Annual Sidney B. Sperry Symposium.* Salt Lake City: Deseret Book Company, 1994. 118–135.

Reis, Pamela Tamarkin. *Reading the Lines: A Fresh Look at the Hebrew Bible.* Peabody, Massachusetts: Hendrickson Publishers, 2002.

Ricks, Stephen D. "The Garment of Adam in Jewish, Muslim, and Christian Tradition." In *Temples of the Ancient World: Ritual and Symbolism.* Ed. Donald W. Parry. Salt Lake City: Deseret Book and FARMS, 1997. 705–741,

----------. "Kingship, Coronation, and Covenant in Mosiah 1–6." In *King Benjamin's Speech: 'That Ye May Learn Wisdom.'* Eds. John W. Welch and Stephen D. Ricks. Provo, Utah: FARMS, 1998. 233–276.

----------. "Olive Culture in the Second Temple Era and Early Rabbinic Period." In *The Allegory of the Olive Tree.* Eds. Stephen D. Ricks and John W. Welch. Salt Lake City and Provo, Utah: Deseret Book Company and FARMS, 1994. 460–476.

Ricks, Stephen D. and John J. Sroka. "King, Coronation, and Temple: Enthronement Ceremonies in History." In *Temples of the Ancient World: Ritual and Symbolism.* Ed. Donald W. Parry. Salt Lake City: Deseret Book and FARMS, 1997. 236–271.

Riddle, Chauncey C. "Code Language in the Book of Mormon." Transcript. Provo, Utah: FARMS, 1992.

Ritmeyer, Leen and Kathleen Ritmeyer. *Secrets of Jerusalem's Temple Mount.* Washington, D.C.: Biblical Archeology Society, 1998.

Robinson, Stephen R. "The Book of Adam in Judaism and Early Christianity." In *The Man Adam.* Eds. Joseph Fielding McConkie and Robert L. Millet. Salt Lake City: Bookcraft, 1990. 128–147.

Romney, Marion G. "Satan—The Great Deceiver." *Ensign*, June 1971, 35–37.

Rona, Daniel. *Israel Revealed Tour.* September 2005.

Ross, Allen P. *Creation & Blessing: A Guide to the Study and Exposition of Genesis.* Grand Rapids, Michigan: Baker Books, 1998.

Rushdoony, Rousas John. *The Institutes of Biblical Law*. United States of America: The Presbyterian and Reformed Publishing Company, 1973.

Ryken, Leland, James C. Wilhoit, Tremper Longman III, eds. *Dictionary of Biblical Imagery.* Downers Grove, Illinois: InterVarsity Press, 1998.

Sakenfeld, Katharine Doob. *The Meaning of Hesed in the Hebrew Bible: A New Inquiry*. Eugene, Oregon: Wipf and Stock Publishers, 1978.

"San Diego Temple Dedication: Temples—Linking Heaven and Earth." *Church News*, May 8, 1993.

Sarna, Nahum. *Exploring Exodus: The Origins of Biblical Israel.* New York: Schocken Books, 1996.

----------. *The JPS Torah Commentary: Exodus*. Philadelphia: The Jewish Publication Society, 1989.

----------. *The JPS Torah Commentary: Genesis*. Philadelphia: The Jewish Publication Society, 1989

----------. *On the Book of Psalms: Exploring the Prayers of Ancient Israel.* New York: Schocken Books, 1993.

----------. *Understanding Genesis*. New York: Schocken Books, 1966.

Schele, Linda and David Freidel. *Forest of Kings: The Untold Story of the Ancient Maya.* New York: Quill William Morrow, 1990.

Scott, Richard G. "Acquiring Spiritual Knowledge." *Ensign*, November 1993, 86–88.

----------. "Do What Is Right." In *Brigham Young University 1995–96 Speeches*. Provo, Utah: Brigham Young University, 1996. 167–174.

----------. "Learning to Recognize Answers to Prayer" *Ensign*, November 1989, 30–32.

Seow. C. L. "Ark of the Covenant." In *The Anchor Bible Dictionary*, edited by David Noel Freedman. Vol 1. New York: Doubleday, 1992. 386–393.

Skinner, Andrew C. "The Garden Tomb," in *The Savior's Final Week.* Salt Lake City: Deseret Book Company, 2014.

----------."Genesis 22: The Paradigm for True Sacrifice in Latter-day Israel." In *The Old Testament and the Latter-day Saints: Sperry*

Symposium 1986. United States of America: Randall Book Company, 1986. 69–84.

----------. "Jacob in the Presence of God." In *Thy People Shall Be My People and Thy God My God: The 22nd Annual Sidney B. Sperry Symposium.* Salt Lake City: Deseret Book Company, 1994. 136–149.

----------. "Savior, Satan, and Serpent: The Duality of a Symbol in the Scriptures." In *The Disciple as Scholar: Essays on Scripture and the Ancient World in Honor of Richard Lloyd Anderson.* Eds. Stephen D. Ricks, Donald W. Parry, and Andrew H. Hedges. Provo, Utah: FARMS, 2000. 359–384.

Slemming, Charles W. *These Are the Garments: A Study of the Garments of the High Priest of Israel.* Fort Washington, Pennsylvania: Christian Literature Crusade, 1998.

Smith, Dennis E. "Messianic Banquet." in *The Anchor Bible Dictionary*, edited by David Noel Freedman. Vol 4. New York: Doubleday, 1992. 788–791.

Smith, Joseph. *Teachings of the Prophet Joseph Smith.* Ed. Joseph Fielding Smith. Salt Lake City: Deseret Book Company, 1976.

Smith, Joseph Fielding. *Answers to Gospel Questions.* 4 vols. Salt Lake City: Deseret Book Company, 1963.

----------. *Church History and Modern Revelation: A Course of Study for the Melchizedek Priesthood Quorums.* 4 vols. Salt Lake City: Deseret Book Company, 1950.

----------. *Man, His Origin and Destiny.* Salt Lake City: Deseret Book Company, 1954.

Speiser, E. A. *Genesis*, Anchor Bible. New York: Doubleday.

Stacey, Michelle. "How the Sexes Differ." *Real Simple*, June 2006: 179–184.

Stapley, Delbert L. Conference Report. October 1964: 61–65.

Stone, David R. "Zion in the Midst of Babylon." *Ensign*, May 2006, 90–92.

Strathearn, Gaye. "Revelation: John's Message of Comfort and Hope." In *The Testimony of John the Beloved: The 27th Annual Sidney B.*

Sperry Symposium. Salt Lake City: Deseret Book Company, 1998. 281–300.

Szink, Terrence L. and John W. Welch. "Benjamin's Speech in the Context of Ancient Israelite Festivals." In *King Benjamin's Speech: "That Ye May Learn Wisdom."* Eds. John W. Welch and Stephen D. Ricks. Provo, Utah: FARMS, 1998. 147–224.

Tate, George S. "Prayer Circle." *Encyclopedia of Mormonism.* Ed. Daniel H. Ludlow. 4 vols. New York: Macmillan Publishing Company, 1992.

"Temple Open House Exceeds Hopes." *Church News*, December 2, 1989.

Thomas, M. Catherine. "Alma the Younger," *FARMS Book of Mormon Lecture Series.* Transcript. 2 Parts. Provo, Utah: FARMS, 1994.

----------. "Benjamin and the Mysteries of God." In *King Benjamin's Speech: "That Ye May Learn Wisdom."* Eds. John W. Welch and Stephen D. Ricks. Provo, Utah: FARMS, 1998. 277–294.

----------. "The Brother of Jared at the Veil." *Temples of the Ancient World: Ritual and Symbolism.* Ed. Donald W. Parry. Salt Lake City: Deseret Book and FARMS, 1997. 388–398.

----------. "Hebrews: to Ascend the Holy Mount." In *Temples of the Ancient World: Ritual and Symbolism.* Ed. Donald W. Parry. Salt Lake City: Deseret Book and FARMS, 1997. 479–491.

----------. "The Provocation in the Wilderness and the Rejection of Grace." In *Thy People Shall Be My People and Thy God My God: The 22nd Annual Sidney B. Sperry Symposium.* Salt Lake City: Deseret Book Company, 1994. 166–177.

----------. "The Sermon on the Mount: The Sacrifice of the Human Heart." In *Studies in Scripture, Volume 5: The Gospels.* Eds. Robert L. Millet and Kent P. Jackson. 8 vols. Salt Lake City: Randall Book Company, 1985. 247–286.

----------. *Spiritual Lightening.* Salt Lake City: Bookcraft, 1996.

----------. "Zion and the Spirit of At-one-ment." *FARMS Book of Mormon Lecture Series.* Transcript. Provo, Utah: FARMS, 1994.

Thomasson, Gordon C. "What's in a Name? Book of Mormon Language, Names, and [Metonymic] Naming." *Journal of Book of Mormon Studies*, vol. 3, no. 1 (Spring 1994): 1–27.

Thompson, J. A. *The Book of Jeremiah.* Grand Rapids, Michigan: William B. Eerdmans Publishing Company, 1980.

"Thousands Visit Newest Utah Temple, 49th in the Church, During Open House." *Church News*, August 17, 1996.

The Tonight Show. NBC. Burbank, California. June 8, 2000.

Trible, Phyllis. *God and the Rhetoric of Sexuality.* Philadelphia: Fortress Press, 1978.

Turner, Rodney. "Christ's Church in Ancient America." *Ensign*, March 2000, 48–52.

Tvedtnes, John A. "My First-Born in the Wilderness," *Journal of Book of Mormon Studies* vol. 3, no. 1 (Spring 1994): 207–209.

----------. "Olive Oil: Symbol of the Holy Ghost." In *The Allegory of the Olive Tree.* Eds. Stephen D. Ricks and John W. Welch. Salt Lake City and Provo, Utah: Deseret Book Company and FARMS, 1994. 427–459.

----------. "Priestly Clothing in Bible Times." In *Temples of the Ancient World: Ritual and Symbolism.* Ed. Donald W. Parry. Salt Lake City: Deseret Book and FARMS, 1997. 649–704.

----------. "Temple Prayer in Ancient Times." In *The Temple in Time and Eternity.* Eds. Donald W. Parry and Stephen D. Ricks. Provo, Utah: FARMS, 1999. 79–98.

Valletta, Thomas R. "Jared and His Brother." In *The Book of Mormon: Fourth Nephi through Moroni, from Zion to Destruction.* Eds. Monte S. Nyman and Charles D. Tate Jr. Provo, Utah: Religious Studies Center Brigham Young University, 1995. 303–322.

Van Orden, Bruce A. "The Seed of Abraham in the Latter Days." In *The Old Testament and the Latter-day Saints: Sperry Symposium 1986.* United States of America: Randall Book Company, 1986. 51–67.

von Wellnitz, Marcus. "The Catholic Liturgy and the Mormon Temple." *BYU Studies*, vol. 21 (Winter 1981): 3–35.

Waltke, Bruce K. with Cathi J. Fredricks. *Genesis: A Commentary.* Grand Rapids, Michigan: Zondervan, 2001.

Walton, John H. and Victor H. Matthews. *The IVP Bible Background Commentary: Genesis–Deuteronomy.* Downers Grove, Illinois: InterVarsity Press, 1997.

Warner, C. Terry. "Honest, Simple, Solid, True," In *Brigham Young University 1995–1996 Speeches.* Provo, Utah: Brigham Young University, 1996. 131–139.

Welch, John W. "Benjamin, the Man: His Place in Nephite History." In *King Benjamin's Speech: 'That Ye May Learn Wisdom.'* Eds. John W. Welch and Stephen D. Ricks. Provo, Utah: FARMS, 1998. 23–54.

----------. "The Temple in the Book of Mormon: The Temples at the Cities of Nephi, Zarahemla, and Bountiful." In *Temples of the Ancient World: Ritual and Symbolism.* Ed. Donald W. Parry. Salt Lake City: Deseret Book and FARMS, 1997. 297–387.

----------. "Ten Testimonies of Jesus Christ from the Book of Mormon." In *Doctrines of the Book of Mormon: The 1991 Sperry Symposium.* Eds. Bruce A. Van Orden and Brent L. Top. Salt Lake City: Deseret Book Company, 1992. 223–242.

----------. *The Sermon at the Temple and the Sermon on the Mount: A Latter-Day Saint Approach.* Salt Lake City and Provo, Utah: Deseret Book Company and FARMS, 1990.

Welch, John W. and Claire Foley. "Gammadia on Early Jewish and Christian Garments." *BYU Studies*, vol. 36, no. 3 (1996–97): 252–257.

Westermann, Claus. *Genesis 1–11: A Commentary.* Trans. John J. Scullion. Minneapolis: Augsburg Publishing House, 1984.

----------. *Genesis 12–36: A Continental Commentary.* Trans. John J. Scullion. Minneapolis: Fortress Press, 1984.

Widtsoe, John A. "Symbolism in the Temples." In *Saviors on Mount Zion.* Ed. Archibald F. Bennett. Salt Lake City: Deseret Sunday School Board, 1950. 163–168.

Widtsoe, John A. and Leah D. Widtsoe. *Word of Wisdom: A Modern Interpretation.* Salt Lake City: Deseret Book Company, 1950.

Wight, Fred H. *Manners and Customs of Bible Lands.* Chicago: Moody Press, 1953.

Wikipedia contributors, "Self in Jungian psychology," Wikipedia, *The Free Encyclopedia,* "https://en.wikipedia.org/wiki/Self_in_Jungian_psychology." (Accessed February 17, 2016).

Wilcox, S. Michael. *Daughters of God: Scriptural Portraits.* Salt Lake City: Deseret Book Company, 1998.

----------. *House of Glory: Finding Personal Meaning in the Temple.* Salt Lake City: Deseret Book Company, 1995.

----------. "The Temple: Taking an Eternal View." In *Every Good Thing: Talks from the 1997 BYU Women's Conference.* Eds. Dawn Hall Anderson, Susette Fletcher Green, Dlora Hall Dalton. Salt Lake City: Deseret Book Company, 1998. 282–298.

----------. *Who Shall Be Able to Stand? Finding Personal Meaning in the Book of Revelation.* Salt Lake City: Deseret Book Company, 2003.

Wilson, Gerald H. *The NIV Application Commentary: Psalms, Volume 1.* Grand Rapids, Michigan: Zondervan, 2002.

Winder, Barbara W. "Enjoy Your Journey." In *Brigham Young University 1989–1990 Speeches.* Provo, Utah: Brigham Young University, 1990. 101–108.

----------. "Striving Together: Transforming Our Beliefs into Action." *Ensign*, November 1984, 98–100.

Wright, David P. "Holiness (OT)." In *The Anchor Bible Dictionary.* Ed. David Noel Freedman, vol 3. New York: Doubleday, 1992. 237–249.

Young, Brigham. *Discourses of Brigham Young.* Ed. John A. Widtsoe. Salt Lake City: Deseret Book Company, 1954.

Youngblood, Ronald. *The Heart of the Old Testament.* Grand Rapids, Michigan: Baker Book House, 1971.

About the Author

Amy Blake Hardison was born in Phoenix and raised in Phoenix and Mesa, Arizona. She graduated magna cum laude from Weber State University in 1980 with a degree in English. Amy has been a stay-at-home mother, raising four children. She has also taught the gospel for twenty-one years as a volunteer institute teacher at Chandler-Gilbert Community College, Tempe Institute (ASU), East Valley Institute, and currently as a teacher for a midsingles class in the Phoenix valley. She has participated in five Sidney B. Sperry Symposiums and the Conference on Abraham at BYU and has had her articles published in the accompanying volumes. Amy lives in Mesa with her wonderful husband, Steve. They have been married for thirty-eight years. They have six grandchildren.